"I recommend this book in the strongest possible terms. Douglas Harink is a biblical theologian precisely positioned to expound the ways in which the letters of Paul the Apostle speak to our present global moment. As the postwar consensus in the West seems to be breaking down on a hundred different fronts, and bitter battles in search of justice erupt throughout American society, the great questions about what justice might actually mean in reality become ever more urgent. Paul's radical understanding of the Christ event has been expounded by important voices before, but has not yet been fully appropriated. Now is the time of need, and this is a book that can help us."
Fleming Rutledge, author of *The Crucifixion: Understanding the Death of Jesus Christ* and *Not Ashamed of the Gospel: Sermons from Paul's Epistle to the Romans*

"Romans is a rich document encompassing multiple important themes, but the one Douglas Harink traces—justice—is often overlooked. This provocative book will therefore surprise many readers, but they will find it to be an engaging treatment of a neglected yet significant theme, punctuated with stimulating reflection questions. (The section on Romans 13:1-7 is alone worth the price of the book.) *Resurrecting Justice* is especially important for Christians today, who need to understand, proclaim, and participate in the peculiar messianic justice of God."
Michael J. Gorman, Raymond E. Brown Professor of Biblical Studies and Theology at St. Mary's Seminary and University, Baltimore

"What is Romans about? We know the traditional answers: justification by faith, forgiveness of sins, personal salvation. Harink doesn't throw these out the window but puts the spotlight on the thematic thread of justice that runs all through Romans. I admit that I had my initial hesitations and doubts about reading Romans as a treatise on justice, but by the end I was a believer! Harink joins together what has often been torn asunder today—the relationships between personal and corporate, individual and communal, and personal justification and social justice in Christian thought and theology—with the resurrection of Christ at the center of it all."
Nijay K. Gupta, professor of New Testament at Northern Seminary

"Paul's letters are often ignored in calls for justice. All who do not naturally gravitate toward the apostle as a champion of justice will be challenged to rethink Paul's gospel as the power of God's justice to rectify the whole world. Harink's rereading of Romans is a welcome, timely, and accessible study for the classroom and the church."
Carla Swafford Works, Wesley Theological Seminary

"Douglas Harink takes readers to school with Paul's letter to the Romans in order to learn (and learn again) that justification has everything to do with justice because the God of the gospel has designs—at once gracious and righteous—upon our persons, our societies, and our nations. The fruit of long wrestling with Paul *Resurrecting Justice* provides an accessible, instr   eart of the gospel: namely, God's powerful set
Philip G. Ziegler, University of Aberdeen

T0284960

RESURRECTING
JUSTICE

Reading Romans for the Life of the World

DOUGLAS HARINK

Academic

An imprint of InterVarsity Press
Downers Grove, Illinois

InterVarsity Press
P.O. Box 1400, Downers Grove, IL 60515-1426
ivpress.com
email@ivpress.com

InterVarsity Press® is the book-publishing division of InterVarsity Christian Fellowship/USA®, a movement of students and faculty active on campus at hundreds of universities, colleges, and schools of nursing in the United States of America, and a member movement of the International Fellowship of Evangelical Students. For information about local and regional activities, visit intervarsity.org.

Scripture quotations, unless otherwise noted, are the author's own translation.

Cover design and image composite: David Fassett
Interior design: Jeanna Wiggins
Images: apostle Paul stained glass window: © sedmak / iStock / Getty Images Plus

ISBN 978-0-8308-5276-5 (print)
ISBN 978-0-8308-4380-0 (digital)

Printed in the United States of America ∞

InterVarsity Press is committed to ecological stewardship and to the conservation of natural resources in all our operations. This book was printed using sustainably sourced paper.

Library of Congress Cataloging-in-Publication Data
A catalog record for this book is available from the Library of Congress.

P	25	24	23	22	21	20	19	18	17	16	15	14	13	12	11	10	9	8	7	6	5	4	3	2	1
Y	38	37	36	35	34	33	32	31	30	29	28	27	26	25	24	23	22	21	20						

For Jack Douglas Klanke

CONTENTS

PREFACE

Justice is every Christian's concern. There is no avoiding it, since the theme of justice pervades the Bible from Genesis to Revelation. Justice is God's concern.

The trouble is that Christians often disagree about what justice means, whether in the Bible or in contemporary society. Christians also disagree about how they should be "for" justice, and what kind of justice they should be promoting and advancing. For example, among North American Christians, some groups think of justice primarily in terms of retributions and punishments for transgressions and crimes committed. They emphasize law and order, and often advocate for harsher penalties for crimes, including the death penalty. Other groups think of justice primarily as social justice, as equity and fairness in the social and economic spheres of life. Among other things, they advocate for better wages and working conditions, and for less disparity between the rich and the poor. While it is not impossible to hold both of these understandings of justice, often these groups are at odds with one another; to be "for" justice means quite different things to each group.

Christians will naturally turn to the Bible to ground and clarify their understandings of justice. They will discover (if they do not already know) that there is a lot of material on the theme in the Old Testament, especially in the books of the Law (Exodus to Deuteronomy) and the Prophets. Any good study of the biblical idea(s) of justice will spend a great deal of time on this material and will find it rich in dimension and nuance. Just about every aspect of justice is found there: trial and judgment, transgression and penalty, crime and punishment, equity and fairness, judgment against greed and cruelty, protection for the poor and vulnerable, and so on. There is also much about the relation between divine and human justice, and between justice and mercy.

Christians are less inclined to turn to the New Testament to shape their ideas of justice. In the Gospels, Jesus seems to be more concerned about challenging some Old Testament forms of justice than about upholding them. In fact, his teachings on justice—for example, in the Sermon on the Mount (Mt 5–7)—seem extreme and unrealistic, lacking the attention to intent, circumstance, and context that we find in the laws of Moses. Most Christians think of Jesus' teachings as representing a kind of ideal, setting before us something to strive toward, but nevertheless unattainable in the practicalities of day-to-day life and society. Understanding Jesus' teachings on justice as nice but unrealistic ideals is disputed by many recent studies of the Gospels, but it continues to make sense to the majority of Christians in our time.

When it comes to the rest of the New Testament, it seems there is very little discussion of justice at all. Perhaps the letter of James is an exception. As for the letters of Paul, well (so the thinking goes), there is next to nothing on the theme.

It is that last thought, on Paul, that I aim to challenge in this book on Romans. For I will argue that *Romans is centrally concerned about justice.* In this letter Paul asks us to think about justice a lot and to think about it differently, since the life, death, resurrection, and exaltation of Jesus *makes all the difference* in our thinking about justice. Therefore Romans demands our attention as the key New Testament document on justice, which not only makes its own claim about the theme but also requires us to receive the Old Testament understanding of justice in a new way. In this book I aim to think along with Paul, and I invite you, the reader, to think along with Paul and me about this most important of themes. For that reason, scattered liberally throughout the chapters of this book you will find textboxes in which I invite you to reflect on questions related to the dimensions and themes of justice in Romans. I urge you—or better, a group of you—to think about and discuss these questions in order to relate what Paul writes to your own contexts, thoughts, and practices. These questions will often be existentially and intellectually demanding, asking you to reflect deeply on your own commitments and ideas, and on many of the ideas, institutions, and practices we take for granted in our societies and nations. Romans demands nothing less than a fundamental rethinking of all things in the light of the gospel—a "renewing of the mind" that is not conformed to this world but transformed by the reality of God, the Father, Son, and Holy Spirit (Rom 12:1-2). In this way, and with some guidance from me, I hope you will be the one to make the connections between what Paul writes about justice in Romans and your own life in the world.

This book is best understood as a reading of Romans. It is not a technical commentary on all the words and phrases in the letter (there are many such commentaries, and their number increases every year) but an attempt to follow Paul as he thinks justice in relation to Jesus. A reading of Romans is more fluid and more adventurous than a technical commentary, less intent on emphasizing the detailed linguistic and historical issues in interpretation, and more intent on attending to how the text shapes our contemporary understanding. A reading also leaves more loose ends (for example, on some important Christian doctrines) than scholarly commentaries usually do. I do not try to deal with every text and the issues they might raise but with those texts that (in my judgment) have most to contribute to our understanding of justice. That all said, I have been engaged in the study of Paul and Romans for many years, and have been deeply instructed and formed by numerous scholarly books and commentaries on Paul, Romans, and justice. Should you, the reader, wish to follow up on what you read in this book, I have provided at the end of the book suggestions for further reading. For readers who may already be familiar with some or much of the scholarship on Paul and Romans, the scholarly influences on my work may be detected on nearly every page. Indeed, if you are a Paul scholar, you may recognize your own influence here! Yet, I have not documented everything (or even very much) in footnotes, in order not to distract the readers for whom this book is primarily written—ordinary, thinking Christians who want a deeper, gospel-informed understanding of biblical justice.

I must at least acknowledge several scholars whose influences are prevalent throughout this book: first and foremost, J. Louis Martyn (of blessed memory), the foundational figure in the contemporary understanding of the "apocalyptic Paul"; Beverly Roberts Gaventa, whose many essays and articles on Romans (soon to bear fruit in a full-scale commentary) have guided me in many of my interpretations; John M. G. Barclay, whose peerless book, *Paul and the Gift*, came at an opportune time, and with whom I had some crucial conversations on Paul and politics at Regent College several years ago. Others who have significantly shaped my thought in this work include Douglas A. Campbell, Michael J. Gorman, Mark Kinzer, P. Travis Kroeker, Mark D. Nanos, John Howard Yoder, and Philip G. Ziegler. I must also mention the Italian philosopher Giorgio Agamben. It's unlikely that any of these scholars would fully agree with what I have done here with Romans, but I owe them much.

Throughout this book I have usually provided my own translations of the text of Romans. Sometimes these are very literal (and thus at times also awkward), and sometimes they are more like paraphrases. I do this because—as I will show in the first chapter—the very theme of justice itself is lost in most modern English translations of the letter. Not only justice but other themes as well. I always aim to be responsible in my translations, which are themselves informed by lexicons, Greek grammars, scholarly commentaries, and other books and articles on Paul and Romans. Still, I urge my readers to have an excellent modern English translation (or two or three—NRSV, TNIV, NASB) available at all times, to cross-reference with my translations along the way. I provide a glossary and explanations for some of my translations at the back of this book.

ACKNOWLEDGMENTS

I AM GRATEFUL TO THE KING'S UNIVERSITY for supporting my scholarly work and teaching in every possible way over the past three decades, and to the many students through the years who took my course on Paul and his letters, and upon whom I sometimes inflicted portions of the manuscript for feedback. The insightful comments by Joseph Zondervan were especially valuable at an early stage of writing.

I am grateful for invitations from St. John the Evangelist Anglican Church, Christ Church Anglican, Lendrum Mennonite Brethren Church, and Fellowship Christian Reformed Church, all in Edmonton, to present this material in a variety of settings. Lendrum Church provided a remarkable opportunity to teach through the whole of Romans on justice over ten weeks in the fall of 2016, with a lively, engaged, intelligent, and challenging group of learners.

My colleagues at The King's University have given much support, friendship, encouragement, and conversation on this long journey, especially Steve Martin, Brett Roscoe, Elden Wiebe, John Wood, and Arlette Zinck. Arlette, our intrepid dean of arts for much of the time I was working on this book, continually encouraged my work both institutionally and personally. Her indefatigable efforts to support and work for the release of Canadian citizen Omar Khadr, unjustly imprisoned for years in "Camp Justice" (Guantanamo Bay Detention Center), and then her work to foster his (and many others') education in Canadian prisons stands as a concrete and powerful example of sharing in God's justice in Jesus Christ.

I must thank the Whiskey Jacks (you know who you are) for our more than two decades of gatherings to share fine spirits, food, friendship, important conversations, and brotherly love. What a gift you are! My longtime colleague and friend Roy Berkenbosch has been a constant sounding board for many of my thoughts on Romans (and many other thoughts besides). On questions of justice especially, I have counted on Roy to supply some "Reformed" pushback to what I present in this book. When I need enthusiastic encouragement, I seek out Myron (Bradley) Penner, with whose thoughts I have found remarkable resonance and who can always be relied on for the goods on Kierkegaard, Agamben, and Žižek. I am grateful for the friendship and support of Philip Ziegler, for his remarkable theological work that has shaped my own, and for the pleasure of working with him on our explorations in theology and apocalyptic.

At a crucial juncture I was blessed to have Elisa (Benterud) Genuis read the entire manuscript of this book with the critical eye of an (exceptionally talented!) undergraduate student. She did this with immense dedication, providing extensive comments, questions, and criticisms, and many suggestions for clarifying arguments, ideas, and style. This book is much better because of her work. Thank you, Elisa!

I am grateful to Dan Reid, former editor at IVP, who believed in this project from the start, and to Anna Gissing and the others at IVP Academic for their work in making this a better book.

I am sustained in every way by my family. My wonderful parents-in-law, Del and Noreen Reimer, have supported (in so many ways), encouraged, and loved me (and my family of course) for over four decades. God bless you! Thank you to Marcia and Tim for always offering us a lovely retreat and loving friendship. To Elizabeth, Allison, and Tim: thank you for your constant love and encouragement. You are a blessing! To Debby: you bless me and bring me joy in every way, beyond all words, far beyond a simple thank you. Nevertheless, thank you!

This book is dedicated to our first grandchild, Jack Douglas Klanke. Jack, may you and our other grandchildren still to come (we hope) know deeply God's grace, justice, and peace in Jesus Christ, and may you bear witness to it throughout your whole life, only now beginning.

1

TERMS OF JUSTICE

IN THIS CHAPTER

● How the theme of justice in Romans gets lost in translation

● Other vocabulary and translation issues in Romans

● Defining two terms: *apocalyptic* and *messianic*

WHEN CHRISTIANS WANT TO think biblically about justice, they do not usually turn to the letters of Paul. They often look to other places in the Bible, such as the laws of Moses, the biblical prophets, and perhaps Jesus, who links his own mission to both the Law and the Prophets in his inaugural justice-sermon in the synagogue in Nazareth (Lk 4:16-21). Ignoring Paul is a habit even for some of the best writers on biblical justice. For example, Ronald Sider's recent book, *Just Politics: A Guide for Christian Engagement*, includes a chapter that summarizes biblical teaching on justice. Sider unpacks the meanings of the two main Hebrew words for justice, *mishpat* and *tsedaqah*, as they occur in the books of Moses, the Psalms, and the Prophets.[1] But there is no mention of any text from Paul.

Further, if you search the tables of contents and subject indexes of scholarly books on Paul or commentaries on Romans, you rarely find any entry on "justice."[2] These findings seem to confirm the impression that Paul and his letter

---

[1] Ronald J. Sider, *Just Politics: A Guide for Christian Engagement* (Grand Rapids, MI: Brazos, 2012), 77-99. An important exception is Christopher D. Marshall, *Beyond Retribution: A New Testament Vision for Justice, Crime, and Punishment* (Grand Rapids, MI: Eerdmans, 2001), 35-69.

[2] In recent years the situation is changing. Important contributions to the theme of justice in Paul's writings include Neil Elliott, *The Arrogance of Nations: Reading Romans in the Shadow of Empire* (Minneapolis: Fortress, 2008); Michael J. Gorman, *Becoming the Gospel: Paul, Participation and Mission* (Grand Rapids, MI: Eerdmans, 2015); Theodore W. Jennings Jr., *Outlaw Justice: The Messianic Politics of Paul* (Stanford, CA: Stanford University Press, 2013); Gordon Zerbe, *Citizenship: Paul on Peace and Politics* (Winnipeg: CMU Press, 2012).

to the Romans have little or nothing to contribute to the topic. One task of this introduction is to account for the absence of justice in studies of Paul, and the absence of Paul in Christian thinking about justice. The other task is to relearn some of Paul's basic vocabulary in order to change our perception of Paul's message and allow the important theme of justice to surface again. In the remainder of the book I explain Paul's letter to the Romans as a message of justice and show how our ideas of justice might be radically affected by that message.

Lost in Translation

Justice is a central and pervasive theme in Romans. So why is that so difficult for us to see? For English-speaking readers, the most important factor is English translations. When we read through Romans (and other letters of Paul) we encounter the words *righteous* and *righteousness* often. But for the modern reader these words have come to have an almost exclusively individual, moral, and religious meaning, and often not a positive one. One of the most common uses in our popular speech is the term *self-righteous*, describing someone who is too overtly religious, pious, moralistic or judgmental. It carries a negative meaning. Still, if we find *righteous* or *righteousness* used often in Paul's letters, and bearing much important weight, it seems Christians at least cannot avoid them. If they are part of Paul's basic vocabulary, they probably should be part of ours as well, even if they risk being misunderstood. After all, Paul seems to be concerned about righteousness.

> What does *righteousness* mean to you? Do you use this word much in everyday life? If not, why not? What does the word *justice* mean to you? Do you feel more comfortable using it? If so, why?

When Paul's letters were translated into Latin early on, the words we read in English as *righteous* and *righteousness* appeared as *iustus* and *iustitia*. Where we now read in Romans 1:17 of "the righteousness of God," the Latin reads *iustitia Dei*, "the justice of God." This also shows up in translations into languages rooted in Latin: for example: "la justice de Dieu" (French), "la justicia de Dios" (Spanish), "la giustizia di Dio" (Italian), and so on. Each of these is a translation of the Greek phrase *dikaiosynē theou*. The word *dikaiosynē* is one word in a set of Greek words beginning with *dik–*: all of them include the sense of what is just within the social and political order as well as personal uprightness—so, *dikaios* means "just," *dikaioō* means "to justify" or "to make just," *dikaiosynē* means "justice." In ancient Greek there was no separate set of words that meant "righteous" or "righteousness" in the individual, moral, religious sense, in contrast to "just" and "justice." The *dik-* words in ordinary Greek usage included both personal *and* legal-social-political meanings. These words may sometimes indicate what we mean by righteousness and a righteous person; but they also indicate such things as a just ruler, justice in a criminal case, just sharing of power and goods, just relations among groups and peoples, and doing justice.

In Paul's letter to the Romans the Greek word *dikaiosynē* occurs thirty-three times, and other words with the *dik-* stem occur another thirty or more times—more than anywhere else in Paul's writings specifically, and more by far than in any other document in the New Testament in general. When the early believers in Rome heard these words read from Paul's letter, they would not have understood them to mean only "righteousness" or "righteous," separated from the meanings of social and political justice. In the Greek word *dikaiosynē* they would have heard the Latin *iustitia*. Justice is the central and pervasive theme of the letter to the Romans—the justice of God, the just ruler, the just person, the way of justice in relationships, society and the world. It would therefore not be unreasonable to call Romans a treatise on justice.

But Paul's language of justice depends not only on Greek and Roman meanings, but also on the early Greek translation of the Hebrew Old Testament, known as the Septuagint (abbreviated with the Roman numerals LXX), the translation that Paul and other New Testament writers used most often. For them the Greek Septuagint was the Bible. In it we encounter the *dik-* stem words—the justice words—numerous times, where they translate the Hebrew words *mišpāt* and *ṣedāqâ*. Here are just three familiar examples from the Septuagint:

> O God, give your judgment to the king, and your *dikaiosynē* [justice] to the king's son; that he may judge your people with *dikaiosynē* [justice] and your poor with judgment. (Ps 72:1-2)

> The Lord has made known his salvation, he has revealed his *dikaiosynē* [justice] in the sight of the nations. (Ps 98:2)

> But let judgment roll down as water, and *dikaiosynē* [justice] as a mighty torrent. (Amos 5:24)

4

TERMS OF JUSTICE

God is the source of justice, he gives justice to the ruler, he calls for justice from his people, and he reveals his justice before the nations. God's salvation is his justice: this is a persistent theme throughout the Old Testament.[3] It is also, we will see, exactly what Paul too will proclaim in Romans. For Paul, God's salvation and justice are the very meaning of the good news—the good news of Jesus.

Jesus (as we have already noted) preached his first and famous justice sermon about the reign of God from Isaiah 61:1–2, a text that declares the liberation and restoration of the people Israel. Jesus announced this good news to a people in social, economic, and political bondage to an oppressive foreign power, Rome. No wonder, then, that when they heard Jesus' sermon of hope, "all were speaking well of him" (Lk 4:22). But already before his first public sermon of good news for prisoners, the poor and the oppressed, Jesus' birth had stirred up hopes among the Judean underdogs for political liberation and justice, hopes expressed boldly in the songs of Mary (Lk 1:46-55) and Zacharias (Lk 1:67-79). On the other political side, Jesus' birth provoked great anxiety among those in charge—Herod the king, and "all Jerusalem with him" (Mt 2:3). Jesus was dogged by various authorities from the beginning to the end of his ministry, and he was finally publicly executed by the Roman occupiers with the approval of the Judean authorities in Jerusalem. The Gospels make clear that the political authorities (Roman and Judean) believed that Jesus, the Messiah and Son of David, was pursuing political aims that both threatened the bases of their own authority and fostered revolutionary hope among his followers—hope for justice.

The political authorities and Jesus' followers were not wrong about Jesus. What they all found hard to grasp was that he consistently refused to use the usual *means*—coercion, violence, and militant insurgency—to accomplish his revolutionary ends. He refused those means first in his temptations in the desert (where they were proposed by the devil) and finally in his willing submission to public execution. Jesus' revolution in this sense was fundamentally different. He did not refuse politics; rather, he proposed a *political*

---

[3]For more on the meaning of justice in the Old Testament, see Sider, *Just Politics*, 77-99; Bruce C. Birch, "Justice," in *Dictionary of Scripture and Ethics*, ed. Joel B. Green (Grand Rapids, MI: Baker Academic, 2011), 433-37; Christopher J. H. Wright, *Old Testament Ethics for the People of God* (Downers Grove, IL: IVP Academic, 2004), 253-80.

alternative to the way the Romans ruled, and to the way his Judean compatriots hoped to rule when the Messiah came. He called his fellow Judeans to refuse guerilla warfare and military solutions in their efforts to attain their hoped-for justice—the liberation and restoration of Israel in its land. Instead he called them to *trust in God* and to wait for God's time and manner of deliverance. Jesus called his compatriots to love and forgive *both* their fellow countrymen *and* their enemy oppressors. He called Israel even under occupation and oppression to become *the true political community of justice*, a people chosen, ruled, and sustained by God and God's Messiah, their just King. In fact, he claimed, they could be this community of justice without controlling their national territory, security, or destiny. According to Jesus, for the people Israel to trust in God, forgive enemies, and refuse violence was already to share in the reality of God's liberation and restoration, God's justice and salvation—the kingdom of God.[4]

We in the modern Western world are tempted to separate "religion" from politics and "spirituality" from justice. Both the Old Testament and the Gospels show that such separation is not part of the biblical mindset. It would therefore be startling and strange if Paul, who was so thoroughly steeped in the Law, the Psalms, the Prophets, and the gospel of Jesus Messiah, and dedicated to the God of Israel and his cause, were now to propose that Israel's God and God's Messiah are really only directly concerned with the spiritual condition and moral lives of individuals. We will soon see that, starting from the first few sentences of Romans and carrying on to the last, Paul declares the good news of God and God's justice for *all of life*, political, social, economic, and personal alike.

More Vocabulary

Separating religion from politics, economics, and justice was not the mindset among Judeans in Paul's time. Nor was it the mindset of Greeks and Romans. For them, all matters of imperial and political authority, good government of cities, and administration of justice in legal, social, and economic spheres,

---

[4]The perspective on Jesus I have sketched here is developed in the classic work by André Trocmé, *Jesus and the Nonviolent Revolution* (Maryknoll, NY: Orbis, 2004). The other classic works on these matters are by John Howard Yoder, *The Original Revolution: Essays on Christian Pacifism* (Scottdale, PA: Herald, 1977), and *The Politics of Jesus: Vicut Agnus Noster*, 2nd ed. (Grand Rapids, MI: Eerdmans, 1994).

as well as the ordinary matters of success in family, business, agriculture, trade, travel, and war, were thoroughly interwoven with what we think of as religion.[5] In matters great and small, Greeks and Romans honored the gods through offerings, sacrifices, rituals, and festivals. They regularly consulted prophets, shamans, astrologers, and soothsayers; they exorcised demons, read omens, cast spells, and practiced magic. No military general would go to war unless the divine signs (discerned by priests and prophets) were in their favor. Temples were built to gods who secured the safety of cities and the triumph of emperors. Indeed, even some of the great emperors, such as Augustus, were regarded as gods or sons of god and were honored in temples built for them. Life—especially *political* life—and "religion" were one. Thus, many New Testament words that we often think of as having specialized spiritual meanings, such as *dikaiosynē*, were part of the vocabulary of Greek and Roman political life. Here are some examples with their meanings:[6]

- "lord" (Greek *kyrios*): a ruler, emperor, master
- "son of God" (Greek *huios theou*): a ruler or emperor with divine authorization or status
- "good news," "gospel" (Greek *euangelion*): a public proclamation of a military victory, royal birth, enthronement, or benefaction
- "coming" (Greek *parousia*): the auspicious arrival or visit of a ruler/emperor, military commander, or other important official; or the presence or manifestation of a god
- "savior" (Greek *sotēr*): the emperor/ruler regarded as a military or political liberator, victor, or protector; "salvation" (Gk *sotēria*): the beneficial results—for example, peace, security, abundance—brought about by an emperor's rule or military victory
- faith (Greek *pistis*): the loyalty, allegiance, and faithfulness that subjects owed to their lords and rulers, or that citizens owed to their cities or to Rome

---

[5]A Roman citizen or soldier in Paul's time would understand and sympathize with the sentiment of a bumper sticker seen on some cars in modern America: "God, Guns and Guts Keep America Free."

[6]The following list is adapted from Michael Gorman, *Apostle of the Crucified Lord: A Theological Introduction to Paul and His Letters*, second ed. (Grand Rapids, MI: Eerdmans, 2017), 131-32.

- freedom (Greek *eleutheria*): political or ethical autonomy of citizens
- "church" (Greek *ekklēsia*): an assembly of citizens in a city; a business meeting of a club

Other words could be added to this list, such as the Greek words for "grace," "peace," "mercy," "blessing," and so on. Paul does not invent new "religious" words or create special religious meanings for words. He uses what was available in ordinary speech, often from the political discourse and propaganda of the surrounding culture.[7] These ordinary words do undergo a transformation of meaning when Paul uses them to proclaim the gospel, but it is not a transformation from secular or political meanings to religious or spiritual meanings. Rather, Paul brings these common words into the orbit of the story of Messiah Jesus and defines them by that story. The ordinary secular and political meanings are co-opted, taken over, and used by Paul to declare a radically new story about the gods (God), kings (Messiah), nations, political authorities, loyalties, and citizenship.

As we will see, this is also what happens for the word *dikaiosynē* (justice). It is not that Paul simply squeezes the meaning of the gospel into the ideas of justice that were available from Greek and Roman surroundings. On the contrary, Paul takes over the Greek justice words and fills them up, even blows them open with the meaning of the gospel, so that they come to signify a justice almost impossibly more radical and comprehensive than those words could have had in their original context. More important, for Paul the new gospel meaning becomes *the true standard* by which other meanings must be measured. *Justice is only truly justice if it lines up with and looks like gospel justice.* Likewise with *lord, son of God, savior, grace, peace,* and so on. For Paul these words take on a new fullness and normativity of meaning when they are "evangelized"—that is, when they are conscripted into proclaiming the news of God's justice in Messiah Jesus.

Perceptive readers may already have noticed I have been using some other unusual vocabulary in this work. Just now (and earlier) I used the phrases "Messiah Jesus" or "Jesus Messiah." Some readers are likely aware

---

[7]One can see how many of these words were used in Greek and Roman political documents and propaganda in a chapter by Neil Elliott and Mark Reasoner titled "The Gospel of Augustus," in *Documents and Images for the Study of Paul*, ed. Neil Elliott and Mark Reasoner (Minneapolis: Fortress, 2011), 119-73.

that *christos* in Greek refers to the Jewish *messiah*. Messiah is not a second name (as in "Christ" being Jesus Christ's second name); Messiah is a *title*. And it is not a religious title; it designates an anointed one, whether political or priestly. More accurately, it is a *theo-political* title, since for Jews in biblical times God (Greek *theos*) and politics were not held in separate compartments; they belonged together.

> Does using the phrase "Jesus Messiah" bring meanings and connections to mind that the phrase "Jesus Christ" does not? If so, what are some of those meanings and connections?

Many Judeans in the time of Jesus, Paul included, had high hopes that a political ruler, chosen and anointed by God—a messiah—would suddenly and dramatically arrive in Israel. He would appear in Jerusalem bearing God's own authority and mandate to be the one through whom God himself would rule Israel. These hopes were rooted in the Old Testament prophetic writings. *Messiah* came freighted with divine meaning. As God's anointed agent, a messiah would liberate (by divinely empowered military might) the people and the land of Israel from their occupation and oppression by the Romans, purify the people, establish social and economic justice in the land, restore Israel to its rightful place among (or above) the nations of the world, and rule with justice from Jerusalem over the nations of the earth. A careful reading of the temptations of Jesus in Matthew 4 and Luke 4 reveals that the devil tempted Jesus with exactly that vision of messiahship, a vision that truly did tempt Jesus—because he loved his people and remained in fundamental solidarity with them—but one he finally resisted. He determined instead to trust God to show him the shape and path of his own messianic mission as well as the future for Israel. Jesus' path as Israel's Messiah led finally not to a glorious throne in Jerusalem but to a torturous public execution outside the gates. It seemed to be the end of his messiahship.

However, the early messianic believers were convinced by his resurrection that Jesus of Nazareth was indeed Israel's hoped-for Messiah. He was Jesus Messiah, God's chosen, anointed, and empowered royal ruler, in whom God himself was reasserting his claim on Israel and calling Israel to a renewed trust in him for its future. By putting together the name Jesus with the title "messiah," the early believers and New Testament authors, Paul included, were declaring that Jesus now *defines* the meaning of the title messiah. Messiah remains a *theological, royal, and political title*, but the true nature of divine power and human political authority are revealed in who Jesus was, what he did and taught, how he lived and died. This is of crucial importance for understanding Romans. When reading Romans we must understand the Greek word *christos* ("Christ") with its original Judean meaning, "messiah."

Readers may also have noticed that I often use the word *Judean* rather than *Jew* or *Jewish*. The reasons are similar to those for using *messiah*. We are in the habit of thinking that *Jew* designates a religious group and that *Jewish* indicates their type of religion. There were, of course, many aspects of Judean life governed by instructions regarding purity, tithing, worship, and sacrifice—things we might regard as religious. But the law of Moses can hardly be reduced to a code of "religion." The law was a kind of treaty or national constitution given by God on Mount Sinai to regulate matters of social, economic and political order—justice—across the whole range of Israel's life *in the land* which they had been promised. Most Judeans of the first century (not only those who lived in the land) were still deeply committed to that land (known as *Ioudaia*, Judea), to being a people in the land (or returning to it), and to the right to have their own national constitution— the law of Moses—become again the law of the land. They were not content simply to practice their "religion" as individuals in a land now occupied and ruled by a foreign and often oppressive power with its own laws. Judeans, like the Romans, or like Canadians, Americans, and Chinese today, knew themselves as *a people* among peoples, a nation among nations, and hoped sometime—soon—to reclaim their rightful place in the world by *getting back control of their land*. Both Jesus and Paul shared this land hope with their fellow Judeans, even though they differed from their compatriots in how they thought that hope might someday be realized politically. When Paul uses the Greek word *Ioudaios*, as he does often, I will usually render it *Judean* (rather than *Jew*) in order to keep in mind the close association of the Judean people with the land and constitution (law) of *Ioudaia*, Judea—Israel.

Our note about Judeans is important for another reason. Just as that word draws our attention to a people and its land, it should also draw our attention to the reality that Judea was surrounded by other peoples and their lands. In fact, many Judeans in Paul's time did not live in Judea but among other peoples, in the towns and cities of other lands. These Diaspora (meaning "scattered") Judeans lived in the major cities of places such as Babylon, Persia, Syria, Egypt, Asia Minor, Greece, and Italy. There was a significant population of Judeans in Rome. In the Greek language, "peoples" or "nations" are *ethnē* (plural—the singular is *ethnos*: it is easy to see that the word *ethnic* is derived from this). However, in most recent English translations of the New Testament (and so also in Romans) the word *ethnē* is usually translated "Gentiles" rather than "peoples" or "nations." But there are problems with this.

First, like the word *Jews*, *Gentiles* leads us to think in almost exclusively individualistic terms. So, for example, when Paul writes in Romans 1:5 (NRSV) that through Jesus Messiah he has "received grace and apostleship to bring about the obedience of faith among all the Gentiles [Greek *ethnēsin*]," we likely imagine that Paul has in mind preaching the gospel to all non-Jewish individuals, indistinct from one another in terms of their geographical locations and their ethnic, social, and political groupings. But this is not how Paul usually thinks. It is evident from the opening greeting in each of his letters to churches that he has a very clear idea of the *geographical-ethnic-political* definition of the people group to which he is writing. He writes to the messianic assemblies in the city of Corinth (and "throughout the region of Achaia," 2 Cor 1:1), in Galatia (either an ethnic or provincial designation), in the cities of Philippi, Colossae, Thessalonica, and so on. The messianic assemblies in a particular place in some sense *stand for* that place as a whole; though few in number, they represent (before God) the city, region, or people from which they are drawn. This sense of representation is especially visible in Paul's own description of his mission, which he provides in Romans 15:18-26:

> For I will not venture to speak of anything except what Messiah has accomplished through me to win obedience from the [*ethnē* nations] . . . so that from Jerusalem and as far around as Illyricum I have *fully proclaimed* the good news of Messiah. Thus I make it my ambition to proclaim the good news, *not where Messiah has already been named,* so that I do not build on someone else's foundation, but as it is written,

"Those who have never been told of him shall see,
and those who have never heard of him shall understand."
This is the reason that I have so often been hindered from coming to you.
But now, with *no further place in these regions*, I desire . . . to come to you [in
Rome] when I go to Spain. . . . At present, however, I am going to Jerusalem
in a ministry to the saints. *Macedonia and Achaia* have been pleased to share
their resources with the poor among the saints in Jerusalem.

We cannot make sense of this important text if we think of *ethnē* as *individual* non-Jewish persons, that is, simply as "Gentiles" in an individualistic sense. For, in those terms, what could Paul possibly mean when he writes that "from Jerusalem and as far around as Illyricum" (the whole northeast portion of the Mediterranean area) he has "fully proclaimed" the gospel? He certainly cannot be boasting that every individual in this whole area has heard the good news from him. That would be the work of an entire lifetime and much more. He has in fact (as the accounts in Acts testify) moved deliberately from one important urban center to another, preaching in the synagogues, public squares, and marketplaces of those cities, declaring in them *the sovereignty (the name) of Messiah Jesus*. In those cities only small groups of believers in Jesus were formed. Nevertheless, on this basis alone Paul is bold to say that he has "no further place in these regions" to proclaim the good news and that, instead, after a short stay in Rome, he plans to travel on to Spain. Before he does that, however, he will carry resources from Macedonia and Achaia to Jerusalem.

What can Paul mean by these sweeping declarations? It is clear from this text that when he thinks here in terms of *ethnē*, he is thinking not in terms of individual Gentiles but in terms of peoples or nations as a whole, represented by specific major cities or geographical or political regions. He has proclaimed the sovereignty of Messiah Jesus to the various *peoples* or *nations*, in this representative and regional sense, from Jerusalem, throughout Asia Minor, and around to Illyricum.

When I use the word *nations* here, it is important not to think of nation-states as we know them today, but of "peoples in their regions with their rulers, language, customs, and laws." The modern nation-state is understood as a relatively stable political entity with sovereign

rights over a geographical territory marked out by well-defined borders. The political reality in ancient times was more fluid; rulers
claimed sovereignty over regions without clearly defined boundaries.
I will sometimes use *nation* and *people* interchangeably when translat-
ing the Greek word *ethnos*, but I mean by both something like "a
people in its region with its ruler, language, customs and laws."

There is a good reason why Paul thinks in these terms. The Old Testament
texts that Paul quotes and alludes to most frequently in his letters—certainly in
Romans—are Deuteronomy, the Psalms, and (especially) Isaiah. Many of Paul's
references to *ethnē* (for example, in Rom 15:9-12) come from the Septuagint. In
their Old Testament context none of these uses of *ethnē* refer to Gentiles in the
individual sense. They refer to the non-Israelite peoples or nations and are
almost always translated that way (from the Hebrew) in our English Bibles. The
Old Testament is indeed deeply concerned about Israel's place among the nations. Yet it is also concerned about the nations themselves, the gods of the
nations, and what the nations are doing politically and militarily among themselves and with respect to Israel. God is God not only of Israel but also of the
nations.[8] We have little problem seeing that when we read the Old Testament.

Therefore, there is no reason to think that Paul understands *ethnē* indi-
vidualistically as Gentiles when, quoting Psalm 18:49, he writes (in Rom 15:9),
"Therefore I will confess you among the *ethnēsin* [nations] and sing praises
to your name." Or, in Romans 15:12, when quoting Isaiah 11:10 (in the Septuagint version), "The root of Jesse shall come, the one who rises to rule
ethnōn [nations]; in him *ethnē* [nations] will hope." So unless there are
strong indications that Paul is speaking in specifically individual terms,
when we encounter the word *Gentiles* in translations of Romans we should
think of "peoples" or "nations." The difference this makes will become clear
as we make our way through Romans, particularly as we ask questions about
the justice of God.

What role, if any, does the idea of nations play in your understanding
of God's work of salvation in the world?

[8]This point is made clearly and powerfully by Christopher Wright in "Politics and the Nations,"
in *Old Testament Ethics*, 212-52.

Two Technical Terms

Throughout this book I will frequently use two technical terms that in some measure capture two crucial aspects of the good news about God's justice that Paul proclaims. They roughly correspond to the aspect of *divine action* on the one hand and the aspect of *human action* on the other. With respect to divine action, I speak of *apocalyptic*. With respect to human action, I speak of *messianic*. Let me explain.

Apocalyptic. This word often generates thoughts, images and feelings of doom, destruction, and cosmic end-time scenarios. Hollywood produces numerous blockbuster films in the apocalyptic genre, where entire cities or even the whole planet are in imminent danger of massive destruction by some uncontrollable force, whether natural (such as an asteroid or tsunami) or manmade (such as a nuclear bomb).

What is one of your favorite or most memorable apocalyptic films? What world-altering threat has to be averted in it? Do you ever imagine an apocalyptic event as good news?

If we think *apocalyptic* in biblical terms, our minds likely run to astonishing, often frightening texts in Ezekiel, Daniel, Mark 13, and especially the book of Revelation. In fact, the very first word of the book of Revelation is the Greek word *apokalypsis*. It is translated "revelation"—hence the name of the book. However, as we read through the book of Revelation, the word *revelation* seems a rather bland and flat descriptor of what is going on there. In its normal use, revelation means something like a disclosure, perhaps of a secret or of something that lies behind a veil or curtain. Think of the reveal, the moment in reality television shows when the public gets to see how a home has been renovated, how a person has undergone a dramatic makeover, or whom the bachelor has chosen.

There is in the book of Revelation something of that meaning of revelation, but there is also much more. The book is full of high tension and grand, often terrifying, sometimes gruesome and horrifying dramatic action on both the historical and cosmic planes, by divine, angelic, demonic, monstrous, and human actors. When we come to the climax of all of this action in Revelation 21–22, *the whole creation has been altered by God* in the most fundamental way, such that there is "a new heaven and a new earth" (Rev 21:1). This is not mere revelation; it is more like wholesale, cosmic revolution. It is truly apocalypse!

Now, all of this may seem a long distance from the writings of Paul. To be sure, the apostle writes two somewhat obvious apocalyptic passages in 1 Thessalonians 4:13–5:11 and 2 Thessalonians 2:1-12. But for the most part it seems Paul is not much for apocalyptic drama—he is more for doctrine and ethics. Here again, though, our translations may hide more than they reveal. For at crucial junctures in his letters, especially Galatians and Romans, when Paul emphatically introduces the good news he proclaims, he speaks of an apocalypse. In Galatians 1:12 he insists that he did not receive the gospel from a human source, but rather "through an *apokalypseōs* of Jesus Messiah." Further, in Galatians 1:16 he writes that God was "pleased to *apokalypsai* his Son to me." So dramatic and powerful and comprehensive is this apocalypse that Paul claims his previous self and world *came to an end* because of it, and a whole new person and world was brought into being: "I have been crucified with Messiah; and it is no longer I who live, but it is Messiah who lives in me" (Gal 2:19-20). And later in the letter, "May I never boast of anything except the cross of our Lord Jesus Messiah, by which the world [*kosmos*] has been crucified to me, and I to the world [*kosmos*]. For neither circumcision [being Judean] nor uncircumcision [being Gentile] is anything; but a *new creation* is everything" (Gal 6:14-15). World destroying and creating anew are the *apocalyptic work of God*.

Paul makes another apocalyptic declaration in 2 Corinthians 5:14-17. "We are convinced," he writes, "that one has died for all; therefore all have died" (2 Cor 5:14). In other words, the whole of sinful humanity has been drawn by God into the death of Messiah and *put to death there*. Paul's thought here is apocalyptic in two respects. First, to assert that all humankind is already *dead* in Messiah runs radically against the grain of our ordinary human perception: we see people alive all around us, not appearing dead at all. Thus Paul's assertion must necessarily be an apocalypse, that is, an astonishing revelation of something *alongside yet beyond* our ordinary physical vision. The people we see alive around us are in fact dead in Christ.

Second, to assert that "one has died for all, therefore all have died" is to perceive *a radically altered reality* in which nothing remains the same. As in

Galatians, Paul calls this the new creation: "if anyone is in Messiah, there is a new creation" (2 Cor 5:17). The arrival of new creation in Messiah is God's act—God bringing the old world to an end and beginning something new—*the apocalypse* in real time! Paul does not call us simply to believe in the new creation as something we can dream about and wish for, something that might arrive sometime in the future. He calls us actually *to live now* in this astonishingly new reality, brought into being through the apocalyptic death and resurrection of Messiah, in which nothing remains the same:

> And [Messiah] died for all, so that those who live might live no longer for themselves, but for the one who died and was raised for them. From now on, therefore, we regard no one according to our old perception. . . . So if anyone is in Messiah there is new creation: everything old has passed away; behold, *everything has become new!* All this is *from God.* (2 Cor 5:15-18)

An apocalypse indeed.[9]

So when Paul announces in Romans 1:16-17 the theme of the whole letter—the good news of the justice of God—he declares that this good news is "apocalypsed" (Greek *apokalyptetai*). The good news is both the *revelation* and the *reality* of what God *does* to bring about justice in the world (see Rom 3:21, "But now . . . the justice of God has been disclosed . . . , the justice of God through the faith of Jesus Messiah").[10] The good news is also simultaneously the revelation and reality of God's judgment on idolatry and injustice (Rom 1:18, "For the wrath of God is apocalypsed [*apokalyptetai*] from heaven against all ungodliness and injustice"). The whole of Romans is written in the aftershock of the apocalypse of God's coming in Jesus Messiah, which powerfully brings about God's own justice in the world and, in that very act, exposes and undermines regimes of human injustice.

But we are getting ahead of ourselves. I will return to those themes in the following chapters. For now, I have made the point that Paul's vision of God's act in Jesus Messiah in relation to all humanity and the whole world is a divine apocalyptic act. The good news is not (only) that God is stirring up

---

[9]The scholar most responsible in recent years for increasing our awareness of the apocalyptic character of Paul is J. Louis Martyn; see especially his *Theological Issues in the Letters of Paul* (Nashville: Abingdon, 1997).

[10]In Rom 3:21 Paul uses another Greek word, *pephanerōtai*, translated as "disclosed," but with essentially the same meaning as "apocalypsed."

new theological thoughts about him or spiritual feelings toward him. The good news is much more: God is actually *creating* a new justice, new relationships, a new humanity, and a new world order. To keep this point before us in the coming pages I will therefore frequently use the words *apocalypse* (as a noun and a verb) and *apocalyptic*.

Messianic. Once we have it firmly in our mind that the Greek word *christos* means "messiah," it is easy to see that Paul's thinking is messianic through and through. He cannot say enough about Jesus *Messiah, Messiah Jesus*. Jesus Messiah *is* God's apocalypse, God's own arrival and presence, God in truth and in person. God's very own reality, power, and mission in the world hinge on Jesus Messiah. But when I use the word *messianic*—an adjective—I intend to point to something quite specific, that is, to the particular manner in which Jesus of Nazareth enacted his messiahship as a truly human being. We have already seen that the four Gospels, each in its own way, show us in considerable detail how Jesus "does" messiah in his life, from his birth and baptism to his crucifixion and resurrection. We come to know the meaning of *messianic* as a *form of life* by attending to the kind of messianic life that the actual Messiah lived and called his disciples to live. In the Gospels this is what is meant by *following* Jesus; it means to live in a manner that reflects the *way* set forth in the teachings and the very life of Jesus himself.

Paul does not provide us with many details of Jesus' life—hardly any, in fact. But this does not prevent him from returning again and again to one fundamental event in that life, the crucifixion. It is the event in which the core meaning of *messianic* is to be learned and lived. This is explicit in Philippians 2:1-11. Paul begins by calling the Philippians to a life together characterized by unity of mind and purpose, and humility toward one another (Phil 2:2-3). "Let each of you look not to your own interests, but to the interests of others," he writes in Philippians 2:4. Then, to make clear what he means and why this kind of life is to be lived among them, he calls them to share in the mind of the Messiah. This messianic mind is not only a new way of thinking; it is the whole form and pattern of life that the Messiah himself took up and lived out, from his incarnation to his crucifixion: he

emptied himself,
   taking the form of a slave,
   being born in human likeness.

And being found in human form,
    he humbled himself
    and became obedient to the point of death—
    even death on a cross. (Phil 2:7-8 NRSV)

This is the *messianic way* because it is *the way of the Messiah himself*: self-emptying, truly human, giving himself to and serving others, humble, obedient to death, even the unjust and shameful death of an alleged insurgent (Paul emphasizes Jesus' shameful death "on a cross"). When we hear further that this same Messiah was exalted, given the name above every name—that is, he actually receives the name of God—and is worshiped by every human being "in heaven and on the earth and under the earth," this is *because* he took the way of life that he did. "*Therefore* God also highly exalted him" (Phil 2:9). For the Messiah *himself* took no path to exaltation except through humble service, obedience, suffering, and death. This truth is basic for Paul; it is the bedrock of all of his instruction *to us* about what it means to live in Messiah, not only in Philippians but in every letter he writes. Certainly in Romans, as we shall soon see. The way of Jesus is what I mean by *messianic*.[11]

For this reason I will also usually refer to those who are "in Messiah," follow the Messiah, and have the mind of the Messiah as *messianics*. It is another way of saying "Christians," but obviously a bit strange and unfamiliar. That is just the point. We are inclined to think that "Christians" are those who identify with and practice the "religion" of Christianity. That may be acceptable in our ordinary discourse. But what I aim to accomplish by the strange word *messianics* is to liberate readers of Paul for the time being from that meaning. I wish to draw the meaning of *Christian* as close as possible to the reality and pattern of Jesus Messiah, which is what I think Paul does.

So then, *apocalyptic* indicates *God's action* in bringing an end to the old world and bringing about the new creation through the incarnation, death, and resurrection of Jesus Messiah. And *messianic* indicates *human action*, first and normatively the act of Jesus the Messiah as the truly human being

---

[11]My understanding of the meaning of *messianic* is deeply informed by the works of John Howard Yoder, especially *Politics of Jesus*. For the meaning of *messianic* in Paul and Romans, the (difficult) philosophical reading of Romans by Giorgio Agamben, *The Time That Remains: A Commentary on the Letter to the Romans* (Stanford, CA: Stanford University Press, 2005), has been influential, as also L. L. Welborn, *Paul's Summons to Messianic Life: Political Theology and the Coming Awakening* (New York: Columbia University Press, 2015).

and king, and then our own action as it is conformed to the life, death, and resurrection of the Messiah. What all of that means in detail will be explored as we make our way through Romans.

Making Our Way

What follows in the coming chapters amounts mostly to a *continuous reading* of the text of Romans. In other words, I will more or less follow the order of the text as Paul wrote it. However, this is not a commentary on Romans in any detailed sense. Romans is an immensely dense and rich letter. It takes a very large commentary to plumb its depths, and many such commentaries have been written throughout the centuries.[12] Unlike many of those works, I will not pause over and discuss all the words, phrases, sentences, and paragraphs of the letter, as commentaries usually do. My overall purpose is to show that Romans is a letter deeply concerned with justice and to explain what justice means according to the good news that Paul proclaims. I will show how the various sections of the letter contribute to that overarching theme. I will pass over some portions and themes of the letter with very little comment, while I will spend a good deal more time on others. And while I will roughly follow the order of the text, there will be some exceptions in order to make Paul's arguments clearer.

Further, because this book is not a comprehensive commentary in any sense, I do not aim to assert that justice is *the only thing* that Romans is about—far from it! Nor is it my intent to suggest that now we can simply dispense with the theme of righteousness and what it has come to mean for interpreters of Romans—far from it! I offer a reading of Romans, which means that I flow fairly fluidly between Paul's time and our own around matters that I believe are as significant today as they were in the first century. I simply make the humble but insistent plea that we *give Romans a serious hearing on the theme of justice* because on the one hand it is there in Romans, and on the other hand the church and the world so desperately need to hear Paul's word on this, now.

---

[12]In Suggestions for Further Reading at the end of this book, I provide the reader with suggestions of helpful works on Romans, including some commentaries.

Part 1

APOCALYPTIC
JUSTICE

2

APOCALYPSE OF JUSTICE

PAUL LAUNCHES THE LETTER to the Romans by declaring "the good news of God" (Rom 1:1) in three ways: (1) in the greeting (Rom 1:1-15), (2) in a highly condensed thematic statement (Rom 1:16-17), and (3) in an expanded statement about the death of the Messiah (Rom 3:21-26). There is a large chunk of material (Rom 1:18–3:20) between the second and third declarations of the good news that may seem like a lot of bad news. But it is not. When we come to that section in our next chapter I will show how it is another facet of the good news. But in order to make that clear then, I must first show how *everything* within Romans 1:1–3:26 is framed by and manifests Paul's declaration of the good news of God.

God, the Sovereign Messiah, and the Nations (Romans 1:1-15)

In his greeting Paul immediately addresses a fundamental question about justice: What is its foundation? Where does it come from? Paul answers the question by declaring the reality of God. *Justice is founded in God—the God of the gospel.* The world into which Paul announced the good news knew no shortage of gods, lesser and greater, who influenced every sphere of life from the household to the workshop, from the grain field to the battlefield, from the city to the empire. Greek and Roman cultures allowed for a wide plurality of complementary, competing, and even conflicting theological convictions, ritual practices, and philosophies, so long as the supreme authority of Roman rule was not challenged or compromised. But in this context Paul is utterly specific—indeed, exclusive—about what he means by *God*. Paul has been "set apart" for the very purpose to declare the reality, identity, and sovereignty of God the Father, God's Son Jesus Messiah, and God's Holy Spirit. This alone is

> the good news of God, which he [God] promised beforehand through the prophets in the holy writings, concerning his Son, who came from the seed of David according to the flesh, and was designated Son of God in power according to the Spirit of holiness by resurrection from the dead—Jesus Messiah our sovereign ruler [*kyrios*], through whom we received grace and apostleship to bring about loyal obedience among all the nations [*ethnē*] for the sake of his name, among whom you also are the called ones of Jesus Messiah. (Rom 1:1-6)

The question of God—the question of divine reality, identity, and sovereignty—is critical in this letter to *Rome*. Rome was the center of the world of nations in Paul's time, the imperial seat of world power and authority, established and blessed (so it was believed) by the gods who favored Rome. From Rome the caesars—the sons of the gods—for generations had exercised their sovereign power, benefaction, and justice over the peoples of the earth (often by conquest), and by their own accounts had thereby blessed the whole world with salvation, grace, and peace from the gods. *Rome was the good news!* The citizens and peoples of the empire owed their devotion, gratitude, loyalty, and obedience to glorious Rome, to its gods, and to its caesars.

How does Paul's announcement of good news stack up against this? By all appearances—that is, according to the normal perception of the man on the street or the man on the throne in Rome—a certain obvious theopolitical order was in place. To proclaim good news in Rome of a god or a son of god or a lord worthy of "loyal obedience" from the nations would have evoked thoughts of the existing Roman divine and political order. Yet Paul's greeting announces something else altogether, something *not available to normal perception*, unlike the obvious and all-pervasive political regime already in place—a new world order coming from God as life and Spirit. Paul announces that the God of Israel, according to the promise of Israel's prophets and Scriptures, has declared Messiah Jesus, the long-promised royal seed of David, to be Son of God, powerfully raised from the dead by the divine Spirit. On *him* God has bestowed supreme sovereignty over all nations. Through this royal Messiah God is establishing a new reign of sovereignty among all peoples, effective immediately.

Despite its invisibility, Paul does not say wistfully about this new world order, "What if?" or "Wouldn't it be nice?" or "Maybe someday." He declares that this new theo-political reality is now apocalypsed; its reality is not only revealed but also already powerfully present and active by Jesus' resurrection from the dead and exaltation to universal kingship. Although invisible according to the usual criteria for discerning political sovereignty, the sovereign reign of the risen Messiah is *surpassingly real* for Paul—so much so that, in Paul's opening declaration of divine reality and sovereignty, Rome's "divine right" to rule over all peoples—Rome's glory—is completely eclipsed. It has disappeared from view.

> What right, sovereignty, glory, and blessing does your nation claim for itself? If you accept the right, sovereignty, and glory of God and Jesus Messiah over all nations, unmediated by the current political authorities, how does that reflect on and qualify your nation's claims on these things? How does it qualify your own loyalty to your nation?

In the new world order revealed in the gospel, is there any part for imperial Rome to play? Perhaps. But it will not be on its own terms. Paul's mission is to call *all peoples of the earth* to give loyal obedience to the one Sovereign, Jesus Messiah. Rome is not the good news; instead, it must hear and believe an *other* good news. Paul makes this clear in Romans 1:13-15:

> I want you to know, brothers and sisters, that I have often intended to come to you [in Rome] (though I have thus far been prevented), in order that I may do fruitful work *among you* as I have *among the rest of the nations* [*ethnē*]. I owe myself both to Greeks and to barbarians, both to the wise and to the foolish—so when I am able, I am eager to proclaim the good news *to you also who are in Rome.*

The good news even for proud Rome is Jesus Messiah. There is a great political-cultural leveling going on here. Romans—so much in the habit of boasting about their divine destiny of dominion over all nations—are instead graciously called to see themselves as just one people "among the rest of the nations" (that is, among "Greeks" and "barbarians" and Judeans, among wise and foolish peoples, whoever they may be). They also are called to hear the good news, to turn to God from idols, to acknowledge Messiah's divinely appointed sovereignty, and to *bow their knee before this Sovereign in trust, loyalty, and obedience* (compare Phil 2:9-11). Even for Rome this is the only path to true glory.

Everything that follows in the letter to the Romans must be seen in the context of what is written in these first few sentences. The *vision of justice* among the nations which Paul declares is founded in the singular reality of the living and true God the Father, his Son Jesus Messiah the Sovereign, raised from the dead, and his life-giving Spirit of holiness. In other words, *the reality of justice is rooted in the reality of the Holy Trinity.*[1] All justice in heaven and on earth, among the nations, between groups and persons, in the church and in human hearts, is grounded in *this* God and his appointed Sovereign Jesus. The apocalypse of the God of the gospel is the revelation of true justice.

Declaring Justice (Romans 1:16-17)

A treatise on justice (if that's how we want to think of Romans) requires something like a thesis statement. Paul provides this in Romans 1:16-17: "For I am not ashamed of the good news; it is the power of God for salvation to everyone who believes, to the Judean first and also to the Greek. For in [the good news] the justice of God is apocalypsed from faith to faith; as it is written, 'The just one will live from faith.'" This thesis is terse and enigmatic. Its precise meaning is a bit obscure. It might be helpful to think of this text as a rough diamond whose brilliance only becomes evident when it is cut and polished and then its light refracted in the rest of the letter. Still, before we move on it is worthwhile to note some facets of the astonishing claims Paul makes here.

---

[1]On the reasons for and importance of understanding Paul as a trinitarian theologian, see Wesley Hill, *Paul and the Trinity: Persons, Relations, and the Pauline Letters* (Grand Rapids, MI: Eerdmans, 2015).

First, we might wonder why Paul declares emphatically that he is not ashamed of the good news. What's to be ashamed of? we might ask. This question arises easily for us who live on this end of many centuries of Christendom, those centuries (roughly the fourth to the nineteenth) in which the Christian religion ruled hearts, minds, philosophies, cultures, societies, and even political regimes and nations throughout the Western (and a good portion of the Eastern) world. Christianity won! No shame in that!

Now, we might rightly ask what "won" and "no shame" in those assertions might mean—in fact, the whole letter will challenge us to do so. But for now we must move back behind the centuries of dominant Christendom and see the situation from Paul's perspective. It was very different. Three comprehensive visions ruled the day. In Paul's time the Romans, Greeks, and Judeans each had their own form of glory to boast about:[2]

- There was the *glorious history of Roman rule* expanding throughout the entire Mediterranean world and beyond, sovereign over many subject peoples (including the Judeans) and bringing (at least in Rome's estimation) justice, law, political stability, technology, infrastructure, peace, and well-being to all peoples under its sway (Rome called it "Peace and Security," as Paul notes in 1 Thess 5:3, quoting a Roman slogan).

- There was the *glorious tradition of Greek philosophical wisdom*, stretching from well before Plato and Aristotle right up to the lively Stoicism of Paul's time, setting the terms for all serious intellectual reflection on reality and truth.

- Among Paul's own Judeans, there was the *glorious law of Moses*, given to Israel in ancient times from God himself, providing instructions, principles, and practices that aligned everyday Judean life with the very grain of God's created universe.

Three worlds, three glories, three reasons for boasting.

What do you consider especially glorious about your own people or nation and its traditions, institutions, values, and achievements? What is worth boasting about?

---

[2]An in-depth discussion of the glories of Israel, Greece, and Rome is provided by N. T. Wright, *Paul and the Faithfulness of God* (Minneapolis: Fortress, 2013), 1:75-347.

In the midst of all this obvious glory, what does Paul have to offer? Only Jesus, a misfit Judean prophet who suffered *shameful* public torture and execution at the hands of the Romans—an execution so shameful it was not allowed for Roman citizens. No power or glory here. Crucifixions in public (sometimes en masse along major highways) were Rome's brutal billboards, advertising Roman right to rule all peoples, and Roman justice on any who would threaten that right.

Nevertheless, Paul is clear: the crucified Messiah is the very content of the *good news*:

I decided to know nothing among you except Jesus Messiah, and him crucified. (1 Cor 2:2)

It was before your eyes that Jesus Messiah was publicly exhibited [in my preaching] as crucified. (Gal 3:1)

Judeans demand signs [of divine power] and Greeks desire [philosophical] wisdom, but we proclaim Messiah crucified, a stumbling block to Judeans and foolishness to the nations. (1 Cor 1:22-23)

In other words, Paul proclaimed shame! In the eyes of any respectable Roman, Greek, or Judean, Paul ought to be ashamed. As far as glory goes, there is nothing to see here.

Yet Paul is not ashamed. Self-evident power and glory are not his standard. The shameful news of the crucified One raised from the dead exposes other glories as weak, foolish, and impoverished; insubstantial, fading, and passing away. The proclamation of the shameful cross as "the power of God for salvation" immediately liberates us from *visions of self-evident power and glory*, visions that bedazzle and entice especially the well-placed and smart and powerful of this world—"the rulers of this age" who "crucified the Lord of glory" (1 Cor 2:8). Paul is not ashamed of the *shamefulness, hiddenness, and weakness* of God's glory, wisdom, and power apocalypsed on the cross (1 Cor 2:7). Those who are in love with the usual standards of glory are perishing, Paul writes in 1 Corinthians 1:18. But those captivated by the inglorious message of the crucified One—who believe it and are not ashamed—are being saved. They are saved, that is, from the systems and standards of self-evident glory that shame the weak and lowly and poor, and blind the eyes of the "glorious" to the way God is accomplishing his "inglorious" work of justice in the world. This news of justice is more likely to be heard as *good news* by the outcast, the shamed, and the forgotten of the world, the kind of people drawn by the gospel from the streets of Rome and gathered together to hear Paul's letter read in their assembly.

We may also be puzzled by Paul's phrase "to the Judean first and also to the Greek" (Rom 1:16). I will have more to say on this later, but for now I note that Paul always assumes and never loses sight of the fact that Israel is God's chosen people and continues to play a crucial role in the apocalypse of God's justice among the nations. Israel-Judea, small and on the margins of the empire, nevertheless has a definite priority in God's purpose ("the Judean first"), a priority established not in Israel's historical achievements but in God's gracious election of this people. Paul anticipates this theme here and in Romans 3:1-2, but it becomes central and crucial in Romans 9–11, where he returns to the question of God's ongoing purpose for Israel in revealing God's justice among the nations. But since he mostly defers the discussion of Israel's priority until those chapters, I will too.

What comes to mind when you read the phrase "the power of God for salvation"? What do you think *power* and *salvation* mean?

Important for now is the phrase "the power of God for salvation." *Dynamis* is the Greek word for power here. Paraphrasing Paul—and taking out any connotations of violence—we might say that God's salvation explodes like dynamite on the world. The gospel according to Paul is not an offer but a power. When Paul announces the good news, he declares what has *already* happened and is happening—news of God resurrecting and exalting God's *Son* by God's powerful *Spirit* of holiness. God reigning and moving in the world by the Son and Spirit is not bound by the past or present, or by human decisions for or against it. Through Paul's proclamation the dynamite of resurrection and new creation is effective and active, claiming all nations, nullifying old regimes of power, creating faithful and obedient subjects, and bringing into being new theo-political assemblies of the Spirit. God's salvation goes far beyond individual souls "going to heaven." Ultimately, as we will see in Romans 8, God's saving power will resurrect all creation to its promised glorious fulfilment along with the *bodies* of the redeemed. God's redemption, restoration, and renewal—God's justice—begins with Messiah's resurrection and reaches out beyond individual persons to all Israel, all nations, and the breadth and depth of all creation.

> When you hear the phrase "the justice of God," what thoughts most immediately come to mind? What does the justice of God look like to you on the ground, in real life? Does the phrase sound threatening? Promising? How does your life situation (rich, poor, powerful, weak, at the center, on the margins) shape how you receive the phrase?

Salvation is God's work of justice. In the good news "the justice [*dikaiosynē*] of God is apocalypsed" (Rom 1:17). In this sentence Paul echoes the declarations of Psalm 98:1-2 (Ps 97:1-2 in the Septuagint, from which I quote): "Sing to the Lord a new song; for the Lord has done wonderful deeds: his right hand and his holy arm have wrought salvation for him. The Lord has made known his *salvation*; he has *revealed* [*apekalypsen*] his *justice* [*dikaiosynēn*] in the sight of the *nations* [*ethnōn*]." We might even imagine the whole of Romans as a commentary on this text. As the psalm declares and Paul reiterates, justice is not something in addition to God's saving power; it is the very quality, form, and content of that saving power. The *saving* God is the *just* God who reveals *justice* among the nations, who *makes right what is wrong*. That is what it means for God to save. This God, this justice, Paul says, is apocalypsed in the good news.

Two things must be said here. First, the justice of which Paul speaks here and throughout the letter is not an idea that might be derived from nature, culture, human sovereignty, or legal tradition. Like the psalmist, Paul is radical on this point: justice is first in God himself and comes from God; in giving justice God *is utterly true to his own nature, character, and word*. If we carry on in Psalm 98 (97) we read: "[God] has *remembered his mercy* to Jacob, and *his truth* to the house of Israel" (Ps 98:3 [97:3]). God is the original, eternal, and faithful fount of justice. In revealing his justice, God remembers what is his, his own mercy and truth.

Second, the purpose of the proclamation of the good news is to *bring about* justice, because the good news *is the power of God* working salvation. Gospel justice is not an eternal principle that needs to be apprehended and "applied" to real life, nor is it a distant ideal or goal that needs to be incrementally attained. Justice is what God *did* in the world in the death and resurrection of Jesus Messiah; it is what God is *now doing* in the world by the Holy Spirit when the good news is proclaimed, believed, and practiced; it is the work God *will do* when he comes to judge Israel, the nations, and every person through Jesus Messiah.

God's justice, Paul goes on to say, is apocalypsed "from faith to [for] faith" (Rom 1:17). Paul now joins the thought of God accomplishing justice for Israel and the nations intimately to the thought of faith, faithfulness, or trust (the Greek word *pistis*, "faith," may mean any of these things, as well as loyalty, allegiance, or fidelity). He finds a brief quotation from the prophet Habakkuk (Hab 2:4) that brings the words *just, faith/faithfulness/trust*, and *live* right together: "The just one will live from/by faith." Who is the just one? Whose faithfulness, faith, or trust is being spoken of? Paul hints here at several meanings, which he develops later in the letter:

- The just one is Jesus the sovereign Messiah, who was faithful and whom God raised from the dead by the Spirit to rule the nations.

- The just one is Abraham, whom God considered just and even in a sense resurrected to life when Abraham believed and trusted God; just ones are those who trust God as Abraham did.

- The faithful one is God, who, by raising Jesus from the dead, evokes faith/trust from those who hear and believe the good news and thereby become just.

- The faithful one is Jesus, who lived a faithful, obedient, and just life— that is, the truly human life—and now communicates that life to all who believe the good news; the faithfulness of Jesus generates the faithful life of those who believe the good news.

- The faithful one is Abraham and all those who, like him, trust God's promise of life rather than their own power of life.

These hints of multiple meanings—there may be more—are still dense and compact. It is as if at this point Paul simply wants to pile all his key terms on the table—*gospel, power* of God, *salvation, faith/faithfulness/trust, Judean* and *Greek, justice* of God, *apocalypse, life*—and then pick them up later, one or two at a time, for further reflection. We will follow his lead. But here we should take note of something strange about the "justice of God," which is the good news. The strangeness has to do with what is *not* said. Nothing is said about justice as promulgating, enforcing or obeying laws, or as punishment or reward, or as equity or fairness, or as what we should struggle for. These usual ways of thinking about justice are not on this table. In Paul's declaration of the good news in Romans 1:16-17 justice happens in the eventful circle of *God's power, divine and human faithfulness, and human faith or trust.* This is the circle of gospel justice. What kind of justice could this be?

> Suppose you were given—out of the blue, as it were—the three words *salvation, justice,* and *faith/trust* and asked to make sense of them together. What would you say about them in two or three sentences?

The Apocalypse of Justice (Romans 3:21-26)

After a lengthy intervening section (Rom 1:18–3:20) dealing with gods, systems, cultures, and law Paul returns in Romans 3:21-26 to some key themes of his thesis statement—revelation, justice as God's saving power, and faith/faithfulness/trust. In the dense statement of Romans 1:16-17 Paul did not directly name Jesus Messiah. In Romans 3:21-26 he names Jesus explicitly and places him in the center of the picture of God's saving justice. All the themes of the eventful circle of justice (as I called it above) come together in one act, one event, one person.

But why should we jump from Romans 1:16-17 to Romans 3:21-26? A long-standing habit of reading Romans 1:18–3:20 suggests that Paul does not arrive at the good news of God's justice in Jesus Messiah without wading through all the bad news first. If he shows us—empirically, we might say—how desperate things really are, perhaps we will be ready to hear good news. What I want to show by treating Romans 3:21-26 right up against Romans 1:1-15 and Romans 1:16-17 is that Paul's long discussion in the section in between (Rom 1:18–3:20) is in fact *framed* by strong declarations of the good news of God's justice and only makes sense within that frame. The good news is not first declared in Romans 3:21-26 after all the bad news.

The good news is already declared—robustly so—right up front in Romans 1:1-17. Paul's account of God's justice does not begin at Romans 1:18. It begins in the first verse of the letter.

If you want to see evidence of justice being done, where are you inclined to look first (institutions, authorities, laws, etc.)? What does justice look like to you on the ground?

"But now, apart from law, the justice of God has been manifested, being [nevertheless] attested by the law and the prophets" (Rom 3:21). Paul declares that the one God of all peoples now manifests his justice "apart from law." Not law, but the triune God, is the foundation of justice. But how does justice become *visible* "apart from law"? Human rulers, lawmakers, and laws render justice concrete, visible, and doable. Law provides standards and measures for discerning and doing justice. Yet Paul turns our attention away from law to the place where God himself makes justice visible. *God manifests his justice in the death of Jesus Messiah.* It is a strange claim. As we saw above, crucifixion makes it even a shame-worthy claim—except that Paul is not ashamed. Romans 3:21-26 emphatically asserts that the death of the Messiah is the one place where God's justice is genuinely, publicly visible: it "has been manifested" (Rom 3:21); it is "witnessed by the law and the prophets"; God "displayed" (Rom 3:25) Messiah's death as atonement; Messiah's death was a "public proof/demonstration" (Rom 3:25-26) of God's justice and God's making just those who share in the faithful Messiah's death. So somehow Messiah's death is where we are to *see* God's justice.

How Jesus' death is God's salvation and justice is hardly self-evident—a point Paul himself recognizes. For when Roman gods and caesars declared their power to save and to establish justice and peace, there were visible results—measurable outcomes: territories were conquered and claimed, peoples were subdued and brought into Rome's service, rebellions were squashed and insurgents executed, laws were promulgated and enforced, taxes were imposed and collected, and cities, roads, and viaducts were planned and constructed. Things got done in ways that all could see. By contrast, gospel justice must be *believed* in order to be seen; "the justice of

God through the faithfulness of Jesus Messiah [has been manifested] to all who *believe*" (Rom 3:22). To help us believe and see, Paul turns to the Old Testament, for this divine justice is "witnessed by the law and the prophets." He demonstrates with two words from the Old Testament—*redemption* and *mercy seat*—that God reveals his justice as sovereign grace and mercy for all in the death of the Messiah.

First, God manifests and demonstrates and proves his justice in Messiah's death as "redemption" or "deliverance" (Rom 3:24). In Romans 3:21-26 God is the active subject of the verbs. Justice is God's redeeming or liberating power. In the biblical sense the primary meaning of redemption goes back to God's deliverance of Israel from Egypt, when God displayed his supremacy and victory over the human and cosmic powers that held Israel in slavery, and delivered Israel into the freedom of service to God. Israel could not deliver itself; only God's power could. "Israel saw the great work that the LORD did. . . . So the people feared the LORD and believed in the LORD" (Ex 14:13-14, 30-31 NRSV). Redemption means God *delivering from bondage into freedom.*

Bondage to enslaving powers (Sin and Death, as we will see) keeps both Israel and the nations from attaining "the glory of God"—their true destiny (Rom 3:23). The glory of God is not an abstraction. Elsewhere (in 2 Cor 4:3-6) Paul writes of "the glory of Messiah, who is the image of God," and of "the glory of God in the face of Jesus Messiah." Jesus Messiah is the glory of God; he himself is the destiny toward which all peoples are called, yet fail to attain. When God redeems, God brings all—Judean and Gentile alike—out of bondage to Sin and into the glorious reality of Messiah, who is God's justice revealed. In this way "God prove[s] publicly that he is just and that he makes just those who share the faithfulness of Jesus" (Rom 3:26).

The Greek phrase in Romans 3:22, 26, regularly translated as "through faith in Jesus Christ," is familiar to many readers of this text. But there is a growing number of scholars who argue that it should be translated "through the faith (or faithfulness) of Jesus Christ" (also recognized in the notes on these verses in the NRSV). I follow that translation. What difference do these two translations make for how you think of this text?

Second, Paul introduces another (difficult and controversial) Greek term, *hilasterion*: "[All] are now made just as a gift of grace through deliverance in Jesus Messiah, whom God put forward as a *hilasterion* through the faithfulness [shown] in his blood, to be a public proof of justice" (Rom 3:24-25). The Greek word *hilasterion* is often translated with abstract concepts such as "propitiation," "expiation," or "sacrifice of atonement."[3] Those translations are not all wrong, although understanding them properly is important, and propitiation is the least satisfactory. What might *hilasterion* mean? Paul declares that God's justice is made manifest "apart from law"; but (as with "redemption") he says it is "witnessed by the law and the prophets" (Rom 3:21). In other words, Israel's Scriptures attest to God's justice by providing the term *hilasterion*.[4]

In the Septuagint, *hilasterion* (in Exodus and Leviticus) refers to the mercy seat, the gold lid of the ark of the covenant on which the blood of a sacrificed animal was sprinkled in order to purify the tabernacle, the priests, and the congregation of Israel (see especially Lev 16:15-22). It does not refer either to the sacrificed animal or to the altar of sacrifice. Concretely, it designates the *lid of the ark* as *the place* where something of critical importance happens. Darrin Belousak identifies three aspects of what happens on the mercy seat. First, it is the place of God's holy presence. In Leviticus 16:2 God says to Moses, "I will appear in the cloud upon the mercy seat." Second, it is the place from which God speaks his divine word and commandment to Moses for the people of Israel (see Num 7:89). Third, Belousak writes (referring to Lev 16:15-16), it is "the place where God (represented by the priest) cleanses the sanctuary and reconciles the people on account of their transgressions."[5]

What does it mean when Paul, drawing from the books of Moses, says that God displays Jesus Messiah as the *hilasterion*, the mercy seat? Belousak sums it up this way:

---

[3]The meaning of *hilasterion* is discussed in numerous articles, books, and commentaries. See Judith Gundry-Volf, "Expiation, Propitiation, Mercy Seat," in *Dictionary of Paul and His Letters*, ed. Gerald Hawthorne, Ralph Martin, and Daniel Reid (Downers Grove, IL: InterVarsity Press, 1993), 279-84. See also Darrin W. Snyder Belousak, *Atonement, Justice, and Peace: The Message of the Cross and the Mission of the Church* (Grand Rapids, MI: Eerdmans, 2012), 244-64; Fleming Rutledge, *The Crucifixion: Understanding the Death of Jesus Christ* (Grand Rapids, MI: Eerdmans, 2015), 278-82.

[4]See Gundry-Volf, "Expiation, Propitiation, Mercy Seat," 280, for a list of Old Testament texts in which *hilasterion* and cognate words appear.

[5]Belousak, *Atonement, Justice, and Peace*, 257.

First, Jesus is God's holy presence among the people, the place of meeting with God. Second, Jesus is God's anointed prophet through whom God speaks, the place where the people hear God's word. Third, Jesus is God's appointed priest through whom God exercises power to cleanse his people from sin, the place where God purges pollution from his holy presence caused by his people's sins. God thus presents Jesus to the world, Paul is saying, as the one in whom we meet the holy God "face-to-face," from whom we hear God's word, and through whom our sins are cleansed.[6]

In other words, God arrives in Jesus to give himself, to speak, to cleanse and reconcile *all*—Judean and Gentile—without distinction (Rom 3:22). Prior to the coming of Messiah God had patiently "passed over" the history of injustices previously committed (Rom 3:25). But "now by his grace as a gift" God comes among "all [who] sinned and fall short of God's glory" and displays his mercy in Messiah's faithful death. At this "mercy seat" God absorbs the history of injustice that bloodies the Messiah and graciously bestows his own living justice through Messiah, who is God's justice and glory. Paul puts this point starkly in 2 Corinthians 5:20-21: "We entreat you on behalf of Messiah, be reconciled to God. For our sake he made him to be sin who knew no sin, so that in him we might become the justice of God."

So then, God no longer merely passes over injustice; he destroys its enslaving power and bestows his own redeeming justice in Jesus the mercy seat. Jesus is the holy site of God's grace, redemption, and reconciliation in the midst of all peoples, the one through whom God generously gives his own justice as a gift and conforms those who believe to the shape of God's justice in Jesus. In Messiah's faithful death God makes his justice visible, speaks justice, does justice, and creates justice in us: "[God] did this as a public display of his own justice, because in God's forbearance he passed over the sins previously committed, so that in the now-time of fulfillment he might demonstrate that he himself is just, and that he creates justice in those who share in the faithful [death] of Jesus" (Rom 3:25-26). How do we discern and learn God's justice? We look to Jesus, the mercy seat.

---

[6]Belousak, *Atonement, Justice, and Peace*, 258.

For Paul the good news of justice is that God apocalypses justice—both reveals and enacts it—in the incarnation, life, death, resurrection, and exaltation of Jesus Messiah. How does this shift and shape how you think of justice now, in comparison to how you thought of it before you read this chapter?

3

JUSTICE BEYOND SYSTEMS

GOD APOCALYPSES JUSTICE IN JESUS MESSIAH, who is the glory of God against which "all fall short," the mercy seat by which all receive justice. This is the clue to understanding the long and difficult discussion we find in Romans 1:18–3:20. In this text Paul shines the light of the good news on the two comprehensive meaning-systems that constituted Paul's world: the Gentile-Roman system and the Judean system. Each of these systems aimed in some comprehensive way to (1) represent what there is, that is, to account for all existing things in their relationships (the Real); and (2) to embody and promote divine order in the world, to make the world a better place (the Good). The Romans, authorized and blessed by their gods, intended to establish the Roman reality among all nations, by conquest if necessary, in order to spread the blessings of their gods among the nations. The Judeans discerned reality in the Torah, revealed to them by God through Moses. For them Torah was much more than a set of numerous rules and regulations; Torah was the divine ordering principle of all things, the pattern by which God created and governed the cosmos. To live according to Torah was to be aligned with divine truth and goodness. Justice in the world was discerned through Torah.

Paul lifts up each of these systems, the Roman-Gentile and the Judean, to the light of the gospel for critical examination and finds them fundamentally —though differently—flawed, incapable of bringing about divine justice in the world.

Of course, from a Roman point of view the Judean Torah system was anything but a comprehensive vision of the Real. It amounted to the strange, even offensive, set of ideas, traditions, and customs of a minority people who dwelt in a small land on the fringes of the empire, and the few Judeans of the Diaspora who gathered in pockets in major cities of the empire and insisted on maintaining their odd customs and traditions. To Romans, Diaspora Judeans were tolerated (and sometimes despised) as obstinate foreigners who refused to assimilate to Roman-Gentile culture and society, that is, to live in the real world and be "normal." To Romans, the strange Judean minority-society hardly counted for much; it was certainly inferior to the great Roman civilization and perhaps even a marginal threat. The Judean law system was something to be contained and tolerated rather than celebrated.

Gentile-Roman society, including its religion, culture, law, and politics, dominated the world, both because it comprised the vast majority of the population and because the Romans ruled an expansive empire, which included Judea. From a Judean point of view, therefore, the Gentile-Roman cosmic-historical system—the Roman vision of the world and Rome's purpose and destiny in it—could be assessed as a single whole, without attention to the nuances and details that would differentiate the traditions and customs of, say, Athens in Greece on the one hand from those of Lyons in Gaul (France) on the other. From a Judean perspective, the whole of Gentile-Roman society was infected by an awful disease, the worship of false gods. All moral, social, and political problems among the Gentile nations were ultimately the fruit of their abhorrent "impiety" or idolatry. Judeans, by contrast, worshiped the one true God who had revealed his name—his divine reality—to them and given the gift of Torah as their comprehensive way of life. So even if the Judean reality system and social order represented only a small minority people, for them it was by far theologically and morally superior.

Roman Gentiles and Judeans tended to view each other with conde-scension and suspicion. This tendency in both groups threads its way as a theme throughout Romans. One of Paul's primary aims in the letter is to undermine that tendency. As we saw in the previous chapter, God's justice in Messiah utterly transcends the difference between Gentiles and Judeans, even as it continues to recognize that difference in some sense (a theme to which we return later). In Romans 1:18–3:20 Paul challenges the tendency to mutual condescension in another way. He shows that in the light of God's justice apocalypsed in Jesus Messiah neither the Roman-Gentile system nor the Judean system provides any basis for boasting and sneering over the other. Neither society as a whole lives up to the reality of God's justice in Messiah; both fall short of it. The gospel reveals that despite their claims to embody truth and justice more truly and gloriously than the other, each society is in fact captive in its own way under the regime of Sin.

> I just now wrote of the regime of Sin with an uppercase S. For Paul, while there are indeed "sins"—the misdeeds of persons—there is also Sin as a cosmic power or regime that rules over all humankind. In Romans 3:9 Paul writes of Judeans and the nations being under Sin. He will also write of being under Death and under Law as cosmic powers or regimes. What difference does it make to think of Sin as a cosmic regime, in addition to thinking simply of "sins"?

The Apocalypse of God's Wrath (Romans 1:18)

God's justice arrives as Jesus Messiah. But according to Paul, the apoca-lyptic good news of God's justice is *simultaneously* the apocalyptic good news of God's *wrath* against human idolatry and injustice. For in the *good news*, Paul writes, "the justice of God [*dikaiosynē theou*] is revealed [*apokalyptetai*]" (Rom 1:17); and "the wrath of God [*orgē theou*] is revealed [*apokalyptetai*]" (Rom 1:18).

The single event of Jesus Messiah is both the justice and the wrath of God. Paul writes, "The gospel is the *power* of God for salvation" (Rom 1:16). When the gospel invades the world, God's strange justice in Jesus reveals the truth about the social, cultural, and political systems of the nations. In the revealing light of the good news, not only do these systems fall short of justice; they are shown often to *foster* disorder, corruption, violence, and injustice. Their fruits are often not justice and life but oppression and death. The good news powerfully bursts into, breaks open, and lays bare the systems of ungodliness and injustice that hold humans in bondage and wreak havoc in history. The gospel arrives as judgment on the systems of this world *for the sake of justice and life*. We must see then that God's wrath is God's mercy; God's wrath *against* systems of idolatry and injustice is good news *for* those who are enslaved, downtrodden, and destroyed by them. God's wrath liberates! The apocalypse of Jesus Messiah is the arrival of God's justice, wrath, and mercy as a single liberating event.

Paul himself is a personal example of the unity of God's justice, wrath, and mercy. In Galatians he writes that the gospel simultaneously destroyed and recreated him: "I have been crucified with Messiah; I no longer live as what I was, but Messiah lives in me. The life I now live in the flesh I live by the faithfulness of the Son of God" (Gal 2:19-20). The life Paul once lived "as what he was" was his life formed within the context of Judaism and the law of Moses. But his life constituted simply in those terms (the justice system according to which Paul considered himself "blameless," Phil 3:6) could not withstand the apocalypse of God's Son to him (Gal 1:16). It was crucified. That was God's severe mercy. On the other side of crucifixion, Paul in the flesh—still the *Judean* Paul—was raised up by the power of resurrection life, the power of the Son of God in him. The *newly created* Judean Paul became Messiah's emissary to the Gentile nations. Later in Galatians Paul writes, "May I never boast of anything except in the cross of our Sovereign Jesus Messiah, through whom the world [*kosmos*] has been crucified to me, and I to the world" (Gal 6:14). Here not only Paul's own personal life but also the world—that is, *reality* as he understood it in terms of the Judean cosmic-historical system—was brought to an end, crucified in Messiah. Paul's world was mercifully destroyed by the good news so that on the other side of that destruction there might be "a new creation" (Gal 6:15). Likewise, the Real and the Good, as defined by Roman-Gentile and Judean cosmic-historical systems,

must be crucified in their encounter with the good news, and raised up
(fundamentally altered) into new creation.

> Reflect on the thought that Jesus Messiah is God's wrath against systems of idolatry and injustice. Do you agree with this? How would this affect your understanding of how God deals with systems of injustice?

Idolatry: The Systemic Captivity of Gentile Peoples (Romans 1:19-32)

It is important to understand that Paul's point in Romans 1:18–3:20 is not (as
often thought) to come to the conclusion that each and every individual
person is a depraved sinner and therefore condemned by God, "lost." In fact,
we will see in Romans 2:1-16 that Paul provides a nuanced account of good
and evil, justice and injustice, at the personal level. As I have already said,
Paul here is addressing the two *comprehensive reality systems* of his world,
the Roman-Gentile (Rom 1:18-32) and the Judean (Rom 2:17–3:20). When
he concludes in Romans 3:9 that all (*pantas*) are under Sin, he means the
collective all that is caught up under one or the other of two large-scale
systems, the Gentile-Roman idolatry system on the one hand and the Judean
Torah system on the other. Both of these systems (though in different ways)
were captured by and caught up into another uber-system—the system of
Sin. When Paul writes in Romans 3:19-20 that "every mouth" (*pan stoma*) is
silenced, that "all the world" (*pas ho kosmos*) is under judgment, and that
"none of all flesh" (*ou . . . pasa sarx*) is made just through Law, he is speaking
in *systemic* categories. The system of idol worship most certainly does not
generate a just society, but neither does the system of Torah, because both
systems are captive to an overruling system, the cosmic regime of Sin. Because of Sin both systems enslave; both systems create enemies; both systems
blind their subjects to God's justice in Jesus.

In significant respects Paul's apocalyptic critique of the Gentile system in
Romans 1:18-32 would be familiar Judean fare. When Paul writes, "For the
wrath of God is apocalypsed against all impiety [*asebeian*] and injustice
[*adikian*—note the *dik-* stem] of men who squash the truth under injustice"
(Rom 1:18), a Judean might think of the miserable condition of the Gentile

peoples, perhaps especially their immoral rulers and powerful elites. *Impiety* names the collective worship of false gods, which disorders Gentile societies from top to bottom. For example, a Jewish philosopher from about a century before Paul, writing under the name of King Solomon (his work is called the Wisdom of Solomon and is found in Bibles that include the Apocrypha and Pseudepigrapha), penned a lengthy criticism of the Gentile peoples that reads much like what we read in Romans 1:19-32 (although Paul is mercifully briefer).

The philosopher argues that the Gentile peoples (represented by the Egyptians) "were unable from the good things that are seen to know the one who exists, nor did they recognize the artisan while paying heed to his works." They failed in this way despite the fact that "from the greatness and beauty of created things comes a corresponding perception of their Creator." While the Gentiles might be "seeking God and desiring to find him," they are nevertheless "not . . . to be excused; for if they had the power to know so much that they could investigate the world [they were good scientists!], how did they fail to find sooner the Lord of these things?" (Wisdom 13:1-9 NRSV). Instead, they became idolaters. While the Gentile peoples honored the gods so that their societies might flourish, in the mind of the Judean philosopher such idolatry was instead "the beginning of fornication" and "the corruption of life," and led to all kinds of moral and social disorder, which the author lists at length (Wisdom 14:12-31 NRSV).

Had the Gentile peoples rightly followed where their investigative-scientific knowledge of the world should have led them, namely, to *know the Creator* and *the moral law*, they would have been saved from rampant idolatry, violence, and injustice. But that did not happen. Their idolatry and injustice are due to their ignorance, foolishness, and sheer willful denial of the obvious truth. God's judgment on them is inevitable and earned, "For equally hateful to God are the ungodly [*asebōn*] and their ungodliness [*asebeia*], for what was done will be punished together with the one who did it" (Wisdom 14:9-10 NRSV).

In some respects Paul agrees with the Judean philosopher. The Gentile peoples should have come to some knowledge of God. Paul says that God manifested his invisible reality to them (Rom 1:19) through the things God created. God gave signs of his divine reality through created things; but

God must not be thought to be one of them. The Gentiles should have at least discerned the *radical distinction* between the Creator and the creature—God's "eternal power and divine nature" (Rom 1:20). They might have known what God is not: God is *not* visible; he is *not* something made. For Paul, God is not simply much better than the gods, as the Judean philosopher argues (Wisdom 13:3); God is beyond comparison. Perhaps a kind of atheism about the gods might have honored God better than idolatry. Instead, the Gentile peoples attributed divine power and nature to visible creaturely things and things made by human hands. "They did not glorify God as God nor thank him; their reasoning became empty and irrational and their hearts became dark. Promoting themselves as wise, they nevertheless became foolish, and changed the glory of the immortal God into the image and likeness of mortal man and birds and quadrupeds and reptiles" (Rom 1:21-23). These imagined gods were made to serve human purposes and causes rather than the other way around, and were believed to be the divine ground and source of Gentile nations, societies, and political orders.

Unlike the Judean philosopher, however, Paul does not say that the "ungodly" are "equally hateful" to God as their "ungodliness." Paul makes a crucial distinction between the system and the person. For Paul, the "wrath of God" burns against *ungodliness (asebeia)*, not against the ungodly. In fact, we will see that God in Messiah comes precisely *to the ungodly* and dies for them. God is not intent on punishing the ungodly Gentile peoples but on delivering them from their bondage to systems of ungodliness and oppression. That is the justice of God.

But the story of the bondage of the Gentile nations is a complicated one. "Therefore God handed them over [*paredōken*]." Paul repeats this phrase three times in a few verses (Rom 1:24, 26, 28). The Greek verb *paredōken* ("handed over") speaks of a deliberate, intentional act of God, such as a judge would "hand over" a convicted criminal to a jailer for imprisonment.[1] In fact this is what happened, according to Paul. God handed the idolatrous nations over to the gods, whose power over the nations grew through their worship of the gods and through the work of those (rulers and priests) who

---

[1] An important and persuasive discussion of the phrase "God handed them over" is provided in Beverley Roberts Gaventa, *Our Mother Saint Paul* (Louisville, KY: Westminster John Knox, 2007), 113-23.

were deemed mediators of divine power. The nations, rather than being free agents, are subject to these malignant divine powers, which in turn shape their cultures, societies, and political orders. Paul describes in uncompromising terms some of the characteristic features of idolatrous societies: lust and the degradation of bodies, disordered sexual passions, darkened minds, social disorder, systemic injustice, violence, and evil (Rom 1:24-32). The problem is that the nations do not acknowledge their condition as enslaved and disordered but as worthy of emulation. As Paul says, "they not only do these things but even approve of others who practice them" (Rom 1:32).

One scholar, Neil Elliott, suggests that in Romans 1:18-32 Paul describes especially the works and ways of the elites who rule and represent the Gentile nations, in particular the imperial families of Rome, who were notorious for their arrogant, flagrant, and often brutal disregard of ordinary morality and justice—above the law and unaccountable. Do you think the impiety and injustice described in this text (especially Rom 1:28-32) applies more accurately to the powerful, wealthy, and famous elites of societies than to ordinary citizens?

For the Gentile peoples, their gods, rulers, and social, cultural, and political forms of life seem both natural and necessary, providing the conditions in which life can flourish, and they are therefore worth celebrating and promoting. But in the light of the gospel those conditions are revealed to be destructive effects of the powers to which the nations have given themselves in worship and obedience—those powers to which God has handed them over.

We must pause here for a few important comments. First, it may seem strange that Paul would say that the bondage of the Gentile nations to idols and injustice is not only the result of their refusal to honor God as God but also the result of God's own act of handing them over. But Paul is clear that it is not God who *makes* the Gentile peoples into idolaters; idolatry is their own act of exchanging the God-beyond-all for the gods of nature and culture (Rom 1:23, 25). Nevertheless, God turns the nations over into the custody of their self-generated gods. These gods attain actual spiritual and political power over human societies (if not real existence) and effectively become the heavenly wardens of the nations (see Gal 4:1-11). No doubt this is why Paul says in Romans 1:18 that "the wrath of God is revealed *from heaven*."

Whatever status the nations might give the gods and powers, the exalted Son of God nevertheless rules over them with divine authority. So Paul understands that even the subjection of the Gentile peoples under the imprisoning custody of the gods is a condition that God ultimately makes to serve the purpose of the gospel (as Paul will ultimately declare in Rom 11:30-32). The point here is that the Gentile nations, despite their idolatry and injustice, have not slipped away from God. Rather, God has handed them over until such time as he liberates them and claims them back, for they are never *not* ultimately his to have.

> How do you respond to the thrice-repeated phrase "God handed them over" (Rom 1:24, 26, 28)? What assumptions about societal and individual freedom are implicit in your response? How does Paul's phrase challenge those assumptions? What spiritual powers (if not gods, then ideals and ultimate values) move and direct your nation and society? How devoted are you to them? How free are you as an individual within the larger sociocultural systems in which you live to frame life differently?

Second, Paul's understanding of social, cultural, and political power is complex. For him, gods and lords, cosmic structures and principles, spiritual powers and authorities, earthly sovereigns, governments and institutions, social norms and pressures, and ordinary human beings with their hopes and desires are all woven together into a complex fabric of worldly reality—it is "this world" or "the present evil age," as Paul sometimes calls it. In texts such as Galatians 4:8-9; 1 Corinthians 2:6-8; 8:4-5; and Romans 8:38-39 Paul lists complex sets of cosmic principles and powers that may threaten to "separate us from the love of God in Christ Jesus our Lord" (Rom 8:39 NRSV). The nations, taken as collective ethnic-social-political entities, are "enslaved to beings that by nature are not gods" (Gal 4:8). Idolatry in the broadest sense names for Paul what in our time we might call a culture, worldview, or social imaginary, that is, the taken-for-granted understanding of "the way things are" in a society or nation. It includes all those ideals, values, institutions, norms, rules, habits, assumptions, agreements, and personal and social practices that make ordinary life possible and create a measure of identity and stability in and among the peoples of the world. There is not mere chaos and mayhem in pagan societies, and often a good deal of flourishing. A kind of *disordered order* pertains even in those systems of "ungodliness" that do not acknowledge the reign of the triune God and his Messiah Jesus.

When Paul says of the Gentile nations that "God handed them over," he is ultimately saying that God did so in some sense *providentially*. That is, God turned the nations over to disordered orders (the "gods")—God incarcerated the Gentile peoples—until such time as God would apocalypse his *true messianic order of liberation and justice*, the "new creation" that arrives in the death and resurrection of Jesus and the power of the Holy Spirit. Even so, in the worldly time that remains, "impiety and injustice" name the state of the nations in systemic captivity, until the good news of divine justice in Messiah invades, and God in his liberating wrath breaks the prison open. Then another reality becomes imaginable.

Good and Evil Among Ordinary Gentiles and Judeans (Romans 2:1-29)

Because the Gentile peoples fail to acknowledge God and continue to practice idolatry and injustice, the Judean philosopher of the Wisdom of Solomon condemns the nations and their people to the penalties of God's judgment. "But just penalties will overtake them on two counts: because they thought wrongly about God in devoting themselves to idols, and because in deceit they swore unrighteously through contempt for holiness" (Wisdom 14:30 NRSV). But the philosopher's own people, the Judeans, are exempt from such penalties. He writes: "But you, our God, are kind and true, patient, and ruling all things in mercy. For even if we [Judeans] sin we are yours, knowing your power; but we will not sin, because we know that you acknowledge us as yours. For to know you is complete righteousness, and to know your power is the root of immortality" (Wisdom 15:1-3 NRSV). In contrast to the Gentile nations' idolatry and just penalties, the Judeans know God and can count on God's kindness and mercy when they sin—even though, as the philosopher says, they will *not* sin because they know God and God's power. Their true knowledge of God assures the Judeans of justice and immortality.

Paul challenges those assumptions in Romans 2. Paul agrees with the Judean philosopher about God's judgment on evil: "We know that God's judgment on those who *do* such things [the evil things that Paul lists in Rom 1:24-32] is in accordance with truth" (Rom 2:2). But he does not accept the philosopher's argument that the Judean people will escape God's judgment simply because they *know* God. Paul writes that if "you" (an imagined Judean who would embrace the philosopher's perspective) do the same things as the Gentiles, then you too will be judged. God's "kindness and forbearance and patience" is not insurance for those who simply know the true God (the Judeans); it is, rather, meant to "lead you to repentance" (Rom 2:4) and to doing what is good. On the day when God's "just judgment" (*dikaiokrisias*) is apocalypsed (Rom 2:5), neither Judeans nor Gentiles will be judged on the basis of what they *knew* but on what they have *done*.

From a high-altitude perspective, the Gentile peoples, in the collective sense, indeed did not attain to the knowledge of God or worship God. So God handed over the nations to their self-chosen gods and powers, which now rule them. Individual persons, too, are imprisoned within and often victims of those collective idolatrous systems and social orders. Nevertheless, those systems and orders do not necessarily prevent ordinary Gentiles or Judeans from doing the good that God requires. The divine requirement to *do the good* exceeds whatever religious, social, legal, or political systems are in place among the nations. God's call to do the good (which is to say, to love one's neighbor as oneself, Rom 13:9) is addressed to every human being in the concreteness of everyday life among friends, strangers, and enemies. When a person responds to God's (implicit) call by doing good, that person in some measure exceeds their systemic captivity. And so in fact it happens. While sociocultural-political systems are enslaved by Sin and are often oppressive and enslaving, still ordinary people, even among idolatrous nations, often do good and lead good lives. And there are ordinary individuals even among God's chosen Judean people who do evil. It is not only Judeans (who have the divine law) who do good, and it is not only Gentiles (without the divine law) who do evil.

Even though Paul would not have disputed the thought that every person sins, he does not offer a blanket view of individual sin (for example, the idea of total depravity); he takes serious account of the ground-level reality of everyday life among ordinary people. Ordinary people, while always caught up in the overarching systems of history and nations—and often both enamored of and oppressed by them—are *more than* the systems in which they are caught up. They often live at peace with and among their families, friends, and neighbors; they get married and raise children; they care for one another in costly ways; they show hospitality to strangers; they work hard in fields, shops, and businesses; they buy, sell, and trade at fair prices; they mourn, laugh, and celebrate together; they ignore systemic segregations; they hate crime, violence, and war. At ground level—perhaps Paul is thinking especially of slaves, peasants, migrants, laborers, artisans, such as would be found in the messianic assemblies in Rome—people often do good and hope for good things to come. We might call this the everyday messianic. Where is this in Paul's understanding of God's justice?

Paul writes: "To those who by enduring in good work [*ergou agathou*—literally, 'who do the work of good'] seek for glory, honor, and immortality [God] will give eternal life; while for those who are self-seeking and do not obey the truth, but obey injustice, there will be wrath and fury" (Rom 2:7-8). Despite the structures, systems, and powers of corruption, falsehood, and injustice that govern nations and social orders and demand conformity and obedience from ordinary citizens, God requires all human beings to do the good and obey the truth. That is true for Judeans and Gentiles alike: "For God shows no partiality" (Rom 2:11). Paul seems to believe that at least some, perhaps many, ordinary people among the nations do indeed do what God requires of them as they strive toward a higher end, a final destiny that the systems cannot and do not give, but that God can and does give—"glory, honor, and immortality." Those who *do* the good, whether they have the law or not, will be judged to be just (*dikaiōthēsontai*, Rom 2:13).

Consider this comment by another Judean writer roughly contemporary with Paul: "When have the inhabitants of the earth not sinned in your sight? Or what nation has kept your commandment so well? You may indeed find individuals who have kept your commandments, but nations you will not find" (2 Esdras 3:35-36 NRSV). What aspects of this comment do you agree and/or disagree with? Are you inclined to believe that at least your nation or people, as such, does good, even if others do not? Are you willing to grant that numerous ordinary citizens even in enemy nations are intent on doing the good and in fact do it?

The gospel of God's wrath on systemic bondage requires both Judeans and Gentiles to look across the systemic boundaries that define and divide them from one another. Neither side is the province solely of evil or of good. Not everyone on the other side of the ethnic-national divide is simply to be condemned. God alone has the right to judge everyone.

But on this matter of God's judgment, Paul makes a crucially important claim: God will judge everyone *through the one who is just, Jesus Messiah* (Rom 2:16). The Good is Jesus Messiah (Rom 3:21-26). Jesus is the measure of justice; there will be no judgment on any human being apart from him. On the day of judgment, Paul writes, God will "judge the secret things of every person *through Jesus Messiah*" (Rom 2:16). The living, reigning reality of Jesus is both the criterion of the good by which God judges all persons and deeds, and the atoning mercy seat, the place where God reconciles and redeems all humankind for himself. God's *judgment* of all through Jesus Messiah is in fact *the good news*.

Judeans as a people, then, cannot rely on having and hearing the law of Moses to bring about justice, whether among them or for them. The knowledge of God and instruction in God's will, which was given to Israel in the law of Moses, cannot be a cause for Judean boasting with respect to the Gentile peoples (as the Judean philosopher does). Paul does not dispute that in receiving the law of Moses the Judean nation was given a unique and indispensable gift ("the very form of knowledge and truth," Rom 2:20) and a unique calling among the nations (to be "a guide to the blind, a light to those in darkness, an instructor of the foolish," Rom 2:19, recalling Is 42:6-7). In fact, we will see later (in Rom 9–11) that these "gifts and the calling of God" bestowed on Israel are never revoked and will yet be brought to their proper fulfillment (Rom 11:28). But the Judean people—"the circumcision," as they called themselves—though having the law, have themselves been guilty of grave injustices. Despite knowing the commandments of God, some among them are guilty of stealing, adultery, robbing temples of idols (even though they forswear idols), and other crimes and injustices (Rom 2:21-22).

So while having the law of Moses is a unique gift and calling, the law itself is not effective in *producing* a truly just people over against the Gentile nations. On that score the Judeans cannot boast. In fact, because of their injustices, Paul declares, "The name of God is blasphemed among the nations because of you" (Rom 2:24, quoting Is 52:5—a word *Christians* throughout the centuries have not sufficiently heard). Having the law of Moses and being the circumcision (which marks their sociocultural difference as whole) are only of value when the good to which the law testifies is *done*. And even among the "uncircumcised," the peoples without the law of Moses, the good is sometimes or often done. Apart from *doing the good* the law requires (which Jesus Messiah in fact does, Rom 10:4), there is no reason to boast about having the law. A Judean who transgresses the law in injustice becomes effectively a member of the uncircumcision—a Gentile. And a Gentile who does the good that the law requires becomes effectively a member of the circumcision—a Judean (Rom 2:25-29). The one criterion by which God will judge "the secret things of men" (whether Judean or Gentile) is Jesus Messiah (Rom 2:16). He is the Good through whom God will judge the works of all human beings. The cosmic-historical systems—whether Gentile idolatry or Judean law—are not the deciding factor in God's judgment. God's goodness, justice, and mercy in Messiah is the deciding factor.

Law: The Systemic Captivity of the Judean People (Romans 3:1-20)

At this point Paul reintroduces the voice of the Judean philosopher, who, as we can imagine, would have a number of pointed and pertinent objections to Paul's seemingly anti-Judean conclusions so far. We will listen in to their further debate, in paraphrase (Rom 3:1-10):

Philosopher: If what you have just said is true, Paul, then what advantage is there in being Judean? What point is there in being "the circumcision"—being a people set apart and marked off from the Gentile nations by having the revealed law of Moses?

Paul: There is very real advantage, in the first place because the Judeans were entrusted with the words [*logia*] of God—

Philosopher (interrupting): And *what if* some Judeans were unfaithful to the law, as you have pointed out? Does their unfaithfulness simply cancel out God's faithfulness to the Judean nation?

Paul: Absolutely not! Even if every human being were a liar, God is not. God is always absolutely true to his word of faithfulness to Israel. As the psalm says, "Your word will always be vindicated, and your judgments will always prevail" [Ps 51:4]. You cannot assail God's faithfulness!

Philosopher: But if, as you argue, it is exactly faithless injustice by some Judeans that serves to confirm God's faithful justice, then isn't the implication that God is *unjust* to condemn Judean injustices? (God forgive me for just saying that!)

Paul: Absolutely not! It is simply a given that God is always absolutely just. If God were unjust, how could God judge anyone in the world at all?

Philosopher: I'll ask the question again, another way: If the truth of God is made to shine even more gloriously because of my lie, why would I (if I lie) nevertheless be condemned as a sinner? Wouldn't it make sense to say (as some people accuse us of saying), Let us do evil deeds that even more of God's goodness will shine through?

Paul: Well, anyone who says something like that truly deserves condemnation. It's ridiculous!

Philosopher: Still, Paul, you haven't answered the question whether the Judean people have any advantage over the Gentile nations.

Paul: Short answer for now: No, no advantage at all! Let me explain. I have already charged that all peoples—Judean and Gentile alike—are "under Sin" as under a hostile, dominating power—imprisoned by it. But it seems I haven't yet made that case sufficiently with respect to the Judean people. I will now make that case with reference to our own Scriptures—the law. Listen to what is written there.

Paul now draws in a series of quotations from the Old Testament, mostly from the Psalms. In them the law (Rom 3:19) declares in unambiguous terms that the Judean nation falls under the same judgment of ungodliness and injustice as the Gentile nations do. The first quotation from Psalm 14:1-3 (Rom 3:10-12) is especially significant in light of the charge that the Judean philosopher brought against the Gentiles. Recall that while he granted that the Gentile peoples might seek after God and try to find him, they nevertheless turned away from what they should have understood about God from creation and continually descended into idolatry, corruption, and injustice. But the first psalm Paul cites declares (in rather exaggerated terms) about the *Judean* people, "There is no one just, not even one; no one has understanding, no one seeks after God. All turned away and together became worthless; there is no one who does kindness, not even one."

In other words, despite the fact that Israel received both the revelation of the true God and the revelation of the law, the psalmist says the same things or worse about Israel as the philosopher said about the Gentile peoples: like them, Israel fails to live by what it should know, it turns away from the clearly revealed knowledge it received, and it does not seek God. The results are similar too. Among the Judeans (as among the Gentiles) there is lying, deceit, slander, cursing, and bitterness. Among them too there is violence, destruction, and bloodshed. They have not followed "the way of peace" (Rom 3:17, quoting Is 59:7-8). They do not honor ("fear") God as God (Rom 3:18). As the people who have the law, how are they different from those idolatrous peoples without the law?

Paul thus demonstrates *from the Judeans' own Scriptures* that having the law of Moses did not prevent the Judean people itself from coming "under [the power of] Sin" (Rom 3:9). In this respect—getting back to the philosopher's question—what is the advantage of having the law? None at all! *Except* that the law itself, as evident in these scriptural texts that Paul quotes, speaks directly to those "under law"—the Judeans—to prove Paul's point. *It is finally the Judean law that silences the Judean philosopher.* Paul has scriptural proof of the failure of the Judean system to bring about justice. And thus not only the Gentile nations but also the Judean people—together they are "the whole world" (Rom 3:19)—are found equally to be under the regime of injustice and equally under God's judgment. A system of law (whether Judean or Roman) does not bring about the justice that God requires of all peoples. Law only yields up a fuller awareness—an accounting—of injustice (Rom 3:20), and there is plenty of that to go around.

The Journey So Far

It is worthwhile to review the journey that Paul has taken so far in Romans. We will now put Romans 1:18–3:20 back into the sequence of the letter itself. In Romans 1 Paul immediately announces the good news of God and God's Son, Jesus Messiah, raised from the dead and appointed ruler over all nations. He is the supreme sovereign to whom Israel and all nations (including Rome) owe loyal obedience. As apostle, Paul was set apart and sent to the nations to proclaim the reign of the Messiah and to call the nations to trust and obey him. When Paul comes to a preliminary definition of the good news (in Rom 1:16-17) he makes the following declarations about it:

- The good news is the active power of God to deliver the nations from their bondage.

- That deliverance ("salvation") comes to those who believe the good news, whether Judean or Gentile.

- In the good news God "apocalypses" an utterly unique justice—God's own justice—which is salvation.

- God's justice comes to all and is done in the world through God's faithfulness and human faith, embodied uniquely in the Just One.

- It is equally important to note what is *missing* in this announcement of good news for Israel and the nations—*law*.

- Justice does not arrive in the world through law.

The absence of law in this good news of justice would likely have struck many Greeks, Romans, and Judeans alike as strange, as missing the key component of a proper theory of justice. All of these great traditions had thought long and deeply about justice in terms of law. Paul acknowledges just how strange his thought is by declaring that the justice he is declaring is in fact an apocalypse, a revelation. It is not arrived at by ordinary human perception or possession or legislation. This justice comes from somewhere else altogether and is established on a different basis altogether. It comes *from God* and is established *by God* through the resurrecting power of life. It must be believed and trusted in its apocalyptic otherness. The power of this apocalypse itself creates belief and trust, and draws all thinking about justice to itself. This is the good news that Paul declares in Romans 1:1-17.

Simultaneous with the apocalypse of God's justice is the apocalypse of God's wrath against the "impiety" and "injustice" of the nations (Rom 1:18). God's wrath is good news because it exposes and unmasks the idolatrous systems and structures that enslave the nations. Paul does not believe the idolatrous nations were simply left to go their own way, abandoned as it were to the natural consequences of their idolatry and their deserved punishment. In some mysterious way—and Paul would only know this, too, by a revelation of the mystery (Rom 16:25-27)—God himself actively handed the Gentile peoples over to their idolatrous systems, as to incarcerating powers. This systemic captivity comes on the nations as collective ethnic-social-political entities through their devotion to the gods, and is perhaps concentrated especially in their rulers and emperors, who represent, legislate, and enforce the systems. We are not at this point given the reason *why* God handed them over. What is important to Paul is that God in Jesus Messiah reigns over the Gentile peoples even in their idolatry and does not abandon them. In other words, imprisoning powers may currently have custody over the nations, but not without God's definite permission, nor apart from God's definite purpose.

With or without law, Gentiles and Judeans alike must do the good. Law may point toward the good, but law itself does not establish or accomplish the good, which exceeds systems and laws. Only persons do good or evil; and doing these—both good and evil—happens among Judeans and Gentiles alike. The systems do not define the good, or the standard of divine judgment. The criterion by which God judges any person's deeds, whether good or evil, is none other than Jesus Messiah, who is himself the reality and form of the Good (Rom 2:16) and the site of God's redeeming mercy for all. Knowing the true God and having the law, as the Judeans do, does not protect Judeans from God's judgment when they do evil. The law of Moses is useful when it points to the good that must be done; but if the good is not done, having the law is useless on the day of judgment. In fact (as we will see), having the law may itself cause the Judean people to miss the powerful event of God's justice in Messiah, which has occurred in their midst. This sums up Romans 2.

When the question is then raised, not surprisingly (Rom 3:1-9), whether there is any advantage to Israel for having the revealed law of Moses, Paul hints that there may indeed be some advantage, but he does not immediately pursue this idea. If God remains steadfastly faithful to the Judeans, it is neither because they are in possession of the law nor because there is no injustice in their midst. In fact, the law itself testifies otherwise to those "under law," giving the knowledge that they (the Judean people) too are "under Sin," subject to this ungodly power that is hostile to justice. The Gentile peoples and the Judean people stand alike before God's just judgment, and law provides no ground or protection whatsoever. In fact, by the time we come to Romans 3:19-20 law and justice stand opposed to each other.

In Romans 3:21-26 Paul returns to the place from which he started in Romans 1:1-17: the apocalypse of God's justice in Jesus Messiah. Now he declares with absolute boldness: God's justice is revealed, it happens, it is accomplished in the world, *apart from law*. The Law and the Prophets are not the source and power of this justice; instead, they *attest* this justice, give their witness to it. One important way they do so is by providing Paul with a key image, the mercy seat in the inner sanctum of the tabernacle. It is the place where God's liberating justice is done and graciously given as a gift to all who believe. Jesus Messiah himself is the mercy seat, where God comes in person to be with his people, to speak to them, to cleanse them, and to reconcile them to himself. As the mercy seat in person, the faithful Jesus Messiah is the site of God's very own justice, arriving, being done, and redeeming *all peoples*—Gentile and Judean alike—who are imprisoned under the hostile power of Sin. Justice is defined by God's act in Messiah. Justice comes to those who find justice here, receive it, and take their place within it.

4

BEING JUST

JESUS MESSIAH IS THE JUSTICE OF GOD. This is not a truth the Gentile peoples could have arrived at on their own. On the contrary, their honoring of many gods and lords stood opposed to that truth. But neither did the Judeans arrive at this truth from their scriptural resources, for they sought justice through the law of Moses. Only an apocalypse *of God* reveals and establishes that Jesus is the justice of God. But this singular divine apocalypse of the truth is exactly what makes it good news for *all*, not only for Judeans. Paul writes in Romans 3:29-30: "Is God the God of Judeans only? Is he not the God of the nations also? Yes, of the nations also, since God is one." As we saw in the previous chapter, even (or precisely) in "handing [the nations] over" into the custody of their gods, God was always the God even of the nations that did not have the law of Moses. God's justice does not depend either on the law of Moses or on the social-cultural-political systems of the Greeks and Romans—as if Gentile peoples might have something to boast about over against the Judeans. God's justice as Jesus is one, as God is one; it transcends all *ethnē* (nations).

Yet law seems to be the most effective way of getting justice done on the ground. It is how justice gets embedded in social and political orders in cities, societies, and nations, and among nations. If law (singularly represented by the law of Moses) is sidelined in God's doing justice in Jesus Messiah, how does this justice take effect in the daily life of Israel or the nations? How will it make a difference? How do ordinary people participate in making justice real, concrete, and effective? Paul now turns to this question and addresses it by unfolding the meaning of a word he already introduced but so far left mostly undefined: faith—*pistis* in Greek. This word had a variety of meanings in Paul's context, including "loyalty" or "fidelity" (as a subject owes to a ruler), "good faith" or "faithfulness" in keeping an oath or promise, "trust," and so on. What *pistis* (faith) means depends a great deal on the context in which it is used. To explain its meaning for the good news, Paul turns to a story in the law to show that *the law itself testifies to God's justice apart from law* for both Judeans and the nations. We do not "cancel" the law with the good news, Paul says; rather, by the good news "we establish the law" (Rom 3:31), precisely by finding the good news anticipated in it. The revelation of God's justice in Jesus Messiah enables us to discern that very justice at work even in stories from the law.

Abraham the Ancestor: Just Gentile and Just Judean (Romans 4:1-12)

In ancient times (though not only then) the forefathers or ancestors of a people or nation embodied in themselves the original essence of the people, as an oak seed bears in itself the essence of the oak tree. A people could remember its true character by recalling the stories of the ancestors. For the Judean people, Abraham, Isaac, and Jacob were such ancestors. Stories about them in Genesis work like creation stories because they tell how the people Israel came into being and who they are called to be. Later, in Romans 9, Paul will turn to the stories of Isaac and Jacob, along with Abraham. At this point he focuses on Abraham, "our" ancestor "according to the flesh [*kata sarka*]" for the Judean people. The Greek phrase *kata sarka*, "according to the flesh," has a double meaning here. On the one hand, it signifies that Abraham is the *genealogical* ancestor of the people of Israel: Israel is from his genetic seed. On the other hand, *kata sarka* signifies that Abraham is the *figural* ancestor of Israel; he was the first to be marked "in the flesh" by circumcision, which became the sign of a genuine descendent of Abraham.

Circumcision was essential to the identity of the Judean people, signifying their participation in the figural reality of Abraham. Abraham was the *original Judean*: being from, in, and like Abraham and being Judean were the same thing.

> Does your nation or people of origin have acknowledged forefathers (or mothers) who represent something of the essence of that nation or people? What distinctive mark or character do those ancestors bestow on your people, and how is it carried forward into the present?

Remarkably, when Paul engages the story of Abraham in the light of the gospel, what he finds is that the gospel of God's justice *for Gentile peoples* as well as for Judeans was already preproclaimed and operative there (see Gal 3:8); the good news for all was already being heard and lived by Abraham and Sarah long before the arrival of Jesus Messiah. And the first thing Paul sees in the Abraham story is that justice comes to Abraham *apart from law*.

For Paul's fellow Judeans, all of the requirements of the law of Moses were effectively anticipated and signified by the one law given to Abraham (long before the law of Moses), namely, that he and all of his descendants should be circumcised (Gen 17:9-14). If keeping law creates a just person, then Abraham's justice was above all represented by his practicing the law of circumcision. In Abraham's law-keeping form of justice all Judeans could find their own form of justice before God, insofar as they, like Abraham, practiced law keeping, represented especially by circumcision.

But Paul finds something strikingly different in the Abraham story. Reading the narrative sequence of the story in Genesis very carefully, Paul discovers that Abraham was already considered a just person even *before* he received and obeyed the law of circumcision. In Genesis 15:6 (as quoted by Paul) we read, "Abraham trusted [*episteusin*] God, and it [trust] was accounted [*elogisthē*] to him as justice [*dikaiosynēn*]" (Rom 4:3). God accounted Abraham just in the moment when Abraham *trusted the promise of God* to give him numerous descendants from his own body, against all natural capacities in himself and Sarah. It is not until the story unfolds *later* in Genesis 17 that God instructs Abraham to seal the promise with the mark of circumcision. So, Paul asks, "How then was [justice] accounted to Abraham? Was it while being [*onti*] in circumcision or in uncircumcision [literally, in foreskin]? It was not in circumcision but in uncircumcision. He received the sign of circumcision as a seal of his justice of trust while [he was still] in uncircumcision" (Rom 4:10-11). I have translated these sentences literally (and awkwardly) to show how for Paul and his fellow Judeans circumcision and uncircumcision were understood as states of being. From a Judean perspective, being in circumcision meant being in law and counted as being in justice, or being just. Circumcision marked out the human sphere in which God worked justice. The Gentile peoples with their foreskins were simply outside all of this.

But what Paul sees is that while Abraham still had his foreskin he was a Gentile, one of the *ungodly* (*asebē*, Rom 4:5; this is the same word used in Rom 1:18 [*asebeia*] to characterize the idolatrous Gentile nations). Yet God attributed justice (*dikaiounta*, "justified," Rom 4:5) to the ungodly, uncircumcised, Gentile Abraham when he trusted that God would fulfill the promise of numerous descendants. Paul draws on a psalm of David (Ps 32:1-2) to make the point another way: "Blessed are those whose lawless deeds [*anomiai*] were forgiven and whose sins were covered over; blessed is the one against whom the Lord will by no means account sin" (Rom 4:7-8). Here God forgives the lawless and does not count sin against sinners. Despite the ungodliness, injustice, lawlessness, and sin that is accounted among both the Gentile nations and the Judeans according to Romans 1:18–3:20, Paul here makes the stunning claim that *God does not account justice according to the measure of lawless or lawful deeds.* Instead, God *gives* justice according to God's own grace, not according to the measure of law; justice is bestowed as God's gift (Rom 4:4) by God's word. God graciously declares Abraham's *trust* as Abraham's justice. Therefore Abraham, the ancestral figurehead, is the father of *all* who share in God's justice through trust as Abraham did, whether they are "in uncircumcision" or "in circumcision," whether "outlaws" or "inlaws," whether Gentile or Judean.[1] God graciously accounts their trust as justice. This is the gospel of justice.

---

[1] I borrow the term *outlaws* from the aptly titled book by Theodore W. Jennings Jr., *Outlaw Justice: The Messianic Politics of Paul* (Stanford: Stanford University Press, 2013).

We must pause briefly to consider the verb "to account" (*logizomai—* often translated "to reckon"). While it certainly carries the meanings of "to consider," or "to account as," or "to attribute to," the meaning here is more than that. I noted above in the translation of Romans 4:10–11 that Paul uses the language of "being in" or participation. From a Judean perspective, one participates in divine and human justice by obeying Torah (represented by circumcision). For Paul justice comes as a gift from God, as active divine grace that effects the justice that it bestows. When Abraham heard the living voice of God he trusted God and was taken by God into God's own active justice; he was made just. Trust and justice are not two things but one. God's *justice is actively done in the world through Abraham's trust.* So it is with all of those who, as Paul says, "walk in the way of trust [*pistis*] as our uncircumcised father Abraham did" (Rom 4:12). God's justice is fulfilled in them. "Blessed are those [like Abraham] who hunger and thirst for justice, for they will be filled" (Mt 5:6).

If trusting God is the way God's justice is done on earth, how does that reshape your understanding of what it means to do justice? How would justice spread?

Abraham, Heir of the World (Romans 4:13-16)

From the beginning of the story of Abraham in the land of Haran (Gen 12) to its climax with Isaac on the mountain in Moriah (Gen 22), "walking in the way of trust" (Rom 4:12) characterizes Abraham's life. His journey of trust begins suddenly with a voice, a word from the Lord, and a startling command to "go from your country and your kindred and your father's house to the land that I will show you" (Gen 12:1 NRSV). In Abram's context this amounted to a command to walk *away* from all of the established familial, social, economic, and political systems that would visibly provide him with identity, stability, prosperity, and security. But it is also a command to walk *toward* something invisible, a future, and a land God would show him. So Abram walks from God, with God, toward God. *This walking itself is Abram's act of trust in the truth of the voice.* The word of the invisible voice is the power that moves and draws him on his journey.

Just as important is what the voice promises: "I will make of you a great nation, and I will bless you, and make your name great, so that you will be a blessing. I will bless those who bless you, and the one who curses you I will curse; and in you all the families of the earth shall be blessed" (Gen 12:2-3 NRSV). Only a few sentences earlier in the story of Abram and Sarai we heard this: "Now Sarai was barren; she had no child" (Gen 11:30). It is a sentence without promise. Genealogically, Sarai's barrenness is a dead end, a void in the numerous fruitful generations that flow without interruption from Shem to Abram (Gen 11:10-27). A dead end. Yet when Abram heard the voice, "he went, as the Lord had told him" (Gen 12:4). He entrusted himself to the word of promise in all its invisibility and impossibility.

It is striking how Paul construes God's promise in Romans 4. Abraham, he says, received "the promise that he would inherit the world" (or "be heir of the world"). That is a startling way to sum up God's words in Genesis 12:2-3: it sets the promise to Abraham on a *world-historical stage* and places the entire destiny of the world in relation to the destiny of Abraham and his descendants. What could it mean for Abraham and his descendants to inherit the world?

Surely history tells us that receiving a divine promise to inherit the world is a dangerous thing. Consider what it might have meant for the rulers and peoples of Egypt, Assyria, Babylon, Persia, Greece, and Rome in ancient times to have received such a divine promise and mandate—as they surely thought they did. These peoples sought to spread their divinely mandated military and political authority as far and wide as possible and bestow the "blessings" of their rule and justice on the peoples they conquered, while demanding devoted loyalty in the form of tribute, taxation, military service, and honor.

This manner of inheriting the world did not end in ancient times. Consider the times AD when Constantine, Theodosius, Charlemagne, and many other rulers of "Christian" empires and nations spread their reign throughout Europe and beyond. The great imperial powers of the colonial era—Spain, Holland, France, Britain—all with some sense of divine mandate, conquered peoples across the seas, claimed their territories, and "blessed" them with civilization, the rule of law, and Christianity. Even today under conviction of a manifest destiny to inherit the world, the United States and its consort global capitalism spread their influence around the world, bestowing justice, equality, democracy, freedom, prosperity, and peace wherever they go, requiring only gratitude, loyal devotion, and a great portion of the world's resources in return for their benevolence. Such is the history of divine promises and mandates to inherit the world.

> Reflect further on the thought of inheriting the world. Some have argued that it is a good thing that a Christian emperor such as Constantine did inherit the world, or that a nation such as the United States does. Do you agree or disagree? Why? Can you think of other examples of inheriting the world that may or may not be a good thing for the world?

How is the promise to Abraham and his descendants any different? Would not the same dangerous determination to dominate other peoples—all for justice, peace, and well-being, of course—threaten to overtake Abraham, Israel, and the church? But here is where Paul detects a fundamental difference in the story of Abraham. God promised Abraham that he would inherit the world. Abraham received and trusted God's word as a divine *promise*, but not as a divine *mandate*. In fact, had Abraham taken God's word as a mandate to bring about the fulfillment of the promise through his own work he would *not* have been reckoned by God as just. "For if Abraham was made just by works [Greek *ex ergōn*; see English *energy*] he has something to boast about, but not before God" (Rom 4:2). Abraham refused inheriting the world and becoming the father of many nations as a mandate to be achieved through his own energy and might. He simultaneously refused the boasting he would be entitled to as a result—the kind of boasting that arises spontaneously from every triumphant ruler and people in history. Instead, Abraham *trusted God* to bring about and bestow his promised inheritance and his destiny to become "the father of many nations." In *that way* he was "reckoned as just," that is, he was taken up into the just purpose of God and participated in God's mission in the world. His inheritance and destiny would only be received as a "gift of grace" (Rom 4:4), not as the reward of his own power to bring it about.

Abraham's beatitude came through meekness: "Blessed are the meek, for they will inherit the earth" (Mt 5:5).

We might paraphrase Romans 4:4–5 in this way:

> Now to the founding ancestor who aspires to world-historical destiny [always in "the godly cause" over against the ungodly] through striving for it in his own might, the result [inheriting the world and being a great figurehead among the nations] cannot be considered a gift graciously given, but the reward due for all of the strategic political skill and military might expended— something to boast about. But to the founding ancestor who does not strive to attain the divinely promised destiny in his own power, but who trusts God graciously to bring it about and bestow it as a gift, even upon the ungodly, that trust itself is *sharing in God's justice, being just, doing God's justice* in the world.

Such was Abraham. He thus became the ancestral figurehead of divine justice for all peoples.

Abraham and Sarah Between Death and Resurrection (Romans 4:17-25)

God's justice does not move in the world through Abraham's efforts to impose "godly" law on the "ungodly." If the just Abraham is to become the father of many nations and to inherit the world, this will come about through the God who "gives life to the dead and calls into being the things that do not exist" (Rom 4:17). Here Paul gives us a clue to why God chose Abram and Sarai in the first place. As we have seen from the story in Genesis, the one signal we are given about Abram before he heard the divine command and promise is that his wife, Sarai, was barren (Gen 11:30). She had no child and no capacity for having children. With respect to Sarai, Abram's future was at a genealogical dead end. Exactly for this reason, it seems, God chose Abram and Sarai—not for their inherent capacity or potential to create a future for themselves or others but for their lack of it. If God then promises that Abram through Sarai will be the father of many nations and that his descendants will be as numerous as the stars in the heavens and the sands of sea, God promises something that Abram cannot bring about himself. In fact, as Paul tells the story, *both* Abraham and Sarah are at a dead end before the promise is fulfilled:

Beyond all hope, [Abraham] in hope trusted that he would become "the father of many nations" according to what was said, "so shall your descendants be." He never weakened in trust, even considering that his own body, being about one hundred years old, was *as good as dead*, and Sarah's womb was *also dead*. He did not turn against the promise of God through mistrust; rather, empowered by trust, he gave glory to God, being fully persuaded that God is able to do what he promised. (Rom 4:18-21)

Paul's point is this: Abram, lacking power to bring about justice for himself (in the form of an heir) trusts unwaveringly in the God who gives life to dead things and creates things from nothing. Only this God can give to Abram and Sarai the future they are promised but cannot attain by their own potency and act: descendants, the nations, the world as an inheritance. Their unwavering trust in the resurrecting and creating God is accounted as justice, a justice also given to all other "dead ones" (the powerless, the poor, refugees, the sidelined and abandoned and forsaken) who "trust in the one who raised Jesus our Lord from the dead" (Rom 4:24).

Notice this: Paul does not go on to say, "And then Abraham and Sarah had a child, an heir," as if justice for them only arrived at the moment of success. Justice was not accounted to Abraham in the moment of *receiving* what was promised. Paul does not *resolve* the story of Abraham and Sarah in terms of outcomes. Rather, Paul leaves them walking in trust and obedience between their origin and their destination, between their already dead bodies and the promise of resurrection and new creation. He leaves them walking the way of trust—beyond all hope, yet full of hope. This for Paul is the gospel itself: it is precisely *in* Abraham's walking the way of trust and leaving the outcome to God that justice is done in the world. *This* is Abraham's world-historical legacy; this is the way the world will be saved from "benevolent" self-assertion, aggression, conquest, domination, and boasting in the name of "justice." And saved from impatience and speed: Abraham's trusting, walking justice is *slow* justice. It is not fast, furious, and forced. Abraham abides in God's justice, walks patiently in justice, waits hopefully for justice. "The Just One shall live from trust" (Rom 1:17).

We must pause for a moment to reflect on what it means, then, to do justice. There is much injustice in the world, of every kind—personal, social, economic, political, international, environmental. It is often embedded in and given leverage by the systems and laws of the nations, which the powerful use to their own benefit. Christians rightly raise their voices in protest and ask how things might be different. They rightly ask how they might be agents of change to bring about a greater measure of justice. So it might be thought that the way of justice represented by Abraham stands in contradiction to Christian activism on behalf of justice, because it encourages a kind of passivity. It seems to allow Christians to sit back and let injustice take its course without active protest, intervention, or alternative action. Is Abraham's trust in God's resurrecting power an "opiate of the people," as Karl Marx might have thought? This is an important concern that must be addressed.

I have tried to stress both from the Genesis story and from Paul that trust, or faith, is always intrinsically *active*—a walking. The act of walking—faith itself—is generated by the word of God to go from the place of comfort, stability, security—the kind of place often founded by warfare and secured by law and enforcement—to another land, an unseen and untried place of promise that God will show. Had Abram not obeyed the voice, left his homeland, and walked toward that yet invisible place, we could not say that he trusted the divine voice. Trust is only actualized, only real, in obedient walking toward the promised yet unseen goal. God "reckons" such trust as justice. Justice happens in the patient walking, not in attaining the goal. Or, put otherwise, justice happens and is done concretely in the *means*, not in the end achieved. For Abraham as for Paul, the end Paul calls "inheriting the world" (or as we might have it, saving the world) can only be received as a gift graciously given.

There is no mandate in the good news for Christians to force outcomes, to attain the goal of justice by whatever means necessary (which, we often think, must realistically include some measure of coercion, violence, or injustice). Rather, trusting in God in the first place is precisely what draws us *out of* that kind of fateful instrumental thinking. Instead, it puts us on a slow and expectant journey toward a currently unimaginable future, opened up by a promise from the God who creates new things from nothing and raises dead things to new life. On this journey we do the interim good that is given to us to do, knowing that we lack the capacity or potential to secure the big outcome. Where hope in a current situation of injustice seems as dead as

Abraham's one-hundred-year-old body and Sarah's barren womb, we are not driven by necessity to achieve an outcome, but instead we are inspired to walk hopefully, trusting that a way will open and a gift will be given from beyond the dead end of the current situation. We hope for a resurrection—a resurrection of justice, which can only come from God.

For Paul, walking in the way of trust is patient action directed toward an end that arrives as a gift of God. Many (but not all) forms of what Christians think of as actively working for justice might count as walking in this sense. What Paul in Romans wants us to see, however, is that we are not given the mandate to *achieve* the end (which is how we usually think of justice being done, especially if an outcome becomes inscribed in and enforced by law). Rather, we are called to trust God, who graciously gives the end as gift. Our active walking and working in this trust is itself *justice given, justice arriving, justice being done.* And it is enough.

What kinds of action for justice are you engaged in? What are the ends you hope for? How (and how quickly) do you expect to achieve those ends? Does your action for justice display primarily "working for results" or "trusting the gift" (Rom 4:4)?

The End of Just War (Romans 4:25–5:11)

Paul completes his thought about "trusting in [God] who raised Jesus our Lord from the dead" by saying that Jesus "was handed over [*paredothē*] because of our offenses and was raised to bring about our justice" (Rom 4:25). We already noted in the last chapter that in Romans 1:24, 26, 28 Paul says about the idolatrous nations that "God handed them over [*paredōken*]" into the custody of powers and passions, binding them there "under Sin" until the time of the apocalypse of justice in the Messiah. In Romans 4:25 Paul describes Jesus as being subjected under the same condition as the nations—handed over to the powers of Sin and Death. As Abraham was once "in uncircumcision"—that is, considered ungodly and unjust—Jesus was found to be among the ungodly and the unjust, standing not against them but in fundamental solidarity with them in their divinely appointed custody under the powers. Their lot became his lot.

Unlike Abraham, however, who was not *intrinsically* just but whose trust was "accounted" to him as justice by God, Jesus Messiah—as Paul already established in Romans 3:21-26—is himself the justice of God *in person*. He is the very being, arrival, presence, and form of justice. His death and resurrection is the *event* of God's justice being done among the idolaters and unjust, the event *into which they are taken* for the sake of bringing about justice in them. This is not a justice for which anyone can "fight," or in the name of which anyone can fight against the unjust others. Paul has already argued, in fact, that the unjust are *not* those "others" (for example, the lawless Gentile nations) but "all," including the Judean people who possessed the law of God. God himself did not fight against the unjust nations but came among them in Messiah, who, himself being handed over, took on their enslaved condition as his own in his death. Messiah won the fight of justice for them in his reconciling death and life-giving resurrection. Being found in Messiah through trust, the unjust are justified—they become just by sharing in his justice.

In this sense the fight for justice is over: "Therefore, being made just through trust, we have peace before God through our Sovereign Messiah Jesus" (Rom 5:1). If justice is brought about in Messiah, so also is *peace*. The Sovereign himself won the peace on behalf of Gentiles and Judeans by occupying the deadly space of enmity between them, being crucified there, becoming the site of God's justice and mercy to all. By his grace Messiah has brought all to stand in this place of peace, as Paul says in Romans 5:2. In this peace that is not of our own making, the nations and Israel are therefore given to boasting in the hope of *God's* coming glory rather than their own. The peace before God of which Paul speaks here is more than a feeling of inner peace (though it may be that); it is even more than our standing now in a peaceable relationship with God, where enmity with God has been overcome (it is surely that too). But it is also a form of *earthly* peace, because the war of the "just" against the "unjust" is over: as Paul says in Ephesians, the Messiah "is our peace" because by his blood and "in his flesh" he has "broken down the dividing wall of hostility" between the circumcision and the uncircumcision (Eph 2:13-15). The sovereign Messiah Jesus has won the war for justice and peace in his own crucified and risen body.

That is not to say, however, that all warring has ceased; manifestly, it has not. Those who trust God's justice in the Messiah (the messianic community) have stopped warring for justice, but they may find *themselves* under attack from those who, because they do not trust in God's justice, are still warring for some version of their own justice. In other words, while the messianic community is not at war—not even a defensive war—its members may yet be *victims* of war, with all the troubles that brings. They may be (and often have been) persecuted when they refuse to join the wars of the nations. In fact, as Paul reiterates throughout Romans, because the messianic community trusts the justice of God in the Sovereign Jesus Messiah and not its own power to establish justice for itself or others, it can expect that it will often be suffering affliction (Rom 5:3). Its condition in the world is *messianic weakness* (which itself is the power to bring about a "better world," as we will see). And so, precisely because it boasts in God and not its own capacity to bring about justice, it is also given to boasting in its own suffering, not because it enjoys suffering or because suffering is a good thing in itself. It boasts in suffering because *suffering is a sign that it shares in a justice it has not achieved in its own strength.*

While this affliction that comes from trust is not itself something good, good things may be generated from it, things such as endurance, character, and hope. As before with the story of Abraham and Sarah, Paul once again arrives at hope. Messianic life is always lived in the sure hope that the good end toward which our action is directed (if it is truly good) *will be given* from God, even when that end is not yet visible and there is no mandate to attain it in our own power. This hope itself is a gift from God. "And in hope we will not be ashamed [in the condition of weakness and affliction] because the love of God has been poured out in our hearts through the Holy Spirit given to us" (Rom 5:5).

> Is there such a thing as just war among nations and peoples? If you think there is, what makes it just? On whose side does Jesus Messiah stand in such a war?

Paul now shifts the register from faith/trust and hope to love. The entire story of God's *justice* in Messiah Jesus is now set within the even larger story of God's *love* in Messiah Jesus. The language of justice inherently deals with something that has gone wrong and needs to be rectified. Of course that is the case everywhere on the human scene, in and among the nations and across history. Yet in human terms the desire for justice or rectification is often blended or even identified with a desire for revenge, retribution, vindication, or domination. But in what Paul now writes he makes utterly clear that God's justice has no other beginning or end than God's love. Love and justice are *not* in balance or in tension with each other in God, either in the sense that God can only love if his desire for justice is satisfied, or that God's justice somehow qualifies his love. Justice is the form God's love takes in order to rectify the condition of bondage to idolatry and injustice under which the nations and Israel suffer. As Paul makes clear, the end of God's work of justice is deliverance from bondage under Sin and the reconciliation of enemies.

God's love arrives in the Messiah. A few sentences earlier Paul had written that the sovereign Jesus was handed over to death (Rom 4:25), being thus subjected under the same condition as Israel and the nations. Now he writes that the Messiah's subjection to death is a destiny that he freely took up as his own, thereby proving both his own and God's love for those in bondage. The point is this: in order to bring about God's justice in his own death and resurrection, the Messiah was moved by his own love to take up the condition of the enslaved, the ungodly, the sinner, the enemy, *as his own.* Where "justice" would normally demand a war *against* the ungodly, the unjust, sinners, and enemies (Rom 5:6-10)—such as, in Paul's time, a justified war by Judeans against the Roman occupation—the justice enacted in the Messiah is fundamentally different.

First, there is only one side in the human situation. Paul already established in Romans 1:18–3:20 that the whole world is on the side of impiety and injustice. The Judean philosopher may well have thought—not unjustly—that the Judean people were the weaker party among the nations, unjustly enslaved under the ungodly enemy power of idolatrous Rome. Surely a great sovereign, a divinely anointed messiah like David, would come in strength against the Romans to achieve the hoped-for justice for the Judeans. Is this not what Judeans could expect, knowing the true God and having the law of God? But in the revealing light of the *actual* Messiah Jesus, in whom

God's justice is apocalypsed, Paul discerns a revolutionary truth. On the one hand the Romans, despite their vaunted power to rule the world, are themselves enslaved and weak. They have been handed over by God to a power greater than themselves from which they need divine *liberation*. The Romans are "under Sin," which is manifest in their imperious boasting. Being under Sin, they continue in idolatry, injustice, and enmity toward the Judeans. On the other hand, though the Judean people are indeed weak and oppressed in the face of Rome, it is not as if the Judeans are simply the just against the unjust, the godly against the ungodly, the lawful against the lawless. The law itself, that is, the Judean Scriptures, testifies that it is not so. The Judean people are unjust, ungodly, and lawless in their own way. Like the Romans, they are under Sin.

Simple castigation of Rome and the Gentile nations as oppressors and wholly evil is itself a manifestation of Judean sin. It blinds them to the ordinary human goodness that is found not only among the circumcision but also among uncircumcision, and to the evil that might be found not only among the uncircumcision but also among the circumcision (which is Paul's point in Rom 2). More important, it blinds the Judeans to God's strange justice in Messiah, for in the war of liberation for Israel and the nations there is only one side: God in Messiah wars against the enslaving regime of Sin, under which "the whole world" suffers (Rom 3:19).

The Messiah in love takes his place on the one side—the only side there is—in the divine war against the regime of Sin. He comes to the side of the enslaved—the weak, the ungodly, the sinner, even the enemy (Rom 5:6-11). It is the side both the Gentile nations and the Judean people are on—the side of injustice. On *this* side and on its behalf, Jesus Messiah conquers the stranglehold of the regime of Sin by giving himself up freely to death for the sake of all. In his love-driven death, "by his blood" (Rom 5:9), the Messiah brings about the liberating justice that *both* Israel and the nations are in need of. They are "saved through him from the wrath" (Rom 5:9).

"The wrath" here is not an eternal destiny that awaits unrepentant individual humans in the age to come. It is the systemic bondage of the Gentile peoples under the alien power of Sin when "God handed them over." It is the systemic bondage of the Judean people, who claimed its privileged place under law, yet even with the law were nevertheless imprisoned "under Sin."

Being saved from the wrath is being delivered from the imprisoning regime of Sin, which rules over both Israel and the nations and sets them against God.

Because of his love, God's Son, through resurrection from the dead, delivers *all peoples* from the regime of Sin into the regime of God. Israel and the nations are brought again onto God's "side." Together they stand with God rather than against him. They are reconciled to God (Rom 5:10-11) in Jesus Messiah, who is the one Sovereign of Judeans and Gentiles alike. The war between Israel and the nations is over not because they have signed a peace treaty, but because each is no longer permitted to regard the other as the enemy. While regarding each other as enemies, they missed seeing the common enemy, Sin. Together they were imprisoned in Sin's alien regime. Together they have been delivered into the regime of God. Together they are gathered under one ruling Sovereign, Jesus Messiah. In the gospel of God and his Son, Jesus Messiah, justice is done for all. "God was in Christ reconciling *the world* to himself, not counting their trespasses against them" (2 Cor 5:19 NRSV). The real enemy of Israel and the nations is exposed, defeated, and rendered inoperative for all of those who believe the good news. For them the war is over.

5

THE JUST ONE

FROM THE BEGINNING OF ROMANS Paul has presented Jesus Messiah as the justice of God. Justice cannot be thought apart from him. Unlike Abraham and his descendants, to whom justice is accounted or reckoned, Jesus Messiah is *intrinsically* the justice of God, the very reality and form of justice, God's justice in person. In Romans 5:12-21 Paul declares this truth again, but now with a different focus and emphasis. In the core declarations of the gospel in Romans 1:1-5, 16-17; 3:21-26 Paul emphasized that justice is *God's act* in and through Jesus Messiah. He wrote about "the good news of God" (Rom 1:1), "the power of God" (Rom 1:16), "the justice of God" (Rom 1:17; 3:21-22) and "the grace [of God]" (Rom 3:24) by which God displayed his justice in Jesus Messiah's redeeming death as the mercy seat (Rom 3:25). Further, in Romans 4 Paul wrote that God promises, gives life to the dead, calls into being things that are not, raises Jesus from the dead, and accounts as just all those who trust God for justice. The perfection, power, and wonder of God's act in Messiah evoke trust from us, as they did from Abraham.

In Romans 5:12–21 Paul focuses on justice as a *human* act, the fully and truly human act of the Messiah. Divine action and human action come together and coincide in him to accomplish the perfection of justice. Jesus

Messiah is the Just One not by being accounted just, but by *being just* in the entirety of his life and death. God vindicates Messiah's human justice by raising him from the dead, which demonstrates God's justice toward Messiah. Because in Messiah we have the perfect coinherence of God's act of justice and the human act of justice, it is also and only through Messiah that the binding chains of injustice are decisively broken and humankind is liberated for justice and life.

Sin, Death, and Sovereignty (Romans 5:12-14)

The gospel discloses a *radical* enmity: not an enmity between peoples, but between opposing sovereign claims on all humankind. An alien sovereign, Sin, has attained rule over all peoples, Gentile nations and Judeans alike, and stands in fundamental opposition to the sovereign rule of God. Sin has an ally—Death. Together they are the tyrants of the regime of injustice.

I have been using the term *Sin* (with a capital *S*) to indicate that Sin must be imagined as an agent with *active power*. Up until this point Paul has not emphasized that aspect of Sin, but it is already implicit in Romans 3:9, where he writes that "all, both Judeans and Greeks, are *under* Sin" as under a power. In Romans 5, however, Paul reveals the invasive manner in which Sin entered the cosmos and took over human history, and the aggressive manner in which Sin spreads its rule. We might paraphrase Romans 5:12 this way: "Sin surreptitiously invaded the world, God's own realm, and along with Sin Death also invaded, enabling Sin aggressively to spread its reign over all humankind, generating an entire history of Sin." But Paul also makes two other important claims about Sin's invasion and sovereign rule.

First, Sin invades "through one man," Adam, the figural human being (Rom 5:14). But (it is crucial to say) Sin's reign over humankind was not in the beginning. It is not original to creation. It *has a beginning*; it does not go all the way back. Sin first entered creation as sin or transgression, that is to say, as a definite act of human disobedience. Only then did Sin find the place from which to launch its deadly mission to conquer and rule *all peoples*.

Second, this happened before there was any division of humankind into those with and those without the law of Moses, as Paul makes clear in Romans 5:13-14: "Sin was in the world before law . . . ; Death reigned even from Adam to Moses." Sin invaded creation before the division between

Israel and the Gentile nations, and its regime has no respect for those boundaries, no matter how important they might otherwise be. So while Sin's universal sovereignty does not go all the way back, it goes a *long* way back, to before there was the law of Moses to measure it. By Moses' time Sin's deadly rule was already well established in the world. As we have seen from Romans 1:18–3:20, the Gentile peoples were handed over to its power through idolatry, and the Judean people also found itself under Sin through Law. Thus even the greatest and best of nations and peoples are the subjects of a mightier regime over which they have no power. They are the subjects of Sin.

> Can you imagine Sin and Death as active powers in history? How does Sin become something more than personal or collective sins? How does Death become something more than the natural deaths of persons or peoples? Does it help to think of such matters in terms of movements, systems, institutions, structures, and even the world order? (It may help to imagine the role of the Ring of Mordor in The Lord of the Rings.)

Much of this talk of the regime of Sin remains somewhat metaphorical and abstract. How does the sovereign rule of Sin and Death happen on the ground in human history? It is no accident that Paul joins the terms Sin (*hamartia*) and Death (*thanatos*) with the idea of *sovereign rule* (*basileuō*, "to rule as king," Rom 5:14, 21, and frequently in Rom 6). Sin rules as king; Death rules as king. Sovereign rule is at the heart of the matter. This becomes clear when Paul sets up the contrast between Adam and Messiah in Romans 5:15-17, but for the moment we must return to the story in Genesis 2–3. There Adam, the original and representative man, was granted authority to be God's regent and caretaker in the realm of living creatures. In Genesis 1:26 God says, "Let us make humankind in our image, according to our likeness; and *let them have dominion* ['rule,' NIV] over the fish of the sea, and over the birds of the air, and over the cattle, and over all the wild animals of the earth, and over every creeping thing that creeps upon the earth" (NRSV). That would have included ruling over the serpent, which itself was a "wild animal that the LORD God had made" (Gen 3:1 NRSV). The authority to reign over all living creatures as God's regent was *given* to humanity by God; it is what it means to be created in God's own image and likeness. If human beings reigned as God reigns, it would be a reign of *shalom*, with humans exercising their sovereignty as God does, to serve the well-being and flourishing of all living creatures.

In Genesis 1–2 it was *not* given to human beings to reign over one another. Among male and female, between the man and the woman, there was to be only mutual delight and partnership in the tasks of ruling creatures and caring for the earth. However, in Genesis 3 the serpent invites the human beings to consider and seize another form of sovereignty: "You will be like God, knowing good and evil" (Gen 3:5 NRSV). To this point the man and the woman knew only goodness, including the goodness of mutual honor and love; it was sufficient and delightful. To be as God (or gods), knowing good and evil, introduces a moral split in the cosmos and a division within human life. Humans become "free" to make their own sovereign decisions between good *and* evil and to do the one or the other.

This freedom as autonomy immediately generates conflict in the personal and social heart of things. Who now decides what is good and what is evil? Who now determines how things will go in human society? Someone must assume godlike, good-and-evil-determining rule over and among human societies. Sovereignty as lording it over is born. That kind of sovereignty was *not* given by God; it was seized by human beings. As the story goes, the results were disastrous. Immediately after seizing godlikeness, humankind began its cursed history of ruling, one over another. The curse on the man is manifest in his "rule" over the woman; the curse on the woman is manifest in her "desire" for the man—for survival? for security?—which enables the man's rule (Gen 3:16). Then, according to Genesis, sovereignty as lording it over spreads rapidly beyond the man and woman. It brings in its train the destructive history of violence, death, revenge, idolatry, and lawlessness, which we read in Genesis 4 and 6.

In other words, we must speak not only of the sovereignty of Sin but of the *sin of sovereignty*. A certain kind of sovereignty—human rule over other human beings, often with the threat of punishment and death—is itself the reign of Sin. Paul's point about Adam is that this form of idolatrous, death-dealing sovereignty is the nature of Adam's sin and becomes the history of the world. It is present well before and well beyond the kind of limitation that is put on it by the law of Moses (or any other law). As powers, Sin and Death make their way in the world when and as some human beings and peoples—with the gods' authorization—assume sovereign power over others, even as those others may desire or require that sovereign power as protection, or resist and rebel against it as oppression. All humankind has sinned in this regard; the desire to gain the upper hand, to lord it over, is hidden in every human heart and manifest in every social order from the family to the empire.

But the sin of sovereignty is particularly manifest in the political, social, and economic realms. Sin co-opts the powers of the world to its cause, and they become its primary instruments of injustice: emperors, kings, tyrants, warlords, governors, presidents, and prime ministers; armies, nations, states, classes, and ethnic groups; global corporations, banks, industries, media, and the market. They attain their sovereignty over others through promises of security, peace, and prosperity, and sometimes achieve these things. They maintain their sovereignty by requiring vows of allegiance, obedience, and sacrifice, and sometimes receive these things. They assert their power over others with threats of war, deprivation, and death, and sometimes commit these things. Much of this is implicit rather than explicit, but it is real. This is Adam's legacy.

Adam-like sovereignty is woven into even the best and best-intentioned aspects of culture, society, and politics, including religions, national constitutions, legal systems, social contracts, economic structures, parliaments, courts, state bureaucracies, schools and universities, armies, police forces, prisons, and so on. All of these institutions provide a measure of order, stability, and flourishing for peoples and nations, and are not simply to be despised (as we will see in Rom 13). Yet governing through fear and the threat of punishment and death is always operative at some level in worldly sovereignties. Though it is normally hidden from view, this form of sovereignty becomes especially visible in extreme situations. For example, in the political sphere a state of emergency can be declared for the sake of securing or protecting such things as a nation's boundaries, independence, and way of life, or such values as democracy, law, order, justice, peace, and so on, when they are threatened. Emergency situations then "demand" the use of a variety of means of protection or aggression, some of which may otherwise be considered illegal: conscription, military defense, or invasion; suppression of protest and opposition; treatment of political opponents as enemies of the state and terrorists; revocations of citizenship; deportations; detentions without trial; "enhanced interrogations"; extralegal prison camps; mass incarcerations and executions; targeted killings, and so on.

While such measures appear at first to be extreme and extraordinary, ordinary citizens often come to accept and endorse them as valid tools in the sovereignty toolkit (even if distasteful), to be used "if necessary" when normal sovereignty needs be backed up with strength. That reasoning funds the scripts of untold numbers of iconic novels and films, in which an otherwise law-abiding soldier, police officer, or ordinary citizen (or a superhero) "must" go beyond the law in order to get justice done, and "must" kill the evil opponent(s) in order to save ordinary people. In like manner sovereigns and subjects, governors and citizens accept that in states of emergency there "must" be sin (acts that transgress normal legal limits) and there "must" be death in order to hold back the sin and death threatened by another power. Sin and Death rule over all worldly sovereignties, therefore, because human sovereignties must rely on them to gain and hold on to their power.

> To your mind, what kinds of extraordinary measures might you consider legitimate or necessary for your government to use in order to maintain what is right and good in the world? What means would cross the line of what you could accept? What is the line?

Justice, Life, and Sovereignty (Romans 5:15-17)

The Adam-like sovereignty which we have been describing is the historical fruit of Adam's transgression.

"But the gift is not like the transgression" (Rom 5:15). Thus Paul begins a series of radical contrasts between the regime inaugurated by "the one man" Adam, and the regime inaugurated by "the one man, Jesus Messiah." However, at the heart of this contrast is not—as we might expect—a rejection of sovereignty for human beings. At the heart of the contrast, rather, is a fundamentally different kind of sovereignty, which arrives in a fundamentally different way: messianic sovereignty, which comes by *grace* as a *gift*. Only this kind of sovereignty brings justice and life in its wake rather than injustice and death.

The godlike sovereignty that invaded human history in Adam's transgression is rooted in a perceived lack. God had graciously *given* the (figural) first human beings everything they needed for human flourishing, including access to the tree of life (the source of immortality) in the middle of the garden. But the serpent's question to the woman immediately generates a sense of what is *not* given to human beings, a sense of something missing; they are not given the tree of the knowledge of good and evil. They now covet the fruit of that tree *because* it was not given. It could be attained only by taking, in direct disobedience of God's command. Taking what is not given is the characteristic sin of godlike sovereignty; lording it over unleashes the horrors of greed, pillage, conquest, and expropriation into the world.

We see a clear biblical example of this when the people of Israel demand that the judge Samuel should appoint them a king to govern them "like other nations" (1 Sam 8:5 NRSV). What this amounts to, the Lord informs Samuel, is not a rejection of Samuel but of God as their king, a rejection rooted in their idolatry (1 Sam 8:7-8). The Lord says to Samuel, "Now then . . . you shall solemnly warn them, and show them the ways of the king *who shall reign over them*" (1 Sam 8:9 NRSV). What follows (1 Sam 8:10-17) is a long litany of ways in which the king will *take*. "He will take your sons" as soldiers, farm laborers, and manufacturers. "He will take your daughters" as household servants. "He will take the best" of all agricultural produce for his royal court. "He will take one-tenth" of everything else the fields produce for his military. "He will take" slaves, oxen, and donkeys to do his work. "He will take one-tenth of your flocks, *and you shall be his slaves*" (1 Sam 8:17 NRSV). And so it happened in Israel that under the reign of its greatest sovereign, Solomon, Israel's military, political, economic, and cultural glory—so impressive in its own right—was built at every stage on the backs of the people (1 Kings 4:22-28; 5:13-18). The sovereign took; the people became his slaves. The same judgment must be made about the Roman ruling elite and the vast numbers of people living in poverty in Paul's time. Being enslaved to Sin included being enslaved to avaricious sovereign powers.

"But the gift is not like the transgression." In stark contrast to rulers who rob, there is the sovereign Messiah Jesus. Unlike Adam and the whole history of enslaving, death-dealing sovereignty proceeding from him, Messiah Jesus lives from the superabundance of God's life and superabundantly gives life to all (Rom 5:15). The result is an equally stark contrast. The one sin of the one man Adam generated the deadly human history of lording it over, conscripting, confiscating, and enslaving: "By the one man's transgression death ruled" (Rom 5:17). But the gracious gift that arrives—apocalyptically, excessively—into the midst of the long history of transgression immediately creates a new history of justice; *justice itself* is the gift.

The gift of justice is not simply equal and opposite to the history of injustice. Rather, the gift of justice abundantly exceeds the history of injustice; the rule of grace abundantly exceeds the regime of sin; the Messiah exceeds Adam; life exceeds death. "*Much more* will those who receive the abundance of grace and the free gift of justice rule in life through the one man, Jesus Messiah" (Rom 5:17). The gift of justice in Messiah overwhelms the idea that justice is done in human history through coercive power, judgment, condemnation, punishment, and death. Jesus' own justice proceeds from divine abundance and is given abundantly to all. This Sovereign gives rather than takes; he liberates rather than enslaves; he bestows life rather than threatens death.

There cannot be life for all unless there is justice for all. Justice for all cannot be defined and determined by any one human society or its rulers. That is how worldly sovereignty works; it always means flourishing for some and suffering for others. But the good news is that God bestows his own justice in the world through the sovereign Jesus Messiah—the justice of flourishing for all. A new kind of history is opened up by the grace of God and the gift of justice. It is a history of *life*. More specifically, it is a history of *truly human sovereignty in life, for life*. Sharing in Messiah's sovereignty, persons and peoples become sovereign with respect to Sin and its enslaving power, and free from the fear of Death. In Messiah God freely bestows the power of life as gift on all humanity, without reserve. There is *no lack* of divine life, only abundance, and it cannot be seized, only given and received. The ungodly sovereignty of ruling over and taking (the sovereignty of Sin and Death) is overcome in Jesus. In him the human addiction to that kind of sovereignty is broken.

Broken also is slavery to the sovereignties of the world that lay claim to human lives and demand their loyalty. Because the gospel superabundantly restores *life-giving* sovereignty—freedom—among all human beings, the sovereigns of this world no longer have any binding claim on those in Messiah, who are liberated from the compulsive desire for survival and security that worldly sovereignties offer. In Messiah, the deceptive claims of worldly sovereigns to provide justice and life may and must no longer be taken seriously by the "subjects" of those sovereigns. (I shall have more to say about this with reference to Rom 13). For the Messiah himself does not reign by hoarding sovereignty and lording it over others, but by gathering all human beings into his self-offered body of justice and graciously bestowing the power of resurrection life on every human being. Jesus Messiah opens up a new history of justice and life. God gives justice and life as gift; they cannot be seized; they can only be *received*.

What would human sovereignty without lording it over look like? How would it operate? Can you think of concrete examples? Would you describe those examples with the word *sovereignty* or something else? How do the gospel narratives of Jesus' life and death enable us to think differently about sovereignty?

The Just One (Romans 5:18-21)

In Romans 5:18-19 Paul sums up the whole gospel story of Jesus Messiah in a couple of sentences; more specifically, in two brief phrases: "one act of justice" and "one man's obedience." It is important not to focus these phrases narrowly only on the death of Jesus on the cross. That, to be sure, is where the justice and obedience of the Messiah come to their climax. But the justice and obedience of which Paul speaks here extend over Jesus' life from his baptism to his crucifixion. Indeed, they are rooted even further back in the eternal divine Son's willingness to do the Father's will. Jesus' baptism marks the public inauguration and manifestation of his messiahship, the moment when Jesus the Son receives divine power from the Spirit and divine authority from the Father. In the event of his baptism it is *given* to Jesus to be the political sovereign of Israel—the King of the Jews.

But what kind of sovereignty will he enact? Will he seize the opportunity to ascend immediately, dramatically, and violently to the throne in Jerusalem and save Israel? These are the questions asked in the temptations of Jesus. Immediately following his baptism, the Spirit sends Jesus into the wilderness to be tempted by Satan. As we read them in Matthew 4:1-11 and Luke 4:1-13, each of the temptations must be understood as Satan tempting Jesus to seize messianic political sovereignty. He is tempted according to Israel's political hopes, to act for Israel's sake and not for his own. The temptations are real for Jesus the Israelite. They make their appeal to Jesus as Israel's already divinely anointed messianic ruler (at his baptism), who is determined to stand in solidarity with his people, to secure, defend, and advance their cause among the nations. *For Jesus, Israel's cause is truly his own.* Given their oppression under Rome, the people of Israel might justly expect a messianic ruler to seek their economic welfare, liberate them from oppression, and restore their standing among the nations. Jesus is Israel's *king.* What else should be expected of him?[1]

So Jesus was tempted to turn the stones of the desert into bread. This kind of messianic wonder not only would address Jesus' own hunger but would also display his commitment and capacity to provide economic relief, welfare, and abundance for the people of Israel. Jesus was deeply sensitive to the poverty of his people, as he displayed in his many acts of mercy. On at least two occasions he was moved by compassion to feed great crowds of listeners. Yet he did not seek out a powerful administrative position in Israel from which he might provide for their social and economic welfare. That would require the overthrow of the Roman system (which taxed heavily) and an overhaul of the temple system (which also taxed heavily). He was critical of both of those systems. But, refusing to lay hold of such power, he fully committed himself to obeying the word of God; he waited for God to reveal God's economy for Israel through his messianic mission, whatever that might look like.

Jesus was also tempted to make a dramatic and miraculous entrance into Jerusalem by descending into the city from the pinnacle of the temple,

---

[1]The following account of the temptations of Jesus is influenced by John Howard Yoder, *The Politics of Jesus: Vicit Agnus Noster,* 2nd ed. (Grand Rapids, MI: Eerdmans, 1994).

upheld by angels. Such a messianic wonder would immediately and unambiguously have displayed his divine right and sovereign authority. With this authority he could call Israel to arms, lead the Jews in conquering the Romans, assume the throne of David, and rule Israel as king. Jesus did not respond to the devil by denying that he was Israel's king. Later on, when he entered Jerusalem, he was hailed as "Son of David." Though he came in weakness and not as a conquering hero, he did not refuse the title. Jesus waited on God to reveal the shape of his kingly mission, rather than testing God to come to his aid with a host of militant angels. Ironically, his kingly mission was most fully revealed in his crucifixion.

Finally, Satan told Jesus that he would give him political sovereignty over all the nations of the earth, if only Jesus would worship Satan. (Recall that, according to Paul, God in some sense has "handed over" the nations to ungodly powers.) The link between self-assertive political sovereignty and Satan's power is clear. It promises triumphant glory and power among the nations, not only for the Messiah, but for Israel too. By resisting Satan's offer, Jesus refused the satanic way of lording it over the nations, but he did not reject political sovereignty. He determined to receive sovereignty only from God, whom alone he worshiped. In the end Jesus did and does indeed *receive* "all authority in heaven and on earth" (Mt 28:18). For it "has been given" to him by God only after and because he was truly designated "King of the Jews" *as he hung on the cross.* The Sovereign One is he who has relinquished the kind of "power over" that Satan offers. When the crucified Messiah was raised from the dead, he commanded the disciples to announce his strange sovereignty to all nations. The disciples were sent out not as military conquerors but as vulnerable "witnesses" (*martyres*, Acts 1:8; see especially their commission in Mt 10). Their purpose was not to subject others to their sovereignty but to call forth followers of the Messiah, teaching them "to do everything I [Jesus] have commanded you" (Mt 28:20).

How does reading the temptations of Jesus as political temptations change your understanding of Jesus' messianic mission? Given that Jesus was revealed to be the true political leader of the Judeans, how does that change your understanding of what Messiah-like political leadership in the world should look like?

In each temptation Jesus refused the *form* of political sovereignty offered by Satan. He determined instead to obey and trust God alone to show him the true form of messianic kingship. It is important to understand that Jesus did not refuse political sovereignty. He did not say to Satan, "You have it wrong; I am not a sovereign ruler," or, "You misunderstand; I rule hearts, not peoples and nations." Rather, Jesus refused to *seize* political sovereignty on Satan's terms, that is, by public wonders, self-evident divine right, and military triumph. In response to each temptation, he committed himself to obey God, who would show him the way of sovereignty. The form of his sovereignty as Israel's king was revealed and given to him as he walked in trust and obedience from Nazareth to Jerusalem and Golgotha. Nowhere along that path to becoming King of the Jews did Jesus assert his sovereignty as *coercive power over*. Instead he fed the hungry, healed the sick, cast out powers of evil, and raised the dead. He called Israel to trust in God's reign despite its oppression by Rome. In these ways he was in fact Israel's ruler, demonstrating the *true* nature of sovereignty.

Ultimately, the sign on the cross, "This is the King of the Jews," spoke the real and final truth about Jesus. While it was intended to mock Jesus' sovereignty, the sign mocked instead the sovereignty of "the rulers of this age" (1 Cor 2:8) who, in a "state of emergency," displayed *their* kind of sovereignty in their executive power to command the public execution of an innocent man. Jesus' refusal to play that kind of sovereignty game exposed its ungodliness and injustice. The cross and resurrection reveal Jesus' entire life of faithful obedience as *a single act of justice, divine and human*. By trusting and obeying God, Jesus lived God's justice from birth to crucifixion. In his life, death, and resurrection the Messiah conquered Adamic sovereignty. A startling new order of justice and life had begun.

I have spent a good deal of time telling the story of Jesus because it is the story Paul sums up in Romans 5:18-19 (paraphrased):

> So therefore, just as Adam's one act of seizing sovereignty as a human right caught up all humankind into its deadly consequences, so the Messiah's one act of receiving sovereignty as a gift—that is, his total life-act of justice— caught up all humankind into his own living justice. For just as the faithless disobedience of the one man Adam brought forth the history of human injustice, so the faithful obedience of the one man Jesus will bring forth the history of human justice.

At the end of the climactic declaration that God graciously and super-abundantly gives the gift of justice and life through Messiah Jesus, Paul reintroduces the subject of law. What is the role of law in this story? Law does not, he declares, lead to the increase of justice; it only leads to increased sin and injustice. "But then law entered, with the result that transgression multiplied" (Rom 5:20). Law operates in human society by defining, refining, and multiplying the numerous ways in which transgressions might be recognized, judged, and punished. For example, apart from law, a starving person who takes a loaf of bread for survival from someone who has plenty may be doing something that ought not to be done (it is a sin), but the act makes a certain kind of human sense, and may even evoke forgiveness and generosity from the one who has plenty. But (in one scenario) law enters and defines taking the loaf as the "crime" of theft and creates a victim and an offender. In fact, the victim and offender as now defined assume roles virtually in reverse; the one who has plenty is the victim, and the one who has nothing is the criminal. A judgment on the crime is "necessary," and the criminal must be punished (perhaps even by death, as has happened in history). Or (in another scenario) law enters and demands that the one who has plenty relinquish some bread for the benefit of those who do not, not as an act of generosity but as a legal requirement. Withholding the loaf of bread is defined as a "crime"—with an offender and a victim—which must be punished (perhaps even by death, as has happened in history). Law raises the transgression to a new level and introduces punishment as the appropriate response: Sin expands its scope, and Death spreads its reign.

God's response to the ever-expanding sovereignty of transgression fostered by law is not to counterattack by multiplying laws and enforcing the rule of law, as governments often do. God does not respond to injustice by getting "tough on crime," expanding the range of illegality, imposing stiffer penalties, building more prisons, and applying the death penalty more frequently (or bringing it back). Those all-too-human responses, Paul says, amount to increasing the regime of Death through ever more rigorous application of law and its penalties. But according to the good news *God acts as God*, which means God acts *beyond the system of law*. God exceeds law altogether. God overcomes the regime of Sin, Death, and Law with his own inexhaustible justice and life in the crucifixion and resurrection of Jesus

Messiah. Whereas the calculus of law creates crimes and corresponding punishments, God creates beneficiaries of his goodness beyond measure. Where Sin "increased" because of the insertion of Law, God's "grace abounded all the more" (Rom 5:20). Grace abounding is a new sovereignty altogether—the sovereignty of divine generosity (Rom 5:21). Grace rather than Law is the new foundation and power of justice and life in the world. In the apocalyptic event of sovereign grace, God pours out justice and eternal life for all through the one just human being, Jesus Messiah our Sovereign. He is the truly human one, the true image of God. We must find our own humanity in his.

6

BECOMING JUST

IN THE FINAL DECLARATIONS OF ROMANS 5 PAUL set in stark contrast the two regimes that rule human life: on the one hand, the regime of Sin, Death, and Law; on the other hand the surpassingly greater regime of Justice, Life, and Grace. Through the obedience and justice of the one man Jesus, humankind, enslaved under Adam's disobedience and injustice, is graciously liberated for justice and life. Jesus Messiah, crucified and raised to life, is the true human being, the definition of the image of God, the embodiment of true dominion or sovereignty. He *is* justice and eternal life. In order for us to live justly, as he did, we must find ourselves within the Messiah's sovereign sphere. The Messiah's *own body* crucified, risen, and exalted *is* that sphere. Strange as it may seem to us, Jesus takes us into his own body so that we might share in his living justice. This is why Paul now turns to the practice of baptism.

Bodies, whether personal, social, or political, are the place where history happens. As bodied beings we enact obedience or disobedience, work justice or injustice, and love or hate our neighbors. In Jesus' crucified body God destroyed the history of injustice that started with Adam's bodily transgression. In Jesus' resurrected body God brings forth a new history of justice. By the bodily act of baptism, we signal that Messiah has taken us into his own bodily history from his incarnation and obedient life to his faithful death, resurrection, and exaltation as God's sovereign. The new history of human justice begins here.

Becoming the Justice of God (Romans 6:1-12)

By referring extensively to Sin and Death as powers that reign over human life, Paul creates a vivid image of what being "in Sin" (Rom 6:1) means. The whole of humanity is caught up into the sphere of transgression and injustice. The God-given authority to serve creation and one another is distorted almost beyond recognition. Sovereignty since Adam has been exercised as mastery and domination. Individuals and groups, rulers and nations, lord it over one another and over other creatures. They assert their sovereignty for seemingly just causes: national security, self-defense, social and economic well-being, freedom, human rights, values, customs, a way of life. The enemies of those just causes "must" be subdued, subjugated, or eliminated. Realistically (as we say), that is the way the world works. Political rulers must "take responsibility" to bring about justice in an unjust world, even if it requires coercion, violence, and warfare. Otherwise injustice will reign. That is certainly how Rome understood its world mission in Paul's time.

But according to Paul that "realistic" logic is what it means to be in Sin. The whole human race finds itself caught up in Sin's logic, according to which there must be empires and colonies, rulers and subjects, governments and citizens, bosses and employees, masters and slaves, the wealthy and the poor. In fact, these ways of ordering people and societies are often construed as just. If there happen to be subjects and slaves and poor, it is just the way things are and perhaps ought to be. And others are destined by fate or the gods to be rulers; they establish and uphold justice by exercising their rightful power over those who are not made for ruling. This too characterized Rome's self-understanding.

> To what extent do you expect and count on your political leaders (or those you would want to be leaders) to establish and uphold justice? To your mind, where does their right to do so come from?

But according to the gospel, the rulers of this age are hardly a solution to the injustice of the world. Indeed, they are the normal means by which Sin and Death maintain sovereignty and ruin the world. The apocalypse of God's justice in Jesus Messiah exposes the lie in the idea that the leaders of the world somehow stand above and beyond the regime of Sin and therefore in a special position to deal with injustice. They do not. After all, Paul says in 1 Corinthians, it is they who "crucified the Lord of glory" (1 Cor 2:8). The gospel reveals that worldly political power must itself be saved from Sin, delivered especially from its propensity to mask its exercise of coercive sovereignty as justice. That deliverance must come from another power altogether, a divine power not caught up in the system of Sin: *Grace*. As *God's* power, Grace utterly differs from and utterly stands against the sovereignty of Sin and the sin of worldly sovereignty. "Just as Sin reigned in the world with the power of Death, so now Grace ever more triumphantly reigns, bringing justice for the sake of eternal life through Jesus Messiah our Sovereign" (Rom 5:21 paraphrased).

"What then shall we say? Shall we continue in Sin in order that Grace may abound?" (Rom 6:1). So someone might challenge Paul. He answers: "Never!" There is no balance of power, no negotiated settlement, no sharing of sovereignty between the regime of Sin and the regime of Grace. They are mutually exclusive. Nevertheless, in the daily life of humanity there is a real struggle to become free of the dominion of Sin and its prevailing logic of lording over. This struggle will finally require nothing less than a death—the death of a whole way of thinking, relating, hoping, believing, acting, and being in the world under the regime of Sin. It will require death to our normal ideas about sovereignty and justice. That whole imaginary must be crucified in the Messiah, and we must be crucified to it (as happened to Paul himself: see Gal 6:14). But *this* death is, shockingly, the good news. It is liberation. The crucifixion of the Messiah exposes the regime of Sin and its Death-dealing logic of coercive sovereignty as a lie. The resurrection of the Messiah inaugurates the sovereign rule of grace, justice, and life—divine life in the midst of the human struggle for justice. Jesus Messiah reigns. A new order of justice has arrived. Baptism is the sign that we share in this new order.

We must recall from Romans 1:1-6 that *Messiah* is a political term, a biblical designation of the sovereign who would arise from David's lineage to rule not only over Israel but also over all nations. When Jesus was raised from the dead and exalted to God's right hand a new *political* reality came into being. The Messiah, resurrected and ruling, creates a new political community (the *ekklēsia* = "church") in the world, which Paul frequently calls "the body of Messiah." The Messiah's reign makes its way in the world by grace rather than by coercion; it conquers through the persuasive embodied power of the good news. Jesus Messiah makes his own sovereign claim on our lives when the gospel is proclaimed, believed, and practiced. Of course, every person and political community is already subject to Messiah, whether they believe it or not—he reigns as *God's* own Son. However, those who believe the good news freely embrace their new citizenship (Greek *politeuma* in Phil 3:20; *politeias* in Eph 2:10) in the political community created by Messiah, and are called actively to *live and walk* as his loyal, trusting subjects. Sharing in the death and resurrection of the Messiah creates radical new patterns and practices of thinking, relating, and "ruling" in everyday life. These build up a new political community rooted in the Spirit and the Spirit's grace-gifts (*charismata*) rather than in law (as we will see more fully in Rom 12–15).

In Romans 6:5-11 Paul draws out the significance of being joined in baptism to the Messiah and sharing in his living reality—his risen body. In the Messiah's own death Sin as an enslaving power was defeated and the power of justice (resurrection power) was unleashed. Paul writes in Romans 6:7: "For the one who has died [the Messiah] is justified [*dedikaiōtai*] from Sin." We can take "justified from Sin" here to mean "justly liberated by God from Sin's oppressive regime, which was responsible for Messiah's death." We ourselves have not yet literally died (as the Messiah did), but, united with him in baptism, we "grow together in the likeness" (Rom 6:5) of the one who has already died. We might say that the Messiah's death already "contains" our own death in itself (see 2 Cor 5:14, "One has died for all; therefore all have died"). But those who by baptism share "in Messiah" are now *actively conformed to his death*. This means those who share in his death to Sin are also dead to Sin. The sinful sovereignty of the "old humanity" that arrived in Adam was terminated and superabundantly overcome in the Messiah's death and resurrection. Yet that "old [lording-it-over] humanity" must also continuously be "made inoperative" or "rendered powerless" (*katargēthē*,

Rom 6:6) in the (personal and political) body of those joined together under the Messiah's reign, so that they are no longer enslaved by sovereign Sin and the sin of sovereignty. This is possible because a new power of life has come, the very power that raised Jesus from the dead.

> The Greek phrase *palaios anthrōpos* in Romans 6:6 is often translated as the "old self." What difference does it make to translate it as the "old humanity," as I have done here?

Sharing in the Messiah's death means sharing simultaneously in the power of his resurrection (Rom 6:8). The power of divine life unleashed on the dead body of the Messiah is inexhaustible, unstoppable, and unending. Death can no longer lord it over the risen Messiah. He died once—completely past tense. The sovereignty of Sin's deadly power over him ended there. Full stop! By contrast, the *resurrected* Messiah "lives *to God*"—completely present tense (Rom 6:10). The Messiah's indestructible divine life is now the source and sustaining power of life of his new community, his body. Just as he died once to Sin but now lives to God, so also those who share "in Messiah Jesus" reckon themselves "dead to Sin but alive *to God*" (Rom 6:11). It is important to emphasize the phrase "to God" both here and in the previous verse. As we saw with respect to Romans 6:7, the Messiah's death and resurrection is the means by which he is justified or justly liberated from Sin's sovereignty. But that liberation is *not* into a kind of aimless freedom-as-autonomy, as we often regard freedom in our time—the freedom to pursue one's own desires, interests, destiny, or fulfillment through limitless choices. That kind of freedom in fact manifests the power of Sin.

The freedom of the good news is liberation into life lived "to God": we are "alive to God in Messiah Jesus" (Rom 6:11). As we saw in Romans 2, in the light of the gospel we discern that no human person or society or people finds itself in a neutral zone making autonomous decisions about which sovereign power to serve. We are always embedded in systems of sovereignty. We serve either the death-dealing power of Sin or, by God's gracious deliverance, the life-giving power of God. When God comes with liberating power in the death and resurrection of the Messiah, it is to create a people living wholly for the rule of God, having been raised to new life only for this purpose. The "mortal body" (which is simultaneously personal, sexual, social, political) was once claimed by the regime of Sin, "obeying evil desires," oriented to the purposes of that regime: power, domination, lust, acquisition, possession, consumption (Rom 6:12). That very same mortal body is now claimed by God, and the claim of Sin's regime on its desires must be utterly rejected.

Becoming Weapons of Justice (Romans 6:13-14)

Paul introduces another startling image. He asks us to imagine the parts or members (*melē*) of our body as weapons (*hopla*). The body in question here may signify the personal, physical body with its limbs, but it may also signify a social or political body with its individual members, such as Paul develops in Romans 12 when he speaks of the body of the Messiah and its members. While the Greek word *hopla* is often translated rather blandly as "instruments" (NRSV, NIV), in Paul's context it was often used in the military sense of "weapons" and/or "armor," as even Paul himself sometimes does (see Rom 13:12; 2 Cor 6:7; Eph 6:11, 13). That Paul has so far consistently been developing the image of regimes of power should therefore lead us to think in terms of weapons rather than simply instruments. In the regime of Sin, he says, we "yielded" (*paristanete*) our bodies and their members as "weapons of injustice" (*hopla adikias*) in Sin's war.

Adamic-style sovereignty often asserts its power with literal lethal and destructive weapons. Every political sovereign lays claim to our bodies and their capacities in order to pay for, defend, and advance its cause. If we believe the cause is in our (national, economic, social, personal) interests, we might voluntarily yield ourselves over to the sovereign's campaigns of dominion—though we might sometimes even be conscripted. In Paul's image, sovereign Sin conscripts our bodies and wields them as weapons in a rampage of injustice. Against this Paul's word is firm: "Do not yield your members to Sin as weapons of injustice!" Certainly on one level we must take this in a personal-moral sense: do not give your bodies to immorality and wickedness. Sin certainly claims us in this way. But there is also an implicit but strong exhortation to cease offering our bodies as weapons in the deadly campaigns of worldly sovereignties, because our bodies also in this way become weapons in the hands of Sin.

At the same time, Paul does not shrink from using weapon imagery to speak of messianic life: "Yield yourselves to God as those who are alive from the dead, and your members to God as weapons of justice [*hopla dikaiosynēs*]" (Rom 6:13). There is potential danger in this statement if we take it out of context. For example, we might be tempted to think that Paul now encourages us to become militantly and coercively involved in various causes of justice, perhaps even a "just war." Here, however, everything depends on what we have already learned of the meaning of the words *God* and *justice* in Paul's gospel. As we learned from the opening lines of Romans, the "good news of God" *is* the good news of "his Son, Jesus Messiah our Ruler" (Rom 1:1-4). If we declare, "In God we trust," and mean this in the sense of *Paul's gospel*, then we are not trusting in "God" in the abstract, with whatever personal or nationalistic meanings we might wish to give to the word *God*. It is the God apocalypsed in Jesus Messiah, and only this God, whom we trust. God's character and purpose among Israel and the nations is defined messianically: it is revealed in the nonviolent, self-offering death and resurrection of God's Son. Thus any cause to which we yield our members as weapons must conform to the way of *this* God, and to the justice defined by the cross. And the weapons themselves must be appropriate to the Messiah's way of conquering the regime of Sin. Paul is explicit about this in Ephesians 6:10-17.

Are you prepared to yield your body to your nation's purposes as a weapon in its wars? What role do worldly weapons (personal weapons or your nation's) play in your understanding of how God's justice gets done in the world? How does that accord with the gospel?

We learned from the opening thesis of the letter (Rom 1:16-17) and from Romans 3:21-26 that *justice* has a very particular meaning: it is apocalypsed in Jesus Messiah. His life, death, and resurrection is how God does justice and is the measure of all justice: what counts as justice must align with God's way of making right what is wrong through the Messiah's crucifixion and resurrection. By this measure, no violence, no coercive militant action, no worldly war, is ever just: rather, these are the manifestations of Sin's sovereignty. "Our struggle is not against blood and flesh" (Eph 6:12). Worldly weapons, from fists and spears to guns and bombs and cyberattacks, are never the appropriate ones in the Messiah's war: these are the weapons of Sin. The only weapon of messianic justice is the powerful good news itself; as Paul says in Ephesians, "the sword of the Spirit . . . is the word of God" (Eph 6:17). The human body given over to the Messiah—the Messiah's political body—embodies in all its body parts the way of the Messiah. To "offer our members to God as weapons of justice" (Rom 6:13) means, then, that our members must be given to no other cause than that of our Sovereign, Jesus Messiah, in whom God and God's justice for all are apocalypsed. *This* yielding of our members to the messianic cause must be wholehearted and exclusive. As weapons, our bodies serve only God's work of justice revealed in the gospel. In this way "Sin shall not lord it over you" (Rom 6:14). Sovereign Sin and worldly sovereigns can no longer command the members of the Messiah's body, nor can they provide the motive or measure for justice. Sin's claim is decisively broken. The messianic body is free for obedience to God alone.

Becoming Slaves of Justice (Romans 6:15-22)

In still another startling image, Paul now speaks of being "slaves" of justice. Even he seems to be somewhat uncomfortable with this disturbing image, but he says he uses it to get the point across in case we miss it (Rom 6:19). What we might miss is what I have already noted, namely, that we might confuse the freedom of God's justice with the aimless freedom our culture offers. We may think liberation means being set into an open space of personal, economic, and/or political autonomy where we are "free" to determine our direction, defend our interests, maximize our choices, and fulfill our possibilities, even if we concede that the law may limit some of our aims and actions. But in gospel terms freedom is not autonomy but service, so there is no need to limit it with law. "You are not under Law but under Grace" (Rom 6:14). Where Grace reigns Law is not needed.

"May we then sin because we are not under Law but under Grace?" (Rom 6:15). "Never!" Paul's answer again emphasizes the absurdity of a thought not to be taken seriously (see Rom 6:1), but not because he wishes to reassert the rule of law. In fact, he now sets aside further discussion of law until Romans 7. His immediate point here is to say that the regime of Sin laid a direct claim on humanity. It enslaved human beings to itself, whether law was in the picture or not (though it did indeed come into the picture). Yet in Paul's metaphor slaves are *subjects* of the master and offer the master *obedience*. Subjects are not objects (as much as the master might think of slaves as such), and obedience is the act of a subject, not an object. So Paul again uses the word *yield*: "if you yield yourselves as slaves for obedience [to God]" (Rom 6:16). Obedience is yielded; it is *given* in some sense. The point here is that while Sin rules as a master in relation to humanity, setting its conditions, limits, and possibilities, humanity in some measure continues to offer itself obediently to this master. Sin is a sovereign, not a mechanical force. Sin commands; humans obey. They even obey with some sense of their own good in mind.

At this crucial juncture, then, we are caught up by a fundamental decision, though again it is not one that we make in a neutral space. A new master has invaded the realm of the old one. By the justice of God in Jesus Messiah we have *already*—even before we have made a decision—been liberated from the master Sin and been claimed by the master Grace. Far from creating neutral space, God's invasion by Grace creates the very condition for the decision that now stands before us. Once, we yielded ourselves to the rule and command of sovereign Sin that held sway over human life: the end of that yielding is bondage and death. But the good news is that "having been freed from Sin, you were enslaved to justice" (Rom 6:18). As the passive voice of Paul's verbs shows, this is an event of freeing and enslaving that was and could only be brought about by God on our behalf. We do not choose ourselves out of Sin's bondage. *Within* God's decision and liberating act for us, our own decision and act is evoked: we yield ourselves as slaves "for obedience [to God], the end of which is justice" (Rom 6:16).

Paul's next sentence displays this dynamic clearly: "Thanks be to God that, having once been slaves of Sin, you *obeyed from the heart* the pattern of teaching to which you were handed over" (Rom 6:17). By first thanking God, Paul sets all that happens here within the context of God's own working. God frees us from the iron grip of master Sin. And because of God's work we have "obeyed from the heart." We have become not merely passive recipients but *living and active subjects* of the gospel of justice ("the pattern of teaching"), which itself has taken us into its sphere of power ("to which you were handed over"). That last phrase, "were handed over" (see Rom 1:24, 26, 28), again suggests God's action at work through Paul's teaching of the gospel to bring about the obedience from the heart.

In yielding our members as obedient slaves under Sin's sovereignty, the end was impurity and ever-increasing lawlessness (literally, "lawlessness upon lawlessness," Rom 6:19). The term *impurity* or *uncleanness* surely indicates that slavery under Sin results in the kind of personal, moral, and sexual transgressions and disorder brought about because of idolatry, as described in Romans 1:18-27. Such impurity, Paul says, brought forth no fruit, but only shame and an "end in death" (Rom 6:21). However, having now been handed over into the sphere of living justice, and yielding our members as "slaves of justice," the power of justice creates in us a fundamental transformation of personal, moral, and sexual life. By the transforming power of justice there is real fruit. It is called sanctification, or holiness—likeness to God.

But the term *impurity* and its opposite, *holiness*, do not refer only to personal life. For Paul the sphere of the personal is never separate from the spheres of social and political sovereignty. For example, *porneia* ("sexual immorality") and domination go hand in hand; they are often one and the same thing. The idolatry that creates impurity is first manifested when image-of-God dominion (for serving one another and creation) is distorted into domination, with the man "ruling over" the woman. "Impurity" therefore surely also signals our exercise of, implication in, and dependence on worldly acts and systems of sovereignty that stand opposed to the sovereignty of God's grace in Jesus Messiah. Impurity results when we believe that yielding ourselves in obedience to God and God's justice is mediated by yielding ourselves in obedience to worldly political powers—social norms, rulers, governments, constitutions, nations, revolutions. That kind of *blended obedience* to God and worldly rulers is both idolatry and impurity. When Paul preaches the good news that calls for the "obedience of faith [loyalty] among all the nations" (Rom 1:5), that claim on our loyalty and obedience is not mediated by worldly sovereignties. We rightly yield to the claim of the good news—personally, socially, politically—only when we become one with the body politic of the crucified and risen Messiah.

The phrase "lawlessness upon lawlessness" in Romans 6:19 anticipates Paul's discussion of the role of the Law (*nomos*) in Romans 7. Lawlessness (*anomia*) needs to be taken seriously in the legal (*nomos*) sense, rather than being understood more generically as personal "iniquity" or "wickedness." The lawlessness brought about by slavery to Sin suggests unrestrained disorder and injustice in the social and political dimensions of life (such as is described in Rom 1:28-32) and not simply in the personal dimension. However, it is crucial to recognize that for Paul the law cannot eliminate injustice. Ending injustice in social and political life is *not* brought about by a society or people yielding its members as "slaves to law," whether by promoting devout obedience to law, expanding the range of its application, or ramping up on enforcement. Law exposes lawlessness, restrains it, and sometimes punishes it, but law is powerless to create a just person or a just society. Lawlessness is brought to an end in those who yield themselves as "slaves to justice," or—*which is the same thing*—become "enslaved to God" (Rom 6:22). According to the gospel, God's justice in Messiah is the measure, condition, and power of justice in society. Where slavery to Sin is lawless, fruitless, shameful, and ends in death, being "enslaved to God" brings about justice and holiness, and ends in eternal life (Rom 6:22).

The Grace of Divine Life (Romans 6:23)

Paul concludes his discussion of the deadly power of Sin and the living power of justice by leaving behind the image of slavery, which, he admits (Rom 6:19), makes a point but does not adequately represent God's justice. For the fact is that Sin promises a kind of *salary* to its obedient slaves—something they might willingly *work* for, for the sake of their own interest—whether that be survival, pleasure, wealth, advantage, status, sovereign power, glory, life. Why else would anyone willingly yield themselves to Sin's mastery, unless there was imagined benefit in it? The huge shock, however, comes on payday: the salary is not what they expected at all: "For the salary of Sin is Death" (Rom 6:23).

In stark contrast, the reality of being brought within the power of justice is not slavery at all, not even employment for a salary. At the end of Romans 5 and in Romans 6:1, 15, Paul contrasts the sovereignty of Sin on the one hand with the infinitely different sovereignty of Grace on the other. Grace is *absolutely* unlike Sin. If slavery is the appropriate image to speak of humanity in relation to Sin, it must finally be abandoned when speaking of humanity in relation to Grace, to justice, and to God. Grace, justice, and God (these three are one) are the origin, moving power, and final end of human freedom. Here there is *no slavery*, and here there is *no salary*. Beyond every work and every payoff and every expectation, beyond the regime of Sin, slavery, and death, there is grace, freedom, life: "the grace-gift [*charisma*] of God is eternal life through Jesus Messiah our one and only Sovereign" (Rom 6:23). The end is not payday but sharing in excessive divine life.

Justice, then, is God's power of eternal life (the Spirit of holiness, Rom 1:4) unleashed on the body of Messiah, raising him from the dead. We have been drawn into this power of life here and now by the good news, in order that we might yield ourselves in free and ready obedience to justice. To remind ourselves: justice, according to the good news, is not a free-floating idea. Justice is what God graciously does in Jesus Messiah—in fact, it is Jesus Messiah himself. It is gift given; it is eternal life unleashed; it is God in action; it is human life freed for divine life.

7

JUSTICE AND LAW

IN THIS CHAPTER

- Romans 7:1-6: Being married to law does not bear the fruit of justice
- Romans 7:7-13: The good of law is ruined by the rule of law
- Romans 7:14-25: When law changes from servant to lord

IN ALMOST EVERYONE'S MIND, justice and law, if not the same thing, are very closely related concepts. We expect law to define the meaning of justice across many spheres of society and aspects of public life. The Judeans in Paul's time had a long and expansive legal tradition, going back to Moses and developed through the centuries by the Judean prophets, wisdom writers, and rabbis. This tradition of law was the foundation of Judean life. As a Pharisee, Paul inherited the tradition, was devoted to it, and continued to be shaped by it even after Jesus Messiah claimed and commissioned him as apostle. It is no surprise, then, that from Romans 2 onward Paul frequently raised the question of the relationship between law and justice.

If the good news is that God's justice is apocalypsed "apart from law," how, if at all, is the law of Moses relevant to our understanding of justice? As the imaginary Judean philosopher had asked in Romans 3:1, "Is there any point in being (or remaining) Judean, or being circumcised?" Paul answered emphatically, "Much, in every way! In the first place, the Judeans were entrusted with the words [*logia*] of God" (Rom 3:2). Yet in Romans 3:9-19 Paul went on to invoke those very "words of God" (that is, the law) to silence the claim that the Judean people are better than the Gentile nations. The law itself speaks against the claim that the law produces justice; rather, it shows (as Paul reads it) that Judean society, like the Gentile nations, is "under Sin" (Rom 3:9).

But that is not a conclusion Paul came to on the basis of argument or empirical evidence. Paul's conclusion that justice comes *apart from law* is based on the fact that God's justice was apocalypsed in the life, death, and resurrection of Jesus Messiah (Rom 1:16-17; 3:21-26; 5:12-20). If both divine and human justice are revealed and enacted in Messiah, then justice does not happen through law. Paul's logic runs this way: because Jesus Messiah *is* God's justice, the law is *not*. That applies not only to the law of Moses but to any other nations' laws as well. We cannot imagine Paul saying that the law of Moses is not God's means of justice but Roman law is. The same must be said of any other constitutions and laws then and now, whether those of our own nation or any other. We saw further that God "reckoned" Abraham to be just because he trusted God (Rom 4:17). God accounted Abraham just apart from any work of Judean law such as circumcision (Abraham trusted God while he still had the foreskin). But it was also apart from any non-Judean law or custom, such as keeping the foreskin (Abraham was later circumcised as a "sign and seal" of the justice of trust, Rom 4:9-12). If trust is what counts as justice, then justice does not happen through law, whether Judean or otherwise. Law is not the origin, form, and power of justice. God working through Messiah is.

> How do you understand the relation between law and justice? Do you count on law for justice? If so, what do you mean by that? How does law work for justice?

For Paul, law does not produce justice. Instead, it functions to define, count up, and punish human transgressions—thus, the more laws, the more transgressions (Rom 5:13, 20). Paul already hints in these claims that law is not working on the side of justice but on the side of Sin. Somehow law is co-opted by Sin into Sin's sphere of sovereignty, and therefore also serves Death; law becomes "Law" as a power working against the good news. By stark contrast, the good news declares that the sovereign power of Grace ("under Grace," thus uppercase *G*) *delivers* us from the sovereign grip of Law ("under Law" [Rom 6:14], thus *L*).

It seems that Paul's argument may lead to the conclusion that God's justice not only arrives apart from law but is in fact *against law*. Perhaps the gospel cancels or nullifies law altogether. But Paul says, No way! Instead, God's justice in Messiah confirms or sustains law (Rom 3:31). In fact, the real truth and purpose of law is only revealed in the light of the good news. Paul now goes on to explain this thought in Romans 7–8, but only *after* he has made it clear that (1) the way of human justice is trust in God (Rom 4), (2) God's justice is apocalypsed for all in Jesus Messiah (Rom 5), and (3) we become just only by participation in Jesus' death and resurrection (Rom 6).

The Marriage-Bond of Law (Romans 7:1-6)

Paul now draws on the marriage relationship to explain by analogy how the good news fundamentally alters the human relationship to law for those who share in the crucifixion and resurrection of Messiah. The aptness of the analogy of marriage will soon become apparent. Everyone who knows the law, Paul writes, knows that law holds authority over a person as long as they live. Paul puts it more dramatically: Law "lords it over" (*kurieuei*) a person throughout the person's life (Rom 7:1). We have already encountered the Greek verb *kyrieuō*, "lord it over," twice in Romans 6. In Romans 6:9 Paul wrote that Death no longer lords it over the body of the risen Messiah; in Romans 6:14 he declared that neither shall Sin lord it over us because Grace now reigns. We thus see a kind of trinity of lords or sovereign powers at work in Sin's ungodly reign of injustice: Sin itself, Death, and Law (uppercase *L*).

The sovereignty of Law, Paul writes, is like the legal relationship of a wife and husband (in Paul's time). The married woman is bound by law to her husband as long as the husband is alive. If she marries another man while her first husband is still alive, she commits adultery under the law (of Moses). However, if her first husband dies, she is free of the legal bond to that husband and free to marry another man (Rom 7:1-3). Sovereign Law is likened to the husband and humanity to the wife. Like a husband, Law holds binding authority over (lords it over) human society; like a wife, human society is legally bound to Law. Here Paul may be reflecting the shift from Genesis 1:26-28, where the man and the woman *together* were given to rule in service of all living creatures, to Genesis 3:16, where—following human transgression—the man will "rule over" the woman and her "desire" shall be for him. So too, now Law (the husband) rules like a sovereign over humankind, and humankind (the wife) is subject to Law and desires to serve it. There is only one way out of this binding marriage: someone must die.

But the analogy is now reversed. Surprisingly, Paul does not say that husband-Law must die. Rather, it is the wife—humanity—who must die with respect to Law. This is consistent with what Paul said earlier in Romans 6. Sharing in the crucified body of Jesus Messiah, *we* "die to Sin" so that Sin's lordship is fundamentally broken. Sin is not eradicated, but its *power*—its capacity to rule human lives—is canceled when a person dies. Sin struggles to regain that lost sovereignty over us; but our victory in that struggle is won through ongoing participation in the Messiah's own *death* to Sin. So also with respect to Law: Law remains in human life, but "you were put to death to the Law through the body of the Messiah" (Rom 7:4). Humanity bound under Law's *rule* (the "first husband") *dies to the sovereignty of Law* through sharing in the death of the Messiah. In Paul's strange analogy, the wife (humanity) dies in order that, raised from the dead, she "might belong to another"—to the second husband, as it were, who is the Messiah himself raised from the dead—"in order that we might bear fruit to God" (Rom 7:4). When we share in the death of Messiah, our bondage relationship to sovereign Law is severed; when we share in the resurrection of the Messiah, we are free for a new "marriage" that will bear the fruit of justice. If we find ourselves yearning for the fruit of justice, we will not bear that fruit by giving ourselves to lordly Law—whether that is the law of Moses, or the law of the Romans, or any other law. We will produce the fruit of justice only in a living, marriage-like bond with Jesus Messiah.

It is no accident, it seems, that when Paul comes to speak of the human relationship to Law he shifts from the more negative analogies of weapons (Rom 6:13-14) and slaves (Rom 6:15-20) to the more positive analogy of marriage. We do not love Sin and Death. Even though we find ourselves inescapably bound under them as sovereign powers, we hate them and their oppressive bondage, even as we cannot free ourselves from them. Paul will make just this point later in Romans 7. But our relationship to law is different. The relationship of Judeans to the law of Moses provides Paul with the representative example of this difference. For reflective Judeans of Paul's time—such as Paul the Pharisee—the whole of Judean law was much more than a set of rules and commandments to observe. To think of living according to Torah as legalism is to miss the point. Torah for the premessianic Paul was the coherent bond holding all things together. Through Torah God created the world, and by it God governs the whole of the cosmos. We might paraphrase Colossians 1:17 with respect to Torah: "Torah is before all things; in Torah all things hold together." God revealed this cosmic Torah to Moses and the Israelites at Mount Sinai as their concrete *form of life*: their founding history, traditions, polity and legal practices; their social, family, and sexual relationships; their worship, customs, habits, and practices of everyday life. In this comprehensive sense law was Judean reality, life, and culture. For a rabbi such as Paul, to be a Judean apart from Torah was inconceivable.

We should not think that the Judeans were unique in this respect. Most peoples in history (most *ethnē*) bear such a relationship to their own laws. It is well-known that as a people the Romans were proud and jealous of their divine-origin stories (about the gods and the founding of Rome), their republican political system and legal system, their social order, customs, and forms of religious practice and sacrifice, and so on. They believed in the divine right and ultimate goodness of their law (both as a comprehensive form of life and in the narrower sense as a legal system) and were prepared not only to maintain and defend it but also to proclaim it as good news for all, far and wide. They regularly spread this gospel by subduing and colonizing peoples around the Mediterranean and throughout Europe, imposing their law for the greater good (they believed) of all who came under their sway. As they saw it, the Roman form of life was self-evidently *good news for all peoples*. Similar thoughts have motivated many colonizing expansions both before and after the Romans, whether Babylonian, Persian, or Greek, whether Spanish, British, or American, whether communist, capitalist, or Islamist.

The identity of a people or nation and its members is constituted by a people's law, if we take *law* not only in the narrower legal sense but also in the sense of the constitution, customs, and culture of a people—their collective "wisdom." Humans are for the most part inevitably, but also willingly and robustly, bound to law. Every people—not just the Judeans—takes their own law to be "holy, just, and good" (Rom 7:12). Therefore, to imagine our relationship to law with the metaphor of marriage, as Paul does, captures something of its *indispensability* and *intimacy* to human life. Law, like a "husband" (in ancient times), establishes and preserves our place in the world and protects us from threats. But it is also within our hearts as the thing we love because it makes us the distinct society, people, or nation that we are, set apart from others. Like a good husband, law in this broad sense captivates me, makes my world, claims my body, gives me an identity, enables my thinking, and shapes my passions and hopes. As a "wife" of law, I give myself willingly to it and orient my life by it and for it. I am prepared to defend its role and advance its influence in whatever way I can. We two become one.

It is easy to see that to live apart from law would require something like a death—a loss of one's world, culture, and identity, a separation from one's *life*. I would have to "die to the law" of my people or nation in order to "belong [fully] to another."

This kind of binding relationship—this marriage—to law seems not only natural and healthy but also essential to my very flourishing. Nevertheless, Paul fundamentally disrupts this marriage with a disturbing word: the marriage must end because it is sterile; it cannot bear the fruit of justice. "For when we were in the flesh [*sarki*] our sinful passions were energized [*energeito*] through the law in our members to bear fruit for death" (Rom 7:5). *Flesh* for Paul is not simply the biological stuff of our physical bodies. It also means living life "naturally," we might say, that is, fundamentally *trusting* all of the assumptions, practices, patterns, habits, social arrangements, and so on that we take for granted as the way things are. Call all of this "Law." There is no real need to trust God, because God's will is mediated by Law. There is no real need to seek life elsewhere, because life just means being "in Law." Yet Paul says that our natural intimacy with and dependence on Law is flesh. We are caught up in a deadly marriage. How so?

Let's put this in the context of Paul's life under Judean law, before the Messiah claimed him. As Paul confesses in his letter to the Galatians (Gal 1:14), "I was advancing in Judaism way beyond my Judean peers, for I was far more zealous for my ancestral traditions." In other words, he was zealous for a total way of life and culture among the Judeans guided by the law. In Philippians he writes: "If anyone else thinks they can trust in the flesh [*sarki*], I can do so more: circumcised on the eighth day, a member of the people [*genous*] Israel, of the tribe of Benjamin, a Hebrew of Hebrews, a Pharisee in Law, persecuting the messianic assembly with zeal, blameless in justice according to Law" (Phil 3:4-6). "In the flesh" Paul found himself energized by passion ("zeal") for the law, that is, for the "natural" form of life that might constitute the Judeans as a distinct people. God's justice had been revealed and mediated to Israel through the law of Moses, and God would come again in justice to deliver Israel if the Judean people would obey, defend, and advance Torah in all of life. As one devoted to Israel's law as the way of life and justice, Paul was naturally caught up in a life-and-death struggle against any Judeans who would threaten the integrity of that way of life, that marriage. He perceived such a threat in those who believed they "belonged to another," that is, to Jesus Messiah. As one "in the flesh," Paul the Judean Pharisee was therefore ready to "bear fruit for death" (Rom 7:5) for the sake of Torah. He was moved to persecute and destroy the messianic community and its members for the sake of his first love, the Torah.

> Paul is not unusual in his identification with a "given" and "natural" way of life and his zeal to defend it. Good citizenship seems to demand such devotion and action. Defending a way of life is why nations have militaries, secret services, and departments of homeland security. Have you ever considered such good citizenship as living *kata sarka*—"according to the flesh"? What would be some implications of regarding your citizenship in that way?

For Paul this is the problem of law, and not only Judean law: when the life of a people (and one's own life as a citizen) is founded in law (as a comprehensive form of life), passions are energized not only *for* that law, as an end in itself, but also *against* whatever or whomever might threaten it. In defense of "our" people and its way of life (its law in the expansive sense), "we, the people" find ourselves at odds and often at war with others: Romans against Judeans, Judeans against Romans; the West against Islam, Islam against the West; Christianity against secularism, secularism against Christianity, and so on. In this way of thinking, the triumph of "our" law is the triumph of justice and life. But, according to the gospel, this is the deadly operation of the flesh: our natural passion for our way of life (law) is commandeered by Sin into opposition and war against others, and brings forth Death.

A fundamental question was thus forced on Paul early on in his mission. It seems no people can live without law. Some early Judean believers in Jesus Messiah thought that Greek and Roman messianics must die to their (pagan, degraded) ways of life and become married instead to the God-given Judean way of life (the law of Moses)—in other words, they must become Judeans, with the males being marked by circumcision. That agenda threatened to destroy the churches in Galatia. Paul rejects it in his letter to the Galatians. Alternatively, some Gentile messianics in Rome seem to have thought that Judeans should die to their way of life (the law of Moses) and be absorbed instead into Greco-Roman culture—in other words, become Gentiles. That is the core issue in Romans 11:13–24 and Romans 14. Paul will reject that idea too, as we will see when we come to those chapters.

The good news Paul proclaims goes down neither of those roads. Rather, the gospel is that Judeans, Greeks, and Romans are all alike "put to death to the Law through the body of Messiah" in order that they might "belong to another, to him who was raised from the dead," and thereby "bear fruit to God" (Rom 7:4). The Messiah's own death under Law (both Judean and Roman law) put an end to Law's *sovereignty* over life. A particular people's law or culture or way of life is no longer the determining factor for the meaning of life and justice. In the Messiah's death that kind of binding but deadly marriage to a law or way of life is brought to an end. In his risen body the Messiah creates and claims a new people who are now married to him, a people who might bear fruit not to a Judean or Roman way of life but to God, the fruit of justice in the "new life of Spirit" (*kainotēti pneumatos*, Rom 7:6).

From Law to Commandment (Romans 7:7-13)

We have seen how Paul brings together Sin, Death, and Law into an unholy trinity of sovereign powers that bring about injustice and death rather than justice and life for all (Rom 5:18). This trinity constitutes the *antigospel*. So closely does Law thus seem to be aligned with Sin and Death that we may be inclined to conclude that *Law equals Sin*; Law is just Sin by another name.

But to this conclusion Paul utters an emphatic "No! Not at all!" (Rom 7:7). The problem of Law is not law itself, but its relationship to Sin. Law itself has been captured by sovereign Sin and forced into serving Sin's purpose rather than serving the purpose of justice. So, how does Law serve Sin?

Law in the way we have been speaking of it, as a people's form of life, is not *as such* the property of Sin (although law never actually appears *as such*). For the most part the form of life we live remains subliminal in our consciousness; it is natural to us, taken for granted, just the way things are. We dwell within it rather than outside it. It is the cultural air we breathe. For a rather trivial example: while driving our car, we see a traffic light up ahead turn red, we slowly apply the brakes, we come to a stop at the line, we wait for the light to turn green, and then we drive on. This may happen many times a day, maybe hundreds of times in a week of commuting to and from work. For most of us the whole process happens each time virtually without a thought about it; in fact, we are likely thinking about other things, perhaps looking at someone on the sidewalk, coveting the car beside us, listening to the radio or music, possibly talking on a phone (not a good idea), perhaps even texting a friend (a very bad idea). We "naturally" stop at the red light whether or not another car is entering the intersection from the side. While it is our legal duty to stop, and illegal not to do so, this is rarely on our mind. Nor is the great deal of sheer custom that is implicit in the whole event. For example, is there anything *intrinsic* to the color red that means "stop," to the color yellow that means "slow down," or to the color green that means "go"? Only custom has made it so, yet it all seems natural. And then there is all the tacit skill of eye-mind-body coordination (learned by practice over time) by which, without thinking, we know just how hard to apply the brakes to come to a gentle stop, and then the accelerator to drive gently through the intersection, perhaps also skillfully and simultaneously turning the steering wheel to make a turn. This, we might say, is law at work in many ways and many dimensions in a single event that we repeat time after time, day after day. This is law experienced and lived not as "a law" ("Stop at a red light!") but as one simple form of life that gets us and many others to and from work safely every day. If we multiply such experiences by many times and in many dimensions, we get the comprehensive form of life we call a society and culture.

Consider other dimensions of life. We often find our attention drawn to what is true and beautiful and good in the world around us—a shapely tree, a graceful animal, a scenic landscape, an elegant house and yard, a fertile piece of land, a compelling work of art, a useful invention, a well-run and successful business, a peaceful and prosperous nation, an attractive person. Much of the time these things register for us only subliminally, as elements that make up the total world "given" to us by the work of nature and human hands. Sometimes we stop to pay attention, to take in and marvel at the wonder of these things, delighting in the details of their form and being. The thought of possessing them for ourselves does not enter our minds. There is no law against such things. There is no sin in this moment.

But then a commanding word (audibly or inaudibly) comes to us: You cannot have that! Perhaps someone perceives my attention to something of theirs as a desire to possess it and utters the prohibition. Now the thought of possessing comes to mind. The prohibition both awakens the desire to possess and names that desire as sin. As Paul writes, "For I would not have known what it was to covet except that the law [*nomos*] said [now as a commandment], 'You shall not covet.' But Sin, seizing the opportunity opened by the commandment [*entolē*], generated in me every kind of covetousness" (Rom 7:7-8). In the moment that law ceases to be the implicit and subliminal structure and form of a life well-lived (*nomos*) and instead becomes distilled into a commandment (*entolē*), in that moment desire is awakened and Law is experienced as a restraining limit. In the prohibition "You shall not covet," I am taken out of my inattentive or attentive delight in what is simply there as given and I become aware of it as what is *not given*. I now start to think of what it would be like to possess it, and perhaps of what I might do in order to possess it. Sin has risen up and manipulated law into the form of a commandment, which now animates the desire that I must struggle to contain.

Paul writes this story of Law in the first person ("I" = Greek *egō*). But his point is not primarily to provide a personal psychoanalysis of how he once related or now relates to Law. Rather, he is giving us a kind of *history* of Law in relation to human life. Paul's I represents my I and everyone's I. More important, it represents the collective I of a people. In the working of law before it functions as commandment, law functions in "weakness," rooting a people in a form of life in which they are scarcely aware of that form as

"Law"; it is more like ground and atmosphere and framework for life, and very little like rule. We experience it as something that enables us to live and breathe in the free space of not paying attention directly to it, rather than as something that claims and contains us. It is fluid and flexible, adjusting to the ongoing movement of persons, peoples and societies over time. It undergirds, evokes, enables, and gives shape to the ordinary goodness of personal, social, economic, and political life.

In this "weak" form law is therefore closer to wisdom and nearer to justice, neither demanding loyalty nor commanding obedience. In this form it is more like spirit. So Paul can say that "the law [*nomos*] is holy [*hagios*]" (Rom 7:12), that "the law [*nomos*] is spiritual [*pneumatikos*]" (Rom 7:14), and that it is "the law [*nomos*] of God" (Rom 7:25). While he says this directly about the Torah in particular, he might make the same claim, though in a reduced sense, about the laws of other nations. It is also clear that in this "weak" form, Paul never required or expected or desired that the Judean people, including Judeans in Jesus Messiah, should give up their practice of the law of Moses as their distinct—indeed, God-given—way of life.

However, law in the "weak" sense is easily co-opted to destructive ends. It can be (and invariably is) turned also into a legal system backed by sovereign power. This is Law (uppercase *L*) in the strong sense. At its best, even such a system is generally aimed toward specifying and protecting the order and ordinary goodness of everyday life. The laws of a legal system are not always by intention the instruments of death (Rom 7:13). Paul can even say, "The commandment [*entolē*] is holy [*hagia*], just [*dikaia*], and good [*agathē*]" (Rom 7:12). But "strong" Law now asserts itself in the form of legal requirements, demands, prohibitions, restraints, and penalties. Commandments and laws (plural) become inscribed in legal decrees and documents, which take on a life of their own and become the basis for legal judgments. Transgressions are defined and made explicit. Penalties and punishments are specified and imposed.

In demanding our obedience and in exposing and judging transgressions and injustices, Law starts to look less like an implicit form of life and more like lording it over in the way that Sin and Death do. Far from tackling Sin in its fundamental character as a destructive power, Law becomes fixated on *sins*. It seeks to identify and classify sins, and curb and manage them with threats of punishment enforced by power, including in some cases the threat of death. In this way Sin's effect in specific transgressions (sins) is exposed, to be sure, but Law now seems also to be caught up in Sin's powerful gravitational pull, gaining strength from Sin rather than serving human life. "In order that Sin might be clearly manifest as Sin, it [Sin] worked Death in me through what was good, that is, through the commandment, by which Sin is exposed in its fundamental character as Sin" (Rom 7:13).

The original "weakness" of law as the wisdom of ordinary life recedes. Separating itself from natural life, Law now demands our attention, obedience, and loyalty as an end in itself. For example, something such as respect for others becomes political correctness and moves toward sanctioning certain types of speech and behavior. The rule of law comes to dominate human relationships. We are now faced with two options in relation to "strong" Law: *Either* we submit ourselves to the system of Law in obedience, even trust, and celebrate Law as an end in itself, as the rules for all, and expect "the Law" to come down on all who disobey it. *Or,* if Law itself has become an instrument of oppression and injustice (as it often does), we desire liberation from its domination, a desire that often generates rebellion and lawlessness. For Paul, each of these options is the way of the flesh.

What confidence do you put in the legal system of your society? Do you find yourself primarily affirming and upholding it and its judgments? Or do you find yourself chafing against its dominion? Consider especially your own relative power in your society. Does the power of the legal system seem to work primarily for you or against you? What difference does that make to your response to the legal system?

From Weak Law to Sovereign Law (Romans 7:14-25)

Again writing in the first person, Paul continues to tell the story of how law, which is "holy, just, and good," becomes enslaved by Sin—becomes Law. Most readers agree that Romans 7:14-25 is a very convoluted text, which leads many to conclude that Paul is expressing his own deep inner conflict—his tortured conscience—regarding the Judean law. However, while Paul himself is certainly not absent from this text, I believe we must again take the "I" in a wider sense than Paul's own autobiography, finding in it also something of the ongoing history of law in human societies. Nevertheless, we will draw on Paul's own story to illustrate the point.

Along with the I, there are three other characters in the story Paul tells: Sin, Law, and Flesh (so we also apply an uppercase *F* in *Flesh*). These characters are ranged on two sides of the battle between good and evil. On one side in this war are the weak characters, I and law; on the other side are the strong characters, Flesh and Sin. The outcome is easy to anticipate. In fact, the whole story starts out with the I—the human being, human society— already fundamentally compromised in the battle. Far from being an independent agent, a warrior on its own side in the battle against evil, the I finds itself as Flesh unwittingly on the side of Sin, functioning despite itself as Sin's slave. "I am of Flesh [*sarkinos*], sold [as a slave] under Sin" (Rom 7:14). Recall that we have already defined Flesh as human life fundamentally oriented toward and confident in its own natural human capacities and possibilities, whether personal or societal. But ironically, as Flesh in this sense we are in fact *not* morally capable free agents in neutral territory. By trusting our own capacities and not trusting God, we as Flesh are already within the orbit of Sin's sovereign power. But Flesh is not there alone: Law is right alongside.

As we have seen, law and human life are closely bound together in an intimate relationship like marriage. In its original and best sense, this marriage is a relationship in which law in "weakness" *serves* human flourishing (unlike a dominating, patriarchal "husband"): in this sense "we know that the law is spiritual" (Rom 7:14). But because of Sin (through human sins), Law asserts itself in strength against sins and comes to lord it over humankind. What was a way of *life* now, like a sovereign, *demands* loyalty, service, and patriotism. Law comes *to act like Sin* by lording it over. Law becomes an unwitting ally of Sin, serving Sin's cause. That is why Paul said earlier that we must die to Law just as we die to Sin, in order to be free of the dominating husband, "Lord Law." With Sin backing it, Law asserts itself as a *ruler* of life, which undermines its *service* in forming a way of life; in turn, it breeds resistance. So "strong" Law—upping the rules and enhancing enforcement—is no help in bringing about the good; in fact, it works against it. "For I know that the good does not [naturally] dwell in me, that is, in my

Flesh; the *will* to do the good is within me, but the *power* to work the good is not" (Rom 7:18). Strong Law is strong in its condemnation of sins; it is weak when it comes to producing the good.

How does all of this connect with the theme of justice? Again, the story of Paul's own life helps us with the question. As a Judean Pharisee, Paul intended nothing but good—God's justice, God's honor, and the defense of God's people. As we have seen from his self-descriptions in the letters to the Galatians and Philippians, he was in every sense a true Israelite—ethnically, culturally, legally, loyally, zealously. Indeed, in some sense he never ceased to be so, as becomes obvious in Romans 9:1-5. He was a "blameless" and devoted champion of "justice in the Law [of Moses]" (Phil 3:6). His vigorous persecution of the new messianic movement was rooted in that sense of justice.

In Paul's own mind, the rise and flourishing of the messianic Jesus sect posed a multifaceted threat to the future of the Judean people and God's cause. Its leader had been crucified by the Romans as a Judean political agitator, and according to Judean law he was a blasphemer and cursed by "hanging on a tree" (Gal 3:13; see Deut 21:23). The claim made by his followers, that this agitator and blasphemer was raised from the dead and exalted as God's Messiah over Israel and the nations, was not only absurd but also generated a good deal of dangerous political unrest among Judeans both in Jerusalem and in the cities of Judea, Galilee, and beyond. Justice according to Law and peace for Judeans demanded that this messianic sect be quashed and eliminated by whatever means necessary, including (according to the book of Acts) the arrest, imprisonment, and even execution of its members. To this work of justice and peace Paul radically and militantly committed himself.

Good intentions (zeal for God), a just end (the security of God's people, the eradication of a real threat), and the legal means to achieve it, authorized by the leaders in Jerusalem: What could be wrong about that? Nothing! Nothing, except the *truth* about justice: God's justice was in fact enacted when God raised up the dead body of the Crucified One by the powerful Holy Spirit. When Paul met the resurrected Jesus on the road to Damascus, all of his certainties about the justice of what he was doing were shattered: "I do not know what I do" (Rom 7:15). Suddenly justice looked fundamentally otherwise than his championing of Law. If Paul loved justice as "God's law" had taught him to do (Rom 7:25), then he must now hate the justice he had wanted to do for the sake of that law, because it was revealed to be the very form of injustice. The good he intended ended up working evil through his own violent actions to exterminate the witnesses of justice, those who really were just because they were "in Messiah Jesus."

> What justice and peace agendas (perhaps in God's name) are you es-
> pecially passionate about? What lengths do you think are appropriate
> to go to in order to achieve those agendas? What laws and enforce-
> ments would you like to see enacted for their sake? How does the
> revelation of God's justice in Jesus Messiah cause you to reflect on and
> reevaluate your agendas?

To borrow words Paul will use later, Paul had a "zeal for God" but it was "not enlightened" by the good news of justice (Rom 10:2). How did that happen? How could he not have known? Paul's answer came only in the blinding, revealing light of the sovereign Justice he was seeking to destroy. He was at the mercy of powers—the power of Sin on the one hand and the power of Flesh ("zeal") on the other. These powers conscripted both Paul and "weak" law (the way of life of the Judeans, in which Paul rightly "delighted," Rom 7:22) and turned them into unwitting and unwilling foot soldiers in Sin's deadly war against justice, against the Messiah.

"What a wretched man I am! Who will rescue me from this body of death?" (Rom 7:24). Neither the I (some inherent personal or social will for the good) nor "weak" law (a people's social-cultural-political resources and capacities) are in any way capable of rescuing us from the grips of injustice and its punishing and death-dealing works. Only *Another* can deliver us, someone altogether beyond Sin, Flesh, and Law, beyond the war between good and evil; only God can deliver, through the Just One himself. "Thanks be to God through Jesus Messiah our Sovereign" (Rom 7:25)!

8

THE SPIRIT OF JUSTICE

WITH A CRY FOR DELIVERANCE from bondage to Law and a declaration of God's liberation in Messiah (Rom 7:24-25), Paul attains a decisive breakthrough on the question of law, a question that had already cropped up in various places in Romans. The good news, which Paul declared right from the beginning in Romans (Rom 1:1-5), had consistently put law into question as the source and power of justice. For, as Paul wrote in Romans 3:21, the gospel of God's justice in Jesus Messiah is apocalypsed "*apart from law.*" If that is so, then what of law? What is its place in human life? In Romans 7 Paul took account of the complexity of law, arguing that it is good, though weak; and it is good when it is weak, when it serves rather than dominates life. But in its very weakness it is susceptible to being co-opted and captured by Sin and Death and made a puppet of those destructive powers. In this condition Law has no power of its own to deliver us from injustice, and often becomes the instrument of it. Law itself must be delivered to serve its true end, God's justice in the Messiah (Rom 10:4). Only Jesus Messiah delivers both humanity and Law from Sin and Death.

Sovereignty (political rule) and law are constituent powers of world history. They shape the stories, movements, interactions, and ongoing life of the peoples of the world. They are also responsible for conflicts and wars when sovereigns or governments seek to defend or advance the particular way of life (law) of their people. On such occasions, what we have called weak law, the form of life that gives shape, texture, identity, and dynamism to a people, is co-opted by Flesh—that is, by the desire of a people to control, impose, and dominate. Sovereignty and law become instruments of Sin and Death. This is the human condition. No nation or people, including God's chosen people Israel and the church, has been immune to it. It is the state of the world—the point that Paul already made in Romans 1:18–3:20. Nevertheless, it is exactly to the worldly powers of sovereignty and Law that we continually turn for a new start, a better day, peace in the world, liberty and justice for all. What will save us, we believe, is a new regime, a change of government, a new constitution, an overhaul of the legal system.

Or perhaps a revolution. Revolution is another power in history. Revolutions are driven by the frustration of justice and by the thought that the overthrow of an existing regime will usher in a new era of justice and peace, and give birth to a new history. Those who advocate revolution are convinced that the fundamental problems of an oppressive system of sovereignty and Law will not be solved by tinkering. The bondages and injustices generated by the current system are too profound to be met by incremental improvements. A call to revolution envisages a *new world order*, and those who obey the call enter into the struggle for it. In this respect, revolution is nearer than sovereignty and Law are to the good news of Jesus Messiah, who was himself crucified as a revolutionary. He envisaged, embodied, and enacted a new world order under the reign of God and called followers into his revolutionary movement.

Where do you find hope for justice within world history or your nation's history? Is it in new political leadership? Constitutional amendments? An improved judicial system? How confident are you that such change(s) will bring about a better future or will be lasting? Or are you inclined to think some kind of revolution is the answer to the injustices of the world?

Romans is passionately focused on a revolution in history that will emancipate history from the never-ending cycle of wars and treaties, triumphs and defeats, justices and injustices, crimes and punishments. Paul does not envisage an escape from history. He does not propose abandoning material, bodily, social, economic, and political life in this world. In fact, as we will see, when the gospel claims us, it drives us ever more deeply and intimately *into* history, into its yearnings, movements, and struggles for a new world to come.

But the kind of history making that the gospel announces is fundamentally different from normal history making according to the Flesh. The gospel is at odds with sovereignty, law, and violent revolution as they take place under the regime of Sin and Death. But because the gospel is concerned with history, it does not cancel the very ideas of sovereignty, law, and revolution. Instead, the good news announces an *other* sovereign and an *other* law, which break into the existing world order to create an alternative history through death and resurrection. The gospel announces the *divine revolution* of Messiah and the Spirit. So radically different is this way of history making that, viewed according to what normally counts as history making (history according to the Flesh), this revolution may look like nothing, or almost nothing. It may look like a *crucifixion*. Its revolutionary power is invisible to the Flesh, but to those who believe, the gospel is the only life-giving power of history there is. Even the greatest powers in history—great because of their deadly power over—all eventually come to an end in history. But already the gospel *announces their end* even before they come to it. It announces the power of a new beginning—the power of the Spirit of resurrection.

Justice Revolution: Crucifying Control (Romans 8:1-9)

Hope for history enslaved under Sin and Death comes from beyond history, from God. God delivers history from its sentence of death. "There is therefore now no death sentence against [*katakrima*] those who are in Messiah Jesus. For the law [*nomos*] of the Spirit of life in Messiah Jesus has liberated you from the law [*nomos*] of Sin and of Death" (Rom 8:1-2).

Worldly law aims at defining and enacting justice, but it requires the backing of executive power to see that justice is done. Despite its aims, therefore, law is all too easily co-opted into the service of sovereign power and manipulated by it. Justice then often amounts to what the powerful want. If our hope for justice is tied to law, which in turn is tied to sovereign power, we might ask whether there is any hope for real justice in history at all.

Can you think of concrete examples in history or in our own time, elsewhere in the world or in your own nation, where justice has become defined as what those with power and influence want? In these examples, what is the hope for justice among the powerless?

Will there be justice on earth? Paul says, Yes!

For what law was powerless to do, being co-opted by the Flesh—the passion for ruling over—God did, by sending his own Son in the likeness of humanity under Sin, in order to defeat the sovereignty of Sin; in the death of his own Son God sentenced to death Sin as the desire to rule over, so that the justice aimed at by the law might instead be fulfilled in us who walk no longer confident in worldly sovereignty, but confident in the powerful Spirit of God. (Rom 8:3-4 paraphrased)

Paul thus gives us a further understanding of the character of God's justice in the Messiah. God sent his Son "in the likeness of sinful Flesh." This recalls what Paul wrote earlier about "the one man" Adam and "the one man" Messiah in Romans 5. In the first place, the phrase "in the *likeness* of sinful Flesh" (Rom 8:3) is not at all a denial of the full humanity of the Messiah; on the contrary, it is another emphatic declaration of it. For sinful Flesh is *not* humanity in its truth but distorted humanity under the sign of Adam, who seized and wielded a sovereignty not given to him. Jesus Messiah is not like humanity in this distorted sense. He is in the likeness of Adam insofar as, like Adam, he is none other than a human being. But he is radically different from Adam insofar as his sovereign power as Messiah is *not* the sovereignty of power over but of power to serve. As Paul already declared in Romans 5, the Messiah is the *true human being*. Jesus Messiah is the reality, truth, and pattern of what it means to live humanly—even *before* Adam, and therefore *for* Adam.

Gospel-shaped human action is action conformed to the pattern of the Messiah. Messianic life—life "in Messiah"—is *truly* human life. It is the end of life as power over, that is, as life toward death. Because Jesus Messiah enacted the truly human life in obedience, it brought him into direct confrontation with Sin in the Flesh—the spiritual and human ruling powers that worked together to crucify him. In the dramatic confrontation on the cross with the destructive powers of history, God doomed Sin in the Flesh by exposing the seemingly attractive, persuasive, and compelling appeal of power over—the normal way of making history and doing justice—as the working of Death itself. Sin in the Flesh was absorbed into and crucified in the obedient flesh of the Son of God. In his death he overcame the power of Death. And in the Son's resurrection from the dead God unleashed the eternal power of life—the "Spirit of holiness" (Rom 1:4)—into the world to remake history according to God's justice in Messiah.

In the Messiah and the Spirit, God himself creates the condition for and gives the power that brings forth a *history of justice*. In Paul's words, God sent his Son and doomed Sin in order that the "justice [*dikaiōma*—just requirement] aimed at by the law might in fact be fulfilled in us, that is, in those who walk not according to Flesh, but according to Spirit" (Rom 8:3-4). Here (as in Rom 4 with Abraham) we encounter again the idea of walking. By God's doing *alone* we are taken into the realm of the Messiah's sovereignty and the Spirit's power of life. Apart from God's initiative our own action is simply Flesh; it is self-defined and self-powered. To "walk according to the Spirit" is to have our action defined by the Messiah and powered by the Spirit. Only then is God's justice fulfilled in our action.

Walking according to Spirit means that it is *not* our task to grab the levers of history to make it come out right, or to get justice done in the world by controlling events and ruling over other people. Rather, in Messiah and the Spirit we make history and do justice when we *give up controlling history*. Truly human action, that is, messianic action, in history does not force outcomes; "in Messiah" human action must always be given over—crucified—into the resurrecting power of God. God promises to bring our faithful, patient walking to its completion according to God's will and not our own. Justice is done in history when we participate in the movement of the Spirit, which is the living history of Jesus Messiah, in whom God's justice is apocalypsed and graciously given to us as a gift.

In the first few sentences of Romans 8 Paul condenses a radical revolution in our way of thinking justice, being just, and doing justice. This revolution is so deep and far ranging that it demands a labor of thought and imagination to wrap our minds around it. Does not every instinct and intuition drive us to think that it is up to us (especially us Christians) to turn the ship of history in the right direction by getting our hands on the levers of power as much as we are able? We presume that the greater our (Christian) power and control, the better the outcome will be. The more power and influence, the more justice: it seems to make good sense. But, says Paul, that is "thinking in terms of Flesh," not Spirit (Rom 8:5).

Paul anticipates the real struggle it will take to change our thinking about our historical action in such a fundamental way (Rom 8:5-8). Those who are habituated to Flesh cannot help thinking that the history of justice is achieved by attaining worldly power: by becoming rulers, governors, judges, and CEOs; by creating global corporations, nations of manifest destiny, "coalitions of the just"; by managing, maneuvering, and manipulating social, judicial, and political forces, and so on. But rather than creating histories of justice, that way of thinking has persistently created histories of power, wealth, and privilege for some, and weakness, poverty, and shame for others—locally, nationally, and globally. For the sake of "advancing the cause of justice" the movers and shakers of history commit themselves and their own people to the "necessity" of self-defense, control, aggression, invasion, war, conquest, and punishment, and will continue to do so. "For the way of thinking according to the Flesh has death as its outcome" (Rom 8:6 paraphrased).

But the gospel generates another mind altogether, the mind of the Spirit. That mind is the difficult thought that, whatever our good motives and intentions might be, we cannot by our own powers—nor even "with God's help"—bring justice to fulfillment. We must not imagine the Spirit as divine strength to do whatever we naturally set our minds to do to gain control. God's power in the Messiah and the Spirit accomplishes justice in those who have learned to *crucify control* and wait on God to complete their work of justice (as God raised Jesus from the dead). These are the ones who give shape to a history of "life and peace" (Rom 8:6). They are thinking according to the Spirit.

The stakes in making this fundamental shift of mind from Flesh to Spirit are infinitely high. For, Paul declares, the thinking that aims to control history and rule the world is "actively hostile [*echthra*] to God" (Rom 8:7), in other words, *at war* with God. Far from advancing the cause of "the law of God" in history, the mind of the Flesh does the opposite. It is incapable of submitting itself to God's law at all—"the law of the Spirit of life." Despite its good intentions of getting God's will done in the world, it is incapable of "pleasing God" (Rom 8:8). The prince or president or prime minister who says, "I am a Christian," yet makes history according to the controlling logic of Flesh rather than Spirit, does not in fact belong to the Messiah but rather is the Messiah's enemy.

> What is your current thinking about the relationship between justice and worldly power or influence? Are you convinced that if the "right" people had power, justice would be done? What would it take for you to change that way of thinking, that is, to believe that in order for justice truly to be done, Christians at least must learn to crucify control?

"But *you*," Paul says, now turning his speech directly to those who have believed the apocalyptic good news, "*you* are *not* in Flesh, but in Spirit, since the Spirit of God dwells in you. If anyone does not have the Spirit of Messiah, this one is not of Messiah" (Rom 8:9). And so at this crucial juncture Paul challenges those in Messiah and Spirit to take up the demanding but necessary task of thinking history *messianically*, of conforming our thinking to the Spirit, who dwells within us, and to the Messiah, in whom we dwell. It is a matter of death or life; it is a matter of being an enemy of God or a friend of God. Where are the friends of God in history? We will not find them among the usual suspects. We will have to look among the poor, the weak, the foolish, among the "nothings" of this world who trust God, to see where God's justice is happening (1 Cor 1:18-31).

Justice Revolution: Living Bodies (Romans 8:10-17)

For Paul, a way of thinking is simultaneously a way of being and acting *bodily* in the world. Bodies—personal, social, political bodies—are the site of historical action. A mind of the Flesh works in the world as a body of the Flesh; a mind of the Spirit works in the world as a body of the Spirit. Paul has just written of the difficulty of changing our minds in this regard, a difficulty that requires, really, nothing short of the crucifixion of one way of imagining change or revolution in history, and the resurrection of another. The same goes for the body; in fact, a change of mind is intimately bound up with a change of bodily practices. So, on the one hand, "if Messiah is in you, your body is dead because of Sin" (Rom 8:10). In other words, our way of being and acting in the world according to the Flesh under Sin has *already* been taken up into the death of the Messiah and crucified (as we have seen Rom 6:1-13): that bodily way is *dead* to those who believe the gospel and find themselves incorporated into the crucifixion of the Messiah.

On the other hand, "[the] Spirit is life for the sake of justice" (Rom 8:10). We recall (from Rom 3:21-26) that Jesus Messiah himself is the justice of God revealed and enacted. The Spirit brings alive this messianic justice in us, and creates a new way of being and acting bodily in the world. The same divine power of life that raised Messiah from the dead is the power of life now enlivening our mortal bodies (Rom 8:11), these very bodies of flesh and bone and blood that are always already in the midst of life, encountering other bodies, sharing space, time, and goods with them, working with and among them, enacting personal, social, and political histories together. The Messiah by the Spirit moves *these* historical bodies here and now, generating new habits and practices that look like the "fruit of the Spirit" (Gal 5:22-23), creating in and through them a history of justice that corresponds to God's apocalypse of justice in the crucified and risen body of Jesus.

So, the only hope for a wholly new revolution of justice in history is rooted in the resurrection power of God. But this is not only a hope for a coming day (though it is assuredly that); it is also, emphatically, a hope in the midst of history, for the sake of history, because the resurrection power of that coming day is already at work now, enlivening our mortal bodies through the Spirit of the Messiah (think again of Abraham's and Sarah's almost-dead bodies). If it is a hope *within* history, then it is also a call to life *here and now*. This is implicit in all that Paul says in Romans 8:5-11, in which he writes of a new mind and an enlivened body. Minds and bodies are *also* ours—we are engaged and activated by the gospel; therefore we have the responsibility—the "obligation" (Rom 8:12) to become in our bodies the messianic life given to us.

Yet Paul is more emphatic in these verses about our obligation *not* to live a certain way, that is, the way of the Flesh. That way is death. Though the Flesh has already been put to death in Messiah, *we* must also put it to death in our daily practices: the Spirit enables us to "put to death the practices of the body" (Rom 8:13) that arise from Flesh—those practices that seek control and lording it over, and often result in competition, coercion, violence, and death. As those practices are continually eradicated in us by the Spirit, we begin to live the life of the Messiah.

The revolution of sovereignty and life inaugurated in the crucifixion and resurrection of Jesus Messiah is unleashed into history; the divine power of life that raised Jesus from the dead is unstoppable. The risen Messiah is the Living One who gives his divine life into the world as the Spirit. It is therefore the very nature of that Spirit to move into history, to bring life where there was death, to create a revolutionary messianic community that shares in the Messiah's own revolution. Or in Paul's words, the Spirit creates sons of God: "Those who are conscripted [*agontai*] by the Spirit of God are sons of God [*huioi theou*]" (Rom 8:14). We must let the word *sons* stand for the moment, because it signals our identification with the Son of God, Jesus Messiah (recall that "Son of God" is a messianic title; see Rom 1:3-4). As sons of God we are messianics who have been conscripted into the revolutionary movement of the Messiah.

To be conscripted, of course, seems to suggest a kind of unwilling, even coerced, participation. Yet Paul's word is appropriate when we remember that our condition prior to this conscription was not that of free agents but of slaves not only captured by but also freely offering our service to sovereign Sin, Death, and Law. Unless we are claimed and delivered by the Spirit of God to become sons of God, in the same way that the enslaved Israelites were claimed and delivered from Egypt to become sons of God (a point Paul will return to in Rom 9:4), we are not free at all. The whole point of our messianic conscription is that we might be delivered from "a spirit of slavery to fear" in order to become no longer slaves, but rather sons, sharing through "a spirit of adoption" in the very sonship of the Messiah (Rom 8:15). *From slaves to free sons*: that in itself is a personal, social, political revolution in history of the most fundamental sort; yet, unlike the usual revolutions in history, it is one that was achieved *for* us, not *by* us. Nevertheless, now as free sons rather than slaves, we may become active agents in the Messiah's revolution.

> Reflect on the idea of being conscripted by the Spirit of God, to be delivered from slavery only then to be enlisted in the Son's revolution of justice. What might this mean for you?

The first characteristic of the band of messianic revolutionaries brought into being by the Spirit's conscription is that they are given to share in the Messiah's very own relationship to the God of Israel and all nations. Jesus is God's Son and calls on God as "*Abba*, Father." At the core of the messianic revolution is the prayer "Our Father. . . ." By the Spirit we are given this Name, "*Abba*, Father," to call on the God of all creation, to place ourselves before this God in confidence and trust as the Father's own "children" (*tekna*, Rom 8:16). Apart from this prayer of fundamental trust in the Father, who alone will accomplish his will "on earth as it is heaven," the messianic revolution descends again quickly into Flesh and becomes mere social justice, political activism in search of control.

But there is even more to being conscripted by the Spirit: because we are now God's children by adopted sonship, we are given to share in the very inheritance of the Son of God, the Messiah. The Messiah's inheritance is to reign over Israel and all the peoples of the earth, indeed, over all of creation (Phil 2:9-11). Sharing in that world-historical inheritance now comes to preliminary fruition in the revolutionary community of messianics brought into being in the Messiah by the Spirit. It is an unimaginably great and glorious inheritance; it would stir the heart of any revolutionary who seeks and strives and struggles for a coming new world order of justice and peace.

Nevertheless! Paul has already made clear that God's sovereign power for justice and peace in the world is apocalypsed in Jesus Messiah. It therefore makes its way in the world and in history in a manner that corresponds to the Messiah's own way—the way of emptying himself of power over, of taking up the role of the servant, of entrusting himself obediently to God, of giving himself up to the unjust and to his enemies (that's us; Rom 5:10), for their (our) sake. The messianic revolution of justice makes its way in the world as Abraham's did: Abraham *trusted* God that "he would inherit the world"; that trust was reckoned by God as justice done. *This* kind of revolution makes its way in the world not by ruling and influencing through assertion, coercion, and force of arms, but by the power of weakness. It makes its way in the world, Paul writes, through "cosuffering" with the Messiah (Rom 8:17).

This is *crucial*—in the original meaning of the word. There will be no coglorying (Rom 8:17) with the Messiah in his world inheritance apart from cosuffering with him in the midst of history, for the sake of history. That means coming alongside those who are weak, poor, and suffering, among the foolish and the nobodies, the forgotten and despised, serving them, giving ourselves to them, working with them for their good, entrusting the outcome of our work to God, and patiently bearing the disregard and enmity of the powerful and unjust. This is the difficult way, but *the only way*, in which messianic revolutionaries participate in the historical struggle for the coming new order. This is the unarmed, disarming revolution, which does not look like one according to the usual standards—the standards of Flesh. Yet, precisely in its vulnerability and near invisibility—in the law of the Spirit of life—this revolution in the Messiah stands to inherit the world.

Cosmic Justice (Romans 8:18-28)

The reach of Paul's messianic vision has already begun to stretch out beyond "realistic" historical bounds—so much so that Paul has had to rein it in for a moment to conform it to the way of the Messiah's cross. There is no world inheritance except through the cross. But then he gives way again to the incomparable glory of the vision: "For I reckon that the sufferings of the now-time [*nyn kairou*—the time of messianic history-making] are not worthy to be compared to the coming glory about to be apocalypsed [*apokalypsthēnai*] to us" (Rom 8:18). The gospel is news of *God's* justice arriving into the midst of history in the crucifixion, and it thrusts us into the ongoing sufferings of history as our share in Messiah's sufferings. But those sufferings—of the Messiah, of the victims of worldly sovereignty and law, of the messianic community—are about to be eclipsed by another apocalypse, the apocalypse of a coming glory, the apocalypse of the Messiah inheriting all things, and messianics coinheriting all things with him (Rom 8:32).

This is something else altogether! We are tempted to think the history of Flesh is all there is, with all of its mastery, victory, and self-proclaimed glory—and all of its injustice, suffering, and death. *This* we take to be the comprehensive reality of all of human life, including messianic life, and "realistically" it establishes the conditions and constraints of whatever vision we might entertain and whatever action we might undertake. So, under the constraints of history we may strive for justice, but "realistically" we cannot hope for much. We may aim for a fair distribution of the world's goods, but finally, "It's the economy, stupid!" We may hold off some of the ravages of disease and death, but there will always be another virus or superbug. We may advocate for better laws to control climate change, but there is always more demand for fossil-fuel energy, and the engines of industry must keep running. Every possible solution to the world's misery has its end game. Injustice will go on forever, and destruction and death will have the last word. Indeed, things might seem even more hopeless for messianics, who, because the Messiah is their sovereign, are called to refuse the controlling, coercive, and sometimes violent methods that at least might get the job done.

Into this sense of fleshly history—the seemingly ultimate reality that defines the conditions and constraints of our vision and action—Paul speaks of the apocalypse of a coming glory. The good news is that *it is this coming glory that defines ultimate reality and conditions all of history*; the coming glory will bring an end to the history of Sin, Death, and Flesh. The coming glory determines the conditions and constraints on history as it is, not the other way around; it opens history to eternal justice in the midst of injustice, to unending life in the midst of death. The coming glory creates the time-into-eternity in which messianic revolutionaries both truly act in time, and simultaneously hand their actions over to God—with the cry, "*Abba*, Father"—who will complete their actions in eternity.

The coming glory is already apocalypsed when the power of the Spirit raises up the crucified body of the Messiah. The resurrection is the "crack in everything"; it is how "the light gets in" (Leonard Cohen). The coming glory is already apocalypsed in the event of the Spirit of life overcoming deadly Flesh in us and creating the messianic community. This coming glory, about to be *fully* apocalypsed, is the total context, the final reality within which messianic revolutionaries confidently carry on their patient, hopeful, risky, vulnerable, and mostly invisible work amid the suffering of the world. So, finally, the coming glory will also be the full apocalypse of the children of God, the revelation that the way of messianic suffering and trust in fact embodies the real truth of history, "the law of the Spirit of life," which is the way of *history into eternity.*

> What cosmic or ultimate vision of reality grounds and enlivens (or crushes) your own participation in history? What for you is the end of all things? What difference does it make to your participation in history to know that all of reality and history is ultimately grounded in the living Messiah, is enlivened by the life-giving Spirit, and has its end in the triune God?

By the time we arrive at Romans 8:19 Paul has stretched the messianic vision far beyond human history to encompass the whole creation (*ktisis*). The whole of creation is eagerly anticipating the apocalypse of the children of God. We have already spoken of how history according to the Flesh is regarded as the total self-enclosed human context with its conditions and constraints. We might also be inclined to regard nature as the even wider context. Nature gives us the sheer physical conditions of existence; it makes physical existence and biological life possible at all. On the other hand, nature too sets its own radical constraints on existence. Nature is the magnificent and horrifying sphere of perpetual life and death, death and life, coming into being and passing away.

It is fundamentally important that Paul does not speak of nature. He speaks of *creation.* In other words, he speaks of all that is and was and ever will be as belonging *intrinsically* to God the Creator. There never was nature, if by that we mean a sphere of self-enclosed existence independent of God's gracious "Let there be!" and "It was good." The inner secret of what we know as nature is creation, and that means existence forever coming from, dwelling in, encountering, and being sustained by God's gracious care.

That said, the divine possibilities of creation seem, from all appearances and experiences, to have been radically shut down. What we see is nature.

Paul himself says so; he is no romantic about the "natural" world: "For the creation was subjected to futility, not of its own will, but because of the one who subjected it" (Rom 8:20). Creation is in "slavery [*douleias*] to decay" (Rom 8:21). That looks very much like nature as we have described it above.

However, two things must be noted here. First, despite its subjection to futility and bondage to decay, this is still *creation*, still intrinsically belonging to God the Creator. Paul never slips into the language of nature. Second, and this makes the point more emphatically, the current futile and enslaved condition of creation is neither something it brought on itself, nor a mere happenstance. Its current condition is the result of "the one who subjected it." What can we say about that? There is indeed an unfathomable mystery here, which Paul never explains—just as Paul never explains the mystery of "God handed them over" in Romans 1:24, 26, 28. The point in all of these texts is *not* divine determinism (exactly the opposite—but that is another story). It is rather that, whatever the current condition of creation or history, neither has fallen out of the hands of God, nor slipped away into its own "free," independent existence. God remains the Lord of all things and in all things, including ungodliness and injustice, corruption and decay. Moreover—this is crucial—whatever the current condition of humankind and creation (enslavement, in fact), the *overriding* condition is *hope!* Hope conditions all, because God conditions all. This is not hope in some immanent potentiality inherent in history or nature, but divine hope rooted in the very God who subjected creation to enslaving decay and handed over humankind to the enslaving powers of Sin and Death. It is the hope of divine liberation.

We may think that Paul has now drifted a long way from the theme of justice and from the messianic revolution. But not so. The good news holds out a vision and hope of justice for *all*, in the most comprehensive sense imaginable. The sons and daughters of God—those in Messiah and the Spirit—are themselves nothing other than human *creatures*, and that means *cocreatures* with everything else that exists. Paul (affirming Gen 1–2) has no vision of human life apart from the whole creaturely world, no vision of human liberation apart from the liberation of "all creation" (*pasa hē ktisis*, Rom 8:22). "Even the creation itself will be liberated from slavery to decay, in order to share in the freedom of the children of God" (Rom 8:21). Just as in Messiah and Spirit humankind is opened by and to the power of divine life, so also will all creation be opened by and to that same power. All creation "groans together [Greek *systenazō*] in labor pains" for that deliverance into new creation (Rom 8:22). Just as the groaning (*stenazō*) of messianics (Rom 8:23) is not an end in itself—as if suffering were a good thing—but is suffered in anticipation of the coming glory, so also all creation groans in eager expectation of the apocalypse of glory.

As we have already emphasized, messianics do not yearn for an escape from history but find themselves with Jesus Messiah driven ever deeper into solidarity with the groaning of all peoples yearning for liberation. Here Paul says that messianics are also driven into suffering solidarity with *all creatures*—animate and inanimate, crushed under the injustices of exploitation and destruction—and drawn into messianic work directed toward the liberation of all creation. Creaturely groaning along with messianic groaning is triggered by the Spirit of life already at work bearing fruit in the midst of this suffering. The messianic community, the Messiah's body, experiences something of the power of divine life already now in the midst of history that makes us yearn even more for "the redemption of our *bodies*" (Rom 8:23). Paul imagines no flight of the soul or spirit from the body but hopes only for the resurrection of the body, and along with that the resurrection of *all creation and history* into an unimaginable freedom.

> What is your current thought about the final destiny of all nonhuman creatures, from geckos to galaxies? What about the destiny of your own body? How does the text of Romans 8:18-25 expand your vision of final destiny?

In this hope we join creation's groaning for an end that is not yet visible. Again, we are compelled to recall Abraham, who, hoping beyond all visible hope, trusted in "the God who gives life to the dead and calls into being the things that are not" (Rom 4:17-18). This God of resurrection and creation promises to resurrect an entire creation whose body, like the bodies of Sarah and Abraham, seems barren and "as good as dead" (Rom 4:19). It is an unimaginable resurrection, as yet almost wholly invisible. For now there is only the resurrection of the Messiah, seen by few, and only early signs of the Spirit bearing fruit in the messianic community. Is that enough? It seems so small, so weak, so easy to dismiss. Yet, Paul writes, "in hope we were saved. But hope that is seen is not hope. Who hopes for what is seen?" (Rom 8:24).

The crucial question here for the messianic community, which has already experienced something of the power of life that brings justice, is whether this community and its members will abide in this *hope of the unseen*. Everything within us drives toward demanding visible results, achieving measurable outcomes, getting the job done, showing the fruit of our struggle for justice, whatever that might be: the election of "our" candidate, a law changed, a criminal arrested, a sweatshop closed down, a polluter punished, a terrorist cell destroyed, an attack on our nation thwarted, another struggle for democracy won, and so on. As the saying goes, "Justice must not only be done, but must be *seen* to be done."

With respect to all of that, the messianic way of justice seems almost invisible, like almost nothing at all, because in the first place messianic justice is not something we achieve, but something in which we *abide*. We abide in the justice *already done by God* in the crucifixion and resurrection of Jesus Messiah. In such abiding, where are the results? What are the measurable outcomes? What is there to see? "Nevertheless," Paul says, "even though we do not see what we hope for, in patience we eagerly anticipate it" (Rom 8:25). The revolution of justice, the coming glory, now almost invisible, is surely already on us, about to be apocalypsed in fullness. For this, all creation groans in eager expectation. For this, messianics also groan. In this, messianics patiently abide in their work of justice.

There is, in fact, a three-part (dis)harmony of groaning toward that invisible end: "In the same way the Spirit shares in our weakness, for we do not know how to pray as we ought, but the Spirit himself intercedes on our behalf with groans [*stenagmois*; see *systenazō* and *stenazō* in Rom 8:22, 23] beyond all words" (Rom 8:26). In "not knowing how to pray as we ought," Paul acknowledges the profound difficulty—no matter our intentions—not only in not being able to guarantee the visible outcomes of our actions, but often in even envisaging what a good outcome might be. Where *should* this work for justice lead? What do I think its result should be? Do I even know for sure? How should it be brought to completion? Will it look like what

I intended? What are the unforeseen consequences and collateral damages? How shall I pray in and for this action?

This is the essential moment of messianic weakness. This is the moment of letting go.

Of course, we will act! We *must* act, within the range of action given us in the Messiah. But we will not lock that action down, either within our intentions or our capacities or our time frames—that is, within our own human power—to bring it to its desired end. In the very moment of our action we will open ourselves to the Spirit, whose proper work it is to groan—to groan beyond all words, we know not what. We will give ourselves to the Spirit, who prays for us in such a way that our work is handed over and conformed to the purpose of God, to the good that God intends and will bring to completion. "And [God] who searches the hearts knows the mind of the Spirit, because the Spirit intercedes for holy ones according to the purpose of God. And we know that, to the ones who love God, to those who are called according to God's purpose, God works in all things to bring about good" (Rom 8:27-28). This kind of weak human action, given over to the groaning prayer of the Spirit and to the fulfilling action of God, is just what it means to be messianic.

Ultimate Justice: God's Unconquered Love (Romans 8:29-39)

Paul now sets our messianic weakness within the ultimate reality of all, beyond history and creation altogether: within God. More precisely, within the eternal love of God, or, which is the same thing, the love of Jesus Messiah. To be messianic is to be vulnerable: vulnerable to the futility and decay of creation in its current state, and vulnerable to the ungodliness and injustice of history according to the Flesh. Since the gospel does not call us out of history and creation but ever deeper into them, messianics will characteristically find themselves at risk and living alongside those who are at risk. They will not seek escape from the destructive powers of nature and history, but nor are they given to lord it over those powers. How then shall they go on without fear?

The purpose of Paul's string of big theological words in Romans 8:29-30—*foreknowledge, predestination, calling, justification, glorification*—is not to send us into flights of theological speculation about the relation of free will and determinism or eternity and time or the order of salvation. It is, rather, to say that from all eternity there is a single divine destiny for humankind: "to be conformed to the image [*eikōn*] of [God's] Son" (Rom 8:29). Paul has already made abundantly clear that Jesus Messiah is the truly human one (Rom 5:12-21), that *his* image *is* the image of God in which humankind was formed from the beginning and to which humankind will be conformed in the end. In this sense he is the firstborn of humanity from the beginning and the firstborn of the new humanity from the end. The purpose of the big theological words is to place our own human life between and within this beginning and this end— between "God foreknew" and "God glorified"—and to say that it is *God's work alone* to bring us from the one to the other, and moreover, that God will not fail to do so.

So certain is this that Paul puts all of these big verbs of God's action in the past tense: this is what has *already happened*, including glorification (which previously Paul had said was coming). It has already happened for us because it has already happened for the Messiah, the human one, who is human for all humanity and in whom all human history and destiny is already fulfilled. This, then, is the ultimate divine reality within which messianic revolutionaries (those "many brothers [and sisters]" conformed to the Son: Rom 8:29) find themselves, and find themselves thrust into the midst of history, sharing the Messiah's suffering, becoming vulnerable, putting themselves at risk for the sake of others.

"If God is for us, who is against us?" (Rom 8:31). It is not that nothing or no one is ever against us. On the contrary, Paul will soon provide a whole list of actual and potential powers and adversaries that may be against us, from the supernatural, to the historical, to the natural. Messianic revolutionaries will not be spared from adversity. Encountering adversity is the characteristic way in which they will find themselves conformed to the image of the Son. Because, in fact, God "did not spare his own Son" from his adversaries; rather, God "handed him over" (*paredōken*, Rom 8:32, the same verb as in Rom 1:24, 26, 28) to his enemies "on behalf of us all."

We have all been taken into the glorious destiny of the Messiah; we have also all been taken into the being-handed-over of the Messiah. In fact, we now realize that the Messiah's being handed over to the powers both encompasses and sets the limits in which our being handed over to the powers of Sin and Death and other hostile powers occurs. There is an infinitely greater sovereignty of love ruling and overruling the powerful but ultimately broken sovereignties of Sin and Death. In other words, our being handed over to those powers (Rom 1:24-28) never did occur and never does occur outside the reality of God's love. Because of God's love he handed over his Son "on behalf of us all" in order that "along with him God will graciously give us all things" (Rom 8:32). This, then, is how we shall go on without fear. Every moment of human history, every moment of creation, happens within the greater reality of Jesus Messiah being handed over—in other words, within the reality of God's love.

So, what about the charges—slanderous, legal, political—that might be brought against messianic revolutionaries, involved as they often are alongside and on behalf of the victims of sovereignty and law in the grip of Sin and Death? Perhaps they become victims themselves, which is the case throughout much of Christian history. "Who will lay any charge against God's chosen ones? Who will condemn?" (Rom 8:33-34). It is not that no one will ever charge or condemn messianics! Jesus himself, the Chosen One of God, was charged and condemned in the highest moment of legal, political, and cosmic injustice. The point is not that we will be spared from unjust charges and condemnations. Perhaps messianics should rather expect them, if we are conformed to the image of the Messiah.

But even the Messiah did not justify himself before his accusers. He remained silent, trusting God for his justice, for "It is God who justifies" (Rom 8:33). Nor was he saved from pain and death: he was tortured and executed. But since it is God who vindicates, Jesus was raised to life and enthroned at the right hand of God as sovereign of all things. Justice reigns in Messiah's rising. So if we find ourselves shamed, condemned, or even sentenced to death, Jesus Messiah is at the right hand of God pleading our cause and securing our justice along with his. "Who shall separate us from the love of Messiah?" (Rom 8:35). It cannot happen.

What forces—natural and historical—have you experienced that threaten your confidence in the triumph of God's justice and love? Have you experienced a charge against you in your witness to Messiah? How have you responded to that charge?

Yet Paul does not hesitate to name the actual and potential powers and adversaries still at work in the world, because messianics should not be naive about them. There are of course the general adversities of circumstance and natural disaster: affliction, distress, famine, perhaps nakedness and peril. But there are also those adversities brought about by human opposition: persecution and sword. In the midst of this list, and with the mention of sword, Paul inserts rather awkwardly a telling quotation from Psalm 44 (Ps 44:22). On the one hand, the whole psalm is messianic in character, effectively summing up the shape of messianic life as Paul has parsed it throughout Romans, coming to a climax in Romans 8. On the other hand, Psalm 44 is about the messianic suffering of *Israel*, about the slanders, charges, shame, and condemnation Israel has faced among the nations when it puts its trust in God. Israel cries out to God for vindication.

This psalm, then, anticipates the whole great section of Romans 9–11 in which Paul will address the destiny of Israel in God's purpose. For the moment, however, Psalm 44:22 states the most extreme case of persecution and sword. It is a kind of holocaust: "For your sake we are being killed all day long; we are reckoned as sheep for the slaughter" (Rom 8:36). Yet, even in such an extreme situation, brought on by the powers of injustice against messianic vulnerability and solidarity with the victims of history, there is a resounding declaration of God's triumph: "Nevertheless, in all these things we are more than conquerors through him who loved us" (Rom 8:37). God's vindication is not only near; it is now: we *are* more than conquerors. As it was for the Messiah, so it is for the messianic people of God: the defeat in weakness is the victory of God over the powers. In the work of justice we abide *in* the Messiah's crucifixion and resurrection. This is the ground of hope. This is how we go on without fear.

In his final litany of adversaries Paul touches on almost every imaginable power that might be ranged against the messianic community. These powers traverse the boundaries between the natural and the supernatural, the political and the cosmic: "neither death, nor life, nor angels, nor rulers [*archai*—these are both political and spiritual—for Paul, there is no hard boundary between them; they depend on each other], nor things present, nor things to come, nor powers [*dynameis*—both historical and cosmic], nor height, nor depth [these in their cosmic proportions], nor any other creature" (Rom 8:38-39).

The deep, broad, and uncontrollable dimensions and powers at work in the world are named here in all of their mysterious complexity and their potential threat to justice and life. These are the spiritual and cosmic and historical powers that, we are so often convinced, really determine all things, limit all things, and finally bring all things to an end—a dead end. These are the powers that so often, therefore, seem *divine*, and so we are drawn to revere them with fear and awe. And we try to control them, at whatever cost. Every injustice in history is born of this *fear* and *awe* and *desire* to control. That was Paul's point in Romans 1:18-32. In the midst of all of this, however, Paul declares the revolutionary good news: perfect love casts out fear. Nothing in all creation has the power "to separate us from the love of God in Messiah Jesus our Sovereign" (Rom 8:39). This divine love is the beginning and end of justice. In this love messianics abide and have their hope. This love is the beginning and end of messianic life for all.

9

JUSTICE AMONG
THE NATIONS

Israel

IN ROMANS 8:36 Paul dropped an ominous quote from the Old Testament into a litany of powers, including the sword, that might threaten to separate us from God's love: "As it is written, 'For your sake we are being killed all day long; we are accounted as sheep to be slaughtered'" (NRSV). By quoting this verse (Ps 44:22) Paul anticipates the theme of the next three chapters—the suffering, witness, and destiny of Israel within the justice of God in Messiah. Paul's public proclamation among the Gentile nations of the news of the sovereign Messiah gave birth to small communities of messianic believers in the cities of Greece and Asia Minor. But while there were messianic Judeans in many or most of those communities, they were predominantly composed of non-Judeans—that is, Gentiles. That was also true in Rome.

At the end of Romans 8 Paul made some emphatic statements: "If God is for us, who can be against us?" "Who will bring any charge against God's chosen ones?" "Who shall separate us from the love of Messiah?" Nothing—no circumstance, no adversary, no power—nothing in all creation "will be able to separate us from the love of God in Messiah Jesus our Sovereign" (Rom 8:31-39). But if the good news of God's love in Messiah is heard and believed mostly by non-Judeans, it raises an important question: What then of that *original* messianic community rooted in Abraham's and Sarah's flesh, Israel? Shall Israel, God's chosen people—which continues to suffer under Roman occupation and oppression, including the sword, and appears to be separated from the justice of God in Messiah Jesus—shall Israel finally be separated from the love of God in Messiah Jesus? Could that actually happen? Paul's ultimate answer is a resounding No! Nevertheless, he takes us on a long journey over several difficult terrains of argument to that ultimate answer.

Paul's vision in these chapters of how God is at work in Israel is no less an apocalypse than anything else he has written so far. The history of Israel (if we may call it that) he provides is in the end a discernment of a deep divine mystery, a glimpse into God's "unsearchable judgments" and "inscrutable ways" (Rom 11:33). The cause-and-effect movement of this history lies beyond the grasp of research; it lies in the realm of revelation. But why is this strange history of Israel so important to Paul, or rather, why is it an essential aspect of the divine apocalypse of justice? Paul devotes more space to the place of Israel in God's work of justice in Jesus Messiah than he does to any other theme in Romans. Clearly something of great importance is at stake here.

Israel Among the Nations

We read back in Romans 2:17-21 that the Judean people understood itself to possess a unique gift and have a unique mission in the world: to "know God's will and determine what is excellent because [they] are instructed in the law"; to be "a guide to the blind, a light to those in darkness, a tutor to the foolish, a teacher of infants, having the very form of knowledge and truth in the law." They were not wrong in this self-understanding; this was the gift and calling God gave to Israel at Mount Sinai, where the Lord said:

"If you obey my voice and keep my covenant, you shall be my *treasured possession* out of all peoples. Indeed, *the whole earth is mine*, but you shall be for me a priestly kingdom and a holy nation" (Ex 19:5-6 NRSV, emphasis added). Here Israel's reason for being is spelled out clearly. God declares Israel's unique place among the nations. Israel is a people dear to God, God's treasured possession out of all the peoples, just as God is *at the same time* the God of the whole earth and therefore of all peoples. Israel as God's treasured people has a specific calling *in the midst* of the nations: to be "a priestly kingdom and a holy nation."

As a priestly kingdom Israel mediates God's purpose to the nations and represents the nations before God. From its beginning in Abraham, Israel was called out not only to receive God's blessing for itself but to be that people through which the divine blessing would spread out into the world: "I will make you a great nation, and I will bless you, and make your name great, so that you will be a blessing . . . and in you all the families of the earth shall be blessed" (Gen 12:2-3 NRSV). In fact, in and through Israel's obedient covenant life the nations should be able to perceive the reality, wisdom, and justice of God, as Moses tells them:

> See, just as the LORD my God has charged me, I now teach you statutes and ordinances for you to observe in the land that you are about to enter and occupy. You must observe them diligently, for this will *show your wisdom and discernment to the peoples*, who, when they hear all these statutes, will say, "Surely this great nation is a wise and discerning people!" For *what other great nation has a god so near to it as the LORD our God* is whenever we call to him? And what other great nation has statutes and ordinances *as just as this entire law* that I am setting before you today? (Deut 4:5-8 NRSV)

It is for this purpose that Israel was called to be a holy nation, a nation *set apart* (the core meaning of holiness) in the midst of the nations to be a clear, visible sign—a *sacrament*—of God's own holiness to the nations. Through Israel the nations were to know the reality of God in some measure. In this sense God stakes the divine destiny of all the nations of the earth on the destiny of Israel. Without Israel the nations are "without hope and without God in the world" (Eph 2:12). Paul remains fundamentally true to that conviction.

Just as important is the fact that God graciously *binds himself* to Israel in loyal love, a love first established in God's covenant with Israel's ancestors. Again, Moses:

> You are a people holy to the LORD your God; *the LORD your God has chosen you* out of all the peoples on earth to be his people, his treasured possession.
>
> It was not because you were more numerous than any other people that *the LORD set his heart on you and chose you*—for you were the fewest of all peoples. It was because *the LORD loved you* and *kept the oath that he swore to your ancestors*, that the LORD has brought you out with a mighty hand, and redeemed you from the house of slavery, from the hand of Pharaoh king of Egypt. Know therefore that the LORD your God is God, *the faithful God who maintains covenant loyalty* with those who love him and keep his commandments, to a thousand generations. (Deut 7:6-9 NRSV, emphasis added)

Throughout Romans 1–8 Paul declared that Jesus, God's Messiah, is the radical, ultimate reality and demonstration of God's justice and love for all humankind without exception. Far from God's love in Messiah excluding Israel, nothing can separate Israel from it. That conviction is what moves Paul into and through the extended struggle over the meaning of Israel in Romans 9–11:

> Who will bring any charge against God's chosen people? God himself justifies them. Who will render a final judgment [against them]? It is Messiah Jesus, who died, indeed, who was raised, who is also at the right hand of God, who also advocates our case before God. Who will separate us from the love of Messiah? . . . [Nothing] in all creation has the power to separate us from the love of God in Messiah Jesus our Sovereign. (Rom 8:33-35, 39)

> As regards [Israel's] election they are beloved [by God], for the sake of their ancestors [see Deut 7:8]; for God's gracious gifts [bestowed on Israel; see Rom 9:4-5] and God's calling [of Israel] are *irrevocable*. (Rom 11:28-29)

For Paul, everything hinges on God's love and justice being proven with respect to Israel. Israel *by its very being* continues to testify to God's reality and purpose. If God's love in Jesus Messiah does not ultimately triumph for Israel's sake as a people, then the Gentile peoples have little reason to trust this God. And they will have little reason to look to Israel to discern how God works in the life of a nation. In fact, the nations might then be justified in contemptuously turning away from Israel to discern the works and ways of God (as they invariably have done), and proudly looking instead to their own histories for signs of divine power and purpose (as they also have invariably done); in other words, they would be justified in continuing in idolatry. If the nations might know how they are to be saved (as nations), they must know how God saves his chosen nation Israel through Messiah, and what is required of Israel in that light. The salvation of nations depends on the salvation of Israel.

Paul the Israelite (Romans 9:1-5)

Paul begins by expressing his "great and unceasing grief" over Israel (Rom 9:1). He wishes that if it were possible he could sacrifice his own being in Messiah for the sake of Israel. Being in Messiah has not loosened Paul's fundamental bond of solidarity with his "brothers," his "natural birth family" ("kin according to flesh," Rom 9:3). In fact, it has made that bond stronger than ever. We are used to Paul calling the fellow members of the messianic community his brothers and sisters (whether Jew or Gentile) because with him they are members of the adopted family created by the Messiah and the Spirit. Yet here Paul speaks unreservedly of the members of his natural birth family as his brothers. They have never lost that status in his eyes. They are the Israelites (Rom 9:4). So in the first place when Paul speaks of Israel, he means his natural (*kata sarka*) kinsfolk, his people of origin, his extended tribe. While *Israel* means more than this for Paul (as we shall see), it never means less. Whatever other meanings there may be, the meaning of Israel includes the flesh (*sarx*) of Israel—that is, Israel as an *ethnic-national reality in history*—which is also undeniably Paul's own flesh.

But Paul's identification with Israel "according to the flesh" is not simple tribalism, not simple ethnic blood ties. Radical identification with Israel is for Paul *theologically inescapable* because Israel "according to the flesh" is simultaneously "the Israel of God" (Gal 6:16). Israel is *theologically constituted*. It is created by God to be Israel and to receive those divine gifts that God intends not only for Israel but for all the nations, indeed for all creation. Paul can hardly be more clear and emphatic about this: "by way of" (*hōn*) the Israelites comes "the sonship and the glory and the covenants and the receiving of law and the worship and the promises" (Rom 9:4)—in other words, all of those gifts that the new community of messianics (mostly Gentile in Rome) now share through Messiah and the Spirit. God gave these gifts *first* to Israel, and only *through* Israel to the nations. That is why Paul says "to the Judeans first, and also to the Greeks/nations" a number of times—starting in Romans 1:16-17.

But there is a twist to this story. The founding ancestors of Israel (Abraham, Isaac, Jacob) also come "by way of" (*hōn*, Rom 9:5) Israel. Paul seems to be saying, somewhat counterintuitively, that even Abraham arises *from* Israel rather than the other way around. While the genetic patriarchs and matriarchs give physical birth to the people Israel, nevertheless Israel in some sense *precedes* the founding ancestors. That is because the reality of Israel is rooted first in God's choice (election) before it is birthed in history. God then chooses the flesh of Israel's founding fathers and mothers to make Israel's prior reality actual in history. This dual but not separable reality of Israel, as both rooted in God's election and generated by human beings, is crucial to understanding what Paul writes throughout Romans 9–11. For now, however, we can see from Paul's claims in Romans 9:4 that Israel is unlike any other people or nation on earth. No other nation has been given the divine gifts Israel has been given. No other nation has its origin and constitution in God's election the way Israel does. Therefore no other nation can legitimately appropriate the idea of Israel for itself, as, for example, England and the United States have done. Israel is theologically unique.

Israel's uniqueness is unmistakable in Paul's next point: "out of" (*ex*, Rom 9:5) Israel "according to the flesh" comes the Messiah. That is clear enough. Jesus is an Israelite. But Paul says more. Just as Israel theologically precedes its founding fathers and mothers, so the Messiah theologically *precedes* Israel. In fact, he precedes *all* things. Paul declares that the Messiah who comes from Israel is "over all things" because he is "God blessed forever" (Rom 9:5). So the Messiah, while generated in time (*kata sarka*) from Israel, is himself the eternal divine reality that ultimately chooses and establishes Israel. Israel is chosen and created by God as the womb that gives birth to the Messiah, even as the Messiah (as God before all things) ultimately gives birth to Israel. Paul cannot think Messiah and Israel apart from each other. That is why Paul's being in Messiah binds him ever more radically to the historical destiny of his birth family Israel, to the Israel of God. It is no accident that the good news of God's justice apocalypsed in Messiah leads Paul to this place in his letter. The question of Israel is at the very heart of the gospel of the Messiah. The "power of God for liberation" (Rom 1:16) and the "love of God in Messiah Jesus our Sovereign" (Rom 8:39) will bring about justice in and for God's people Israel just as surely as they do in and for the other peoples of the earth.

God Divides Israel from Israel (Romans 9:6-29)

Paul grieves over his people. But he does not grieve because the word of God has failed (Rom 9:6). The word of God, the good news of the Messiah "who is over all," will not fail to bring about deliverance and justice for Israel. Rather, Paul grieves because Israel is *divided*—divided, as we know, between those few from Israel who heard and believed the news about God's justice in Messiah, and those—the greater portion of Israel—who heard and did not believe it. What is the meaning of that division? Will God's justice apocalypsed in Messiah finally be accomplished for a few messianic Judeans but not for *all* Israel? Will the division in Israel be final, or will God bring it to an end? Those are the questions for Paul.

Paul begins with a startling declaration: "For not all those of [*ex*] Israel are Israel" (Rom 9:6).

> This is the most literal translation. Readers of Romans should be wary when translations too freely add meanings to "clarify" Paul's terse phrasing. For example: "For not all Israelites truly belong to Israel" (NRSV). The word *Israelites* rather than *Israel* immediately individualizes the meaning of Israel. And the words "truly belong" end up separating the larger reality of Israel from what is "truly" Israel—making the larger reality *not* "truly" Israel. But Paul does not say that. As we will see, Paul is intent on making a distinction *within* Israel on the one hand, while retaining the thought of a single Israel on the other.

Paul's sentence is an odd construction. On the one hand there is Israel, and on the other hand there is Israel. These are both one Israel and not one.

They are one in the sense that *Israel* is the encompassing term that includes both the "all Israel" and the less-than-all. They are *not* one in the sense that within the larger encompassing category of "Israel" another Israel is distinguished. How can this be?

Paul explains by recalling the stories of the patriarchs and matriarchs of Israel. Abraham—the father of Israel—had "children [*tekna*, plural] of the flesh" (Rom 9:8), that is, children by straightforward human generation. Paul does not name these children (that is, Ishmael and a number of others [Gen 16; 25:1-2]), but instead says "not all" of those children are Abraham's seed, but only the one promised to Sarah. Paul makes a distinction here between children (*tekna*) and seed (*sperma*), which parallels his distinction between all Israel and the less-than-all Israel. The designation "seed" is reserved for Isaac, according to the word of Genesis 21:12, which Paul quotes (Rom 9:7): "In Isaac your *seed* will be *called*." To be called indicates an effective and creative act of God. As Paul wrote in Romans 4, God "makes dead ones live and *calls* into being what is not" (Rom 4:17). Sarai was barren. Isaac is anything but the result of natural human procreative powers. He is the result of God's calling into being—in other words, God's creative power. The specific distinction of Abraham's and Sarah's one seed from Abraham's other children is determined by God. So too is the distinction between Israel and all Israel. Note that Paul does not imply a *negative* evaluation of Abraham's other children, only a *distinction* between the many children and the one "seed."

Paul explains further by referring to Rebecca, Isaac's wife (Rom 9:10). She conceived two children, twins, by the "one man" Isaac. But God chose only one of those children. Further, God did not choose according to the expected criterion of birth order (by which one would expect the elder Esau to be chosen), or according to a criterion of moral worth: God chose Jacob "before they were born or had done anything good or bad" (Rom 9:11). God made the radical distinction between the twins only according to God's own electing purpose and calling: "I have loved Jacob, but I have hated Esau" (Rom 9:13, quoting Mal 1:2-3). Jacob was chosen. Esau was not.

Paul's point in the love-hate language of Romans 9:3 is not to focus on God's "emotions," or to explain God's rationale for the decision, but to emphasize the *radical distinction* that *God* makes according to his own decision between the two sons of Rebecca. Further, Paul prohibits us from making any moral judgment for Jacob and against Esau, or, for that matter, from determining that Jacob is "saved" and Esau is not.

What role does God's choosing or election play in your understanding of how God works in your life or in the movement of history? If you have a sense that God has chosen you, or the people Israel, what does that mean (in your mind) for those whom God has not chosen?

The point of these stories from the matriarchs and patriarchs comes to this: if God (in Paul's time) makes a distinction between a part of Israel and all Israel, it simply follows the ancient pattern of how God works. Paul is saying that if we want to know how God's justice is working with respect to Israel in Paul's own time, we have to understand the pattern that begins with Abraham and Sarah, Isaac and Rebecca, Esau and Jacob. God works according to God's own electing, creating, and resurrecting logic. If Paul in his time discerns that a part of Israel is in some sense set apart from all Israel because of Jesus Messiah, it is not because God has rejected the greater portion of Israel, or even because of moral failure by that portion of Israel that has refused the messiahship of Jesus. It is because God is *creatively at work.*

Paul recognizes that it is hard to see how such a pattern of divine working can be construed as justice. A loyal Israelite could surely ask, "What then shall we say? Is that not *injustice* [*adikia*] on God's part?" (Rom 9:14). If God simply does not take account of things such as birth priority and morality when God makes such fundamental decisions that determine Israel's history, how does that accord with any normal standard of justice? It is a good question. Yet, apart from responding with "By no means!" to the very thought of God's injustice, Paul does not answer the question with an explanation. In fact, he *radicalizes* the offensiveness of the argument. He now writes about God's mercy and God's hardening.

First, in Romans 9:15 he quotes Exodus 33:19: "I will have mercy on whom I have mercy, and I will have compassion on whom I have compassion." It is indeed God's right to decide between Isaac and Ishmael, between Jacob and Esau, between all Israel and a part of Israel, because *God is God*. The decision is rooted in God's mercy and compassion. There is no hint of injustice in it—or so Paul declares.

Paul next quotes Exodus 9:16, in which God speaks to Pharaoh: "I have raised you up for this very purpose, that I may demonstrate my power in you and that my name may be declared in all the earth" (Rom 9:17). "So then," Paul writes, "[God] has mercy on whomever he chooses, and he hardens the heart of whomever he chooses" (Rom 9:18). God hardens hearts? The exodus story speaks a number of times about Pharaoh's hardened heart. Early in the story of the plagues Pharaoh seems to be the agent of his own hardened heart. Later on, however, God declares himself to be the agent of Pharaoh's hardened heart.

The complex dynamics of hardening in the exodus story are nicely summed up in Exodus 9:34–10:1:

> But when Pharaoh saw that the rain and the hail and the thunder had ceased, *he sinned* once more and *hardened his heart*, he and his officials. So the heart of Pharaoh *was hardened*, and he would not let the Israelites go, just as the LORD had spoken through Moses.
>
> Then the LORD said to Moses, "Go to Pharaoh; for *I have hardened his heart and the heart* of his officials, *in order that* I may show these signs of mine among them."

How do you respond to the idea that God hardened Pharaoh's heart?

Paul focuses exclusively on God's agency in hardening. But Paul also emphasizes God's *purpose*. God "raised up" Pharaoh to reveal God's power (*dynamis*) and in order that God's name should be declared in all the earth (Rom 9:17). Paul does not claim either that Pharaoh was wicked (and thus deserving of God's hardening), or that God's purpose was *against* Pharaoh. Rather, Pharaoh simply served as God's instrument for the sake of revealing God and spreading the news of God among all peoples. (In Rom 1:16: "The good news is the *power* of God for salvation . . . to the Judean first and also to the Greek"—that is, to the whole earth.) For Paul, both mercy and hardening serve a *single* divine purpose: that the whole earth and all its peoples might know God's reality (his name) and God's liberating power. If a portion of Israel receives God's mercy (in believing in Jesus Messiah) while the larger portion is hardened, Paul can only imagine it is for that same purpose, to reveal God and spread the good news.

Still, Paul again has to ward off the criticism of injustice. God divides people up according to his will: some receive mercy, others receive hardening. That division has nothing to do with merit or morality. Again a loyal Israelite might ask, Does that not remove all responsibility from the human sphere? Can God still "find fault" (Rom 9:19) with Israel if God alone is making the decisions? Where is the justice in that? Once again Paul does not explain God, nor does he answer the question about human responsibility—in fact, he simply drops the question of fault. If Isaac, not Abraham's other children, is Abraham's seed; if Jacob is chosen and not Esau; if some receive God's mercy while others like Pharaoh are hardened—well, that is simply the right of the divine potter over the human clay (Rom 9:20-22). The only important question for Paul is what *purpose* is being served by these divine decisions and divisions. About this he is clear: through these decisions and divisions God is revealing his own divine purpose, power, and glorious reality (Rom 9:22-23): in other words, God is making known the good news of God.

Throughout this passage Paul contends with some forceful objections about divine justice and injustice. Any loyal Israelite (Paul himself, for example!)—even Israel itself as a character—could be raising those objections. The larger portion of Israel is being lumped with the other children of Abraham rather than with Isaac, with the unchosen Esau rather than with Jacob. It is being lumped with Pharaoh, whom God hardened. This is Israel in the historical ethnic-national sense, which would certainly (and rightly) have understood itself as God's people, God's chosen and beloved, those who have received God's mercy. Yet Paul has lined up this Israel with the unchosen, the unbeloved, the heart-hardened. Paul even lumps them together with the "vessels of wrath" (the Gentile nations), which the divine potter "endures with much patience" rather than destroying them (Rom 9:22; see Rom 3:25). That would certainly be offensive to Israel. Given all that *Israel* means, even according to Paul in Romans 9:1-5, how does any of this make sense?

Again without answering the question, Paul turns instead to what he calls the "vessels of mercy." These are the called ones, Paul writes, "including us whom he has called, not only from Judeans but also from nations" (Rom 9:24). In other words, messianics. Here again (quoting Hos 2:23; 1:10) Paul stresses God's creative power to call into being that which was not (see Rom 4:17). According to Hosea, those who were once "not [God's] people" (the Gentile nations) God calls "my people" and "sons of the living God." The one who was once "not beloved" God calls "my beloved." From these texts in Hosea Paul now argues that by his call alone God creates a people of God *from the Gentile nations*. These messianic Gentiles are now lumped together with Isaac the seed and with Jacob the chosen and beloved. They are also lumped together with the smaller subset of Israel, which Paul now for the first time calls "the remnant" (Rom 9:27, quoting Is 10:22) that receives God's mercy. So, on the one hand there is Israel as an historical ethnic-national whole whose number may be as many "as the sand of the sea" (Rom 9:27). On the other hand there is by God's mercy a smaller number, a *remnant* of Israel, which Paul identifies as seed (*sperma*, Rom 9:29, quoting Is 1:9) saved from destruction.

Again, we need to watch the translations: The NRSV translates Paul's quote from Isaiah 10:22 (in Rom 9:27) as "only a remnant of them will be saved" (so also TNIV: "only the remnant will be saved"). *Only* suggests that the remnant will be saved *to the exclusion of* the rest. Paul does not use the word *only*; the destiny of the rest is left open.

This remnant-seed Israel is those Judeans whom God in Paul's time is setting apart and "saving" in Messiah Jesus. They, along with Gentile messianics, are together the "vessels of mercy" that "make known the riches of [God's] glory" (Rom 9:23).

What then will become of Israel as an historical ethnic-national reality? That remains to be seen.

God's Justice in the Midst of
Israel (Romans 9:30–10:21)

In Romans 9:30-33, Paul finally comes around to responding to the question of justice and begins to explain why all of this matters in the first place. While up to this point in the argument it may seem that God is making decisions and divisions arbitrarily—according to some mysterious divine whim and seemingly unjustly—that is not the case. In fact, those decisions and divisions come about precisely *because of God's justice*. For we have seen that God's justice *according to the good news* is anything but an abstract idea. From the beginning of Romans Paul has not allowed us to think of God's justice as anything other than the divine-human reality of Jesus Messiah— his life, atoning death, resurrection, and sovereign rule—and our sharing in that reality through trust. Jesus Messiah, God's justice in person, creates the distinction within Israel by his very presence. Because of *him* there is Israel the remnant (Judeans who believe in him) on the one hand, and Israel the historical ethnic-national whole ("the rest") on the other. This latter Israel stumbles over the very being and form of divine justice itself:

> What then shall we say? Gentiles who did not pursue justice have nevertheless laid hold of justice [i.e., Jesus Messiah], the justice of trust. But Israel, pursuing law-justice, did not arrive at it. Why? Because they pursued [justice] not through trust but through striving. They stumbled on the stone of stumbling, as it is written, "Behold, I lay in Zion a stone of stumbling and a rock of scandal, and the one who trusts in him will not be put to shame." (Rom 9:30-33, quoting Is 8:14; 28:16)

The boundary that (for the time being) divides Israel from Israel is the Messiah—the *shamed, crucified* Messiah. He is the scandalous rock that God has thrown onto Israel's path in its pursuit of justice. Demanding divine justice, but not willing to share the Messiah's shame, Israel stumbled over him. No wonder! The Messiah declared in Paul's good news does not look anything like justice according to Israel's hopes. After his coming, even after his resurrection and exaltation as sovereign Ruler, Israel remained an occupied land and a subjugated people, shamed and humiliated among the nations. If (as Paul believes) the Messiah bears Israel's meaning and destiny in himself, does that mean ethnic-national Israel is also called to the messianic path of shame and crucifixion? Is Israel called actually to *embrace* its current weakness and humiliation, and to trust God in it? Is that its path to justice?

Paul says, Yes! Precisely! The scandalous rock and stumbling stone—the shameful Messiah—is the reality, form, and power of God's *justice* in the midst of Israel, for the sake of Israel. Will Israel believe this and trust God?

This is a hard thing to ask of a nation whose expectations of justice, messianic liberation, and glory were profoundly different. What nation on earth would believe such a message? A nation survives, thrives, and arrives at its place among nations only through its works (Rom 9:32), its capacity to possess its land, define and determine itself, establish its constitution and laws, pursue its way of life, flourish and grow politically and economically, defend its borders against enemies, expel alien powers. Could Israel be any different? Would not the way of justice for Israel run down that road, with God blessing and empowering Israel's best efforts to establish itself as a nation among the nations? Yet Paul knows that God's will for *this* nation— God's chosen nation—has now been revealed and defined in Israel's Messiah.

Thus Paul's "heart's desire and prayer to God" (Rom 10:1) is that Israel might come to acknowledge the way of justice apocalypsed in its midst. Paul's solidarity with Israel is unshaken. He has no doubt that Israel has a "zeal for God" (Rom 10:2)—a passion for justice—but it is not a zeal moved by the justice of God in Messiah. Hoping to establish (or reestablish) its existence, land, and way of life among the nations through its own power— as any nation would—Israel does not trust God's way of giving Israel justice through Messiah (Rom 10:3). In the gospel God reveals that the normal worldly road to justice is a dead end for Israel. Israel's purpose is not to secure its land and way of life (the law) among the nations through its own capacity. According to the good news, that is not Israel's *justice*. "For," Paul declares, "Messiah is the end [*telos*] of law, so there may be justice for *all* who *trust*" (10:4). Messiah stands beyond the law, and defines the justice meaning of the law for Israel. That meaning is *trust*—trust in God who graciously gives Israel justice now in Messiah, and will give Israel restorative justice in messianic time (Rom 11:26).

Paul turns to the law itself (Leviticus and Deuteronomy) to make the case: he finds that the law testifies to the divine-human reality of God's justice in

Messiah for all.[1] But the law is not simply straightforward on this matter. On the one hand Paul finds in Leviticus 18 a text in which "Moses writes about law-justice" (Rom 10:5): According to Moses, "the sons of Israel" (Lev 18:2) must not practice the ways of the Egyptians, among whom they once dwelt, nor the ways of the Canaanites, among whom they were about to dwell; rather, Israel must walk in the laws and instructions of the Lord alone (Lev 18:3-4). In other words, according to this text Israel will attain justice by practicing its own particular way of life among the nations, distinct from the nations. Keeping the law of Moses both defines Israel and sets it apart from the other nations (whose practices they are forbidden to do).

It appears in Leviticus that the law of Moses is the way of life for Israel (Lev 18:5, which Paul quotes in Rom 10:5). In quoting Leviticus 18:5 Paul acknowledges that historical ethnic-national Israel is on scriptural ground when Israel zealously defends justice through law and believes that it will live through law. Paul is not quick to criticize Israel for believing that. The text was written by Moses. The problem with the vision in Leviticus is that the way of justice through the law of Moses promises life to *Israel alone* through its law, and leaves the other nations on the outside, dead to life. In fact, Leviticus 18:1-5 seems to set Israel *against* the nations.

But—as he did with the story of Abraham—Paul finds another text in Scripture that he believes speaks a different word from Leviticus 18. He turns to Deuteronomy 30:11-14, providing what is surely a creative reading of that text. Here, Paul says, "the justice of trust" *speaks*. Paul personifies Justice-of-Trust as a speaking character. We may be warranted in thinking that for Paul this speaking character is the Messiah himself (in contrast to Moses, who wrote Lev 18). Now, whereas in Deuteronomy 30:11-14 it is the commandment that is near and accessible to Israel, in Paul's interpretation of the text it is the living reality of Messiah that is graciously near and accessible to Israel: "But the Justice-of-Trust says, 'Do not say in your heart, Who will ascend into heaven?'" (to bring Messiah down from there) "or, Who will descend into the abyss?" (to bring Messiah up from the dead). "But what does [he] say? 'The word is near you, on your lips and in your heart'" (that is, the word of trust that we proclaim; Rom 10:6-8). The Messiah is *present* to Israel. The

---

[1]My reading here is influenced by Francis Watson, *Paul and the Hermeneutics of Faith* (London: T&T Clark, 2004), 315-23, 329-41.

law itself (in Deuteronomy) testifies that Israel does not have to search for him in the heights and depths. Justice-as-Trust—Messiah—is in Israel's midst right now. He has already come (from heaven), was crucified (into the abyss), and was raised up by God from the dead. He now lives and speaks in and to Israel through Scripture and the word of the apostles. All that remains for Israel to do is confess with her mouth and trust in her heart that it is so (Rom 10:9). That trust would be Israel's *justice* (as it was for Abraham); that confession would be its liberation. In other words, it would result in what Israel had hoped for from the justice of law. "Messiah is the *telos*—the justice meaning—of the law" (Rom 10:4).

There would be no shame in Israel's trust (Rom 10:11), because the Messiah in whom they would trust is the living, saving Sovereign of all peoples. He is not only the shameful crucified one; he is also the glorious risen one. Further—which is the point Paul emphasizes—the divinely given *gift* of justice for Israel would not set it *against* the Gentile nations, but join it *with* the believing Gentiles in a common confession of God's justice in Jesus Messiah: "For there is no difference between Judean and Greek; for the same Lord is over *all* and is richly generous to *all* who call on him. For, 'Everyone who calls on the name of the Lord shall be saved'" (Rom 10:12-13, quoting Joel 2:32). Israel's justice consists in its joining Gentiles in calling on the God whose justice is given in Jesus.

Nevertheless, the divine gift of justice that should unite Israel and the nations remains for Israel precisely what not only divides Israel internally but also divides Israel from the nations. For not all of Israel has "obeyed the good news" proclaimed by the apostles (Rom 10:16). It is not the case that Israel has not *heard* the good news. In fact, Paul says (quoting Ps 19:4), the apostles' message about Messiah "has gone out to all the earth, and to the ends of the world" (Rom 10:18). But Israel did not grasp that message. It did not see that even the writings of Moses (Paul quotes Deut 32:21) and Isaiah (Paul quotes Is 65:1) testify that God would make Israel "jealous" and "angry" by the "foolish" Gentile nations—those nations that were not even searching and asking for God (Rom 10:19-20) but are now trusting in him. God revealed himself to those nations through the apostolic message of the justice of trust, and they found God. Israel stands on the outside, not seeking the justice that the nations have found by God's grace but seeking its justice—its own rightful place among the nations—through self-sovereignty and law.

But that is not the end of the story for Israel. On the contrary, says Paul: God continues "all day long" to "reach out his hands" to Israel (Rom 10:21, quoting Is 65:2). God does not abandon Israel.

> What do you make of the fact that Israel—God's chosen nation—did not (and does not) acknowledge Jesus Messiah as God's justice? Where does this put Israel, then and now, in the larger picture of God's purpose of justice for the world?

God's Justice for Israel, Israel, and the Nations (Romans 11:1-32)

On the basis of the quotation from Isaiah 65:2 (in Rom 10:21) Paul is confident to make his next declaration. For someone might rightly ask Paul, "So then, has God rejected his people?" Paul says, "No way!" (Rom 11:1). For a third time in these chapters (see Rom 9:1-3; 10:1-2) Paul expresses his fundamental solidarity with his people. He is *one of them*: "I myself am an Israelite, from the seed of Abraham, of the tribe of Benjamin" (Rom 11:1). Paul is in fact saying that, as an Israelite who trusts God and is therefore one of Abraham's seed, he alone would be sufficient evidence that God has not abandoned Israel. The one Israelite may stand for the many; Paul the Israelite is alone sufficient to represent the whole people. Therefore, he declares, "God has not rejected his people whom he foreknew" (Rom 11:2). But Paul is not the only one from Israel whom God foreknew and graciously chose to bear the good news. Many other Judeans in Paul's time heard and believed the good news: in them, Paul says, God has created "a remnant" according to God's "gracious choosing" (Rom 11:5).

Paul thus returns to themes he introduced in Romans 9: God's sovereign and gracious choosing, the remnant, and the division *within* Israel. Within the one Israel there are two groups, a remnant that is chosen (those who believe the message about the Messiah), and "the rest" (*hoi loipoi*), which is "hardened" (Rom 11:7). This latter group—what I have been calling the historical ethnic-national Israel—does not attain the justice it was seeking through sovereignty and law. What is crucial to see here, however, is that Paul does not lay the fault for the condition of "the rest" at their own feet. Paul had written in Romans 9:18, with reference to Pharaoh: "So then [God] has mercy on whomever he chooses, and he hardens the heart of whomever he chooses." In Romans 11:7 Paul makes that same point again with quotations from Scripture, but now about "the rest" of Israel: "*God gave them* a comatose spirit, eyes that do not see, ears that do not hear" (Rom 11:8, quoting from Deut 29:4; Is 29:10). Clearly *God* is to "blame" for the condition of "the rest" of Israel. That is also Paul's point when he quotes from Psalm 69:22-23 LXX: "*Let* their table become for them a snare and a trap, a stumbling stone and a retribution; *let* their eyes be darkened so they cannot see, and *let* their backs be always bent" (Rom 11:9-10 NRSV). *God* is the one letting these things happen to Israel by his own decision.

But precisely because God is responsible for Israel's condition described in these texts, it is clear that Israel has not simply chosen its own course and somehow thereby slipped away from God. "No way!" says Paul. Paul adopts the metaphor of a footrace: if Israel has stumbled in the race toward justice (stumbled because of God—see again Rom 9:33), there is nevertheless no way it will fall so as to be excluded from or not complete the race. Israel's stumble serves only one purpose: that salvation—God's justice in Messiah—might go out to the nations; and that Israel, seeing the nations getting ahead, might become jealous and seek out what is giving the nations the advantage in the race—the good news (Rom 11:11). But ultimately God will see to it that Israel completes the race: "Now, if [Israel's] misstep in the race means advantage for the world, and [Israel's] losing ground means getting ahead for the nations, how much more will [Israel's] full completion of the race mean!" (Rom 11:12).[2]

Paul thus anticipates his conclusion but he doesn't rush to it. Instead, he now directly addresses his *Roman-Gentile* audience to remind them of how they fit in this story. We can see from Romans 11:18 that some of them were thinking that the nations (or maybe Rome in particular) had now *become the story of God's purposes*, that Israel is now out of the race for justice, and that only the Gentile peoples would complete it—and thus have boasting rights. (Romans were already in the habit of boasting about themselves and deriding Judeans.) But, No! says Paul:

---

[2]I am grateful to Mark Kinzer for sending me his (unpublished) translation of Romans, which guides mine at this point.

Listen, you Gentile peoples: If for the time being the greater part of Israel
stumbles over the good news, it is *for your sake!* My mission to you Gentiles
is aimed at stirring up desire for the gospel in *them.* Yes, they are running
off-track. But through this, God has brought about nothing less than the
reconciliation of the world in Jesus Messiah. So what will happen when they—
the "rest" of Israel—are brought back on track (as they surely will be)? Nothing
less than resurrection from the dead—new creation! Do not be proud, Roman
Gentiles! The deliverance of the Gentile peoples is completely bound up with
the deliverance of the people Israel. Further, the deliverance of Israel as a
whole is bound up with the remnant of Israel that believes the gospel. Consider
the remnant of Israel as the "firstfruit offering" of bread dough, the part for
the whole: if that remnant offering is sanctified to God, then the whole batch
of dough is sanctified through it; and if the root of the tree of Israel (Jesus
Messiah?) is holy, then the branches of the tree are made holy through the
root. Far from God abandoning Israel as a whole, God has *already sanctified*
it through sanctifying the remnant of Israel. Israel as a whole is not out of the
race! They will finish it. Deliverance and justice for all Israel is assured.
(Rom 11:13-16 paraphrased)

Paul has introduced the image of the root and the branches, which he now
goes on to expand.

The details of the analogy (for example, how accurate is Paul's knowledge
of horticulture?) must not deter from the main point. The redemption of the
Gentile peoples—whom Paul calls "wild olive branches"—depends on their
being grafted in to the nourishing tree of Israel.

Here we encounter another translation issue in the NRSV, which translates *enekentristhēs en autois* in Romans 11:17 as "were grafted *in their
place,"* that is, wild olive shoots (Gentiles) were grafted in the place
where "some branches [of Israel] were broken off." "In their place"
suggests that the ingrafted Gentiles replace the broken-off Israelites.
But *en autois* does not mean "in their place." It means "among them,"
or "in among the others" (so TNIV). In other words, the ingrafted
Gentiles *join* the non-broken-off branches of Israel but do not by that
fact replace the broken-off ones. For as Paul goes on to say, there is
still plenty of room for the broken-off branches of Israel to be regrafted "into their own [*idia*] olive tree" (Rom 11:24).

If some among Israel (those natural branches that do not believe the good news, Rom 11:20) are currently broken off of the good olive tree, it is (again) because *God* has broken them off. Likewise, the wild olive branches—the believing Gentile peoples—have been grafted in by God because of God's *kindness*. They were not capable of grafting themselves in; they have no grounds for boasting. In fact, if they do not acknowledge that God's kindness is the *only* reason they share in the many riches of the tree of Israel (see Rom 9:4-5), they too might be cut off of that tree. While there is hope that the natural branches might through trust be regrafted into the tree, Paul does not hold out the same hope for the boasting wild olive branches. Let the Gentile peoples hear and understand!

Ultimately for Paul there will only be one, united, reconciled, resurrected Israel. The mystery of *the divine strategic distinction* between Israel and Israel, between the part of Israel that received mercy and the part of Israel that was hardened, between the remnant and the rest, *will come to an end* when the fullness (*plērōma*) of the Gentile nations "comes in" (Rom 11:25). What precisely Paul means by that last phrase, "the fullness of the nations," is itself a mystery. But what he is clear about is that "all Israel [*pas Israēl*] will be saved" (Rom 11:26). Indeed, the very source of ("the rest" of) Israel's stumbling and hardening—Messiah Jesus—will also finally be the source and power of "all Israel's" deliverance. The prophet Isaiah testifies to that fact: "Out of Zion will come the Deliverer; *he* will turn away ungodliness from Jacob. And this is the binding covenant *from me* to them, when *I* take away their sins" (Rom 11:26-27, quoting Is 59:20-21; 27:9). Israel will not achieve its own ultimate liberation. Justice for Israel is the gracious work of God through the liberating Messiah. Precisely so, it is a sure thing! In this all Israel may trust and receive God's justice.

Paul once again addresses the Gentiles in Rome to hammer a final nail in the coffin of their temptation to boast:

> With respect to the good news [that is, as a consequence of and in service to the good news] a portion of Israel are "enemies." But that is only for the sake of you Gentiles, and only according to the divine purpose. By divine election Israel remains God's beloved people, because God will never take back his gifts and calling of the ancestors of Israel. There was a time when you Gentile peoples were imprisoned in disobedience to God; yet now you have received

God's mercy through the good news. But that is only because (according to God's will) Israel was disobedient to that good news. That is not the end of the story for them. Far from it! Their disobedience indeed means mercy for you, but ultimately it can only mean mercy also for them. For at one time or another God has bound up *all* in disobedience (first the Gentile peoples, then Israel) in order that ultimately he might show mercy to *all* (the Gentile peoples *and* Israel). (Rom 11:28-32 paraphrased)[3]

Not only does Paul here put an end to all boasting. He unites *all* of the characters in this complicated story—Israel as a whole, the remnant of Israel, the Gentile peoples—under the *single divine purpose* to show mercy to the whole world. That is the final meaning of God's justice. "God was in Messiah reconciling the world to himself, not reckoning their trespasses against them, and entrusting to us that word of reconciliation" (2 Cor 5:19).

> What do you make of the various twists and turns in God's purpose (according to Paul) that end up with Paul's declaration in Romans 11:32? How do you think Paul has been able to discern these twists and turns? What do you make of the idea that God "has bound up all in disobedience in order that he might have mercy on all" (taking "all" here as both Israel and the Gentile nations)?

Paul has—obviously through divine apocalypse—disclosed to us something of God's hidden work behind the visible scene of what happens when the controversial good news makes its way into the world of Israel and the nations, persuading some, hardening others. Paul himself seems somewhat baffled by the mystery of it all and does not claim to know more than what he has declared, nor does he claim to have explained *why* God has chosen to work in this way. Instead, he breaks out into doxology, worshiping God for God's riches, wisdom, knowledge, unsearchable judgments, and inscrutable ways (Rom 11:33-35). What he is absolutely sure about is that "all things" occur within God's purpose for Israel and the nations, and for the sake of an ultimate destiny in the triune life of God: "For from him and through him and to him are all things. To him be the glory into the ages. Amen."

---

[3]In Rom 11:28 the NRSV translates the one Greek word *echthroi* ("enemies") as "enemies of God." Paul does *not* write *echthroi tou theou* ("enemies of God").

An Audacious Vision for the Nations

In these three chapters of Romans Paul has turned his attention to God's chosen nation, Israel—a nation that neither God nor Paul has abandoned, a nation with which both God and Paul continue to stand in fundamental solidarity. Before this in the letter Paul had written extensively about God's justice for "all." Yet even there, in the midst of that universalism, he maintained the distinction between Judeans and Gentiles. In Romans 9–11 he reaffirms and emphasizes the distinction between Israel and the nations (and even marks another distinction within Israel) as the very condition within which God will ultimately show mercy to all. Israel—historical ethnic-national Israel—remains unique to the end, indispensable in God's apocalypse of justice among the nations. As the unique sign and sacrament of God's purpose for all nations (according to Ex 19:5-6), God's messianic vision for Israel as a nation, revealed in Jesus Messiah, is also given as God's messianic vision for all other nations.

Peoples and nations throughout history (particularly in the Christian West and Christian East) have often thought of themselves and their destiny as bearers of God's world-historical purpose. There is no indication in Romans 9–11 that Paul *forbids* that thought. Instead, he draws attention—especially Gentile attention—to what world-historical purpose might look like for a people or nation when that thought is disciplined by the reality of Jesus Messiah and the being and destiny of Israel. Israel *is* God's nation by God's election. As such, Israel is called by God to the way of Israel's Messiah, who is even now immediately present in their midst as their true calling and destiny.

In the time between God's justice arriving in Israel as Messiah Jesus and God's justice arriving in Israel as the Deliverer who comes "out of Zion" (Rom 11:26), Israel's world-historical purpose as a nation is none other than to be conformed to the way of Jesus Messiah—to be a *messianic* people in precisely that sense. As Paul has shown, that would mean being always ready to exist as a nation without self-assertion, without self-sovereignty, without self-defense, without the triumph of its rule and law; in other words, without looking like a nation according to the usual definitions and determinations. As such, Israel would have to be prepared to embrace even shame and humiliation among the Gentile nations as its share in the sufferings of the

Messiah, trusting its faithful God for final vindication. Israel's justice—the justice of trust—among the nations would start there.

In just this way Israel would demonstrate that it is indeed God's world-historical priestly kingdom and holy nation, showing by its own trust what it would mean for *any other nation* to imagine its own existence as world-historical in messianic terms—ready to refuse self-assertion, self-sovereignty, and self-defense; ready to serve other nations rather than impose its own ways; ready to suffer loss and defeat; ready to live vulnerably, humbly, even shamefully (rather than boastfully) as one people among many peoples.

What might God's justice in and among even Gentile nations look like? By reaffirming and reimagining the unique gifts and calling of Israel through the apocalyptic reality of God's justice in Jesus Messiah, Paul has not stopped short of casting an audacious vision of how any nation might participate in the messianic justice of God in the world—indeed, be an instrument of God's peace.

> Given that the truth of God's reality and God's justice are apocalypsed in Jesus Messiah and the Holy Spirit for Israel and all nations, what would it mean for a nation—your nation—to declare, "In God we trust"? What concrete evidence is there that might suggest your nation's declaration is meaningful in messianic terms? What evidence might suggest otherwise? Or do you think it is impossible that Israel or any other nation on the world stage can truthfully make that declaration in the sense that Paul has given it in Romans? What conditions would have to be in place to make it possible?

Part 2

MESSIANIC
LIFE

10

MESSIANIC PUBLIC SERVICE

IN THIS CHAPTER

- Romans 12:1-2: Messianic life in bodies and minds
- Romans 12:3-13: Messianic life in a new body politic
- Romans 12:14-18: Messianic life on the streets and in the neighborhoods

THE PERCEPTIVE READER will notice that for the first time in this book the word *justice* does not appear in the chapter title. There is a good reason for that: the Greek *justice/righteousness* words all but disappear in the last five chapters of Romans, with one exception (Rom 14:17). This may seem strange. We might expect in an extensive treatise on justice (which is how we have characterized Romans) that the author, having given a robust account of God's justice, would now turn to the reader with an exhortation to "do justice" and with an account of what that might look like. But, unlike Micah 6:8, Paul nowhere in his writings instructs messianics to do justice. We have seen in Romans 6 that Paul speaks of messianics as slaves of justice, and their body parts as weapons of justice, but not as self-moved *agents* of justice. Weapons do not wield themselves; slaves do not act according to their own will but according to the will of the master. Messianics have become "slaves of justice" (Rom 6:18), or, which is the same thing, "slaves of God" (Rom 6:22).

What Romans 1–11 has made clear is that *God* is the one who does justice, and God does justice in Jesus Messiah and through the Spirit of life. Messianics are given to share in God's justice through trust and share in

God's life through the Spirit. Paul concludes in Romans 11:32 that God's justice comes strangely to this: God has *mercy* on all. Justice is not given to messianics as an agenda but as the gracious gift of sharing, through trust, in the divine life of God the Father, Son, and Holy Spirit, the God whose justice is mercy. As Paul writes in 2 Corinthians 5:21, "[God] made [Messiah] who knew no sin to be sin for us, so that we might *in him become* the justice of God."

To become the justice of God! It is not as if Paul leaves justice behind. Messianics are called to *become* what God accomplishes and gives in Jesus Messiah, in whose divine-human reality they share by the Spirit. Therefore Paul's treatise on justice continues in the next five chapters of Romans in terms of messianic life. That simple phrase captures three crucial ideas we have already discussed: (1) being just means trusting God who raised Jesus from the dead (Rom 4); (2) becoming just means sharing in the crucified/living Messiah (the focus of Rom 5–6); and (3) living justly means living in the Spirit (the focus of Rom 8). Participating *in* Messiah and the Holy Spirit through trust is how messianics bear God's justice into the world and make it visible.

Messianic Bodies and Minds (Romans 12:1-2)

In Romans 1–11 Paul proclaimed that God's justice apocalypsed in Messiah is God's mercy to Israel and the nations (Rom 11:32). Paul now urges the messianic community brought into being by God's "mercies" (Rom 12:1) to live in and from those mercies. How does a people created by God's mercy and compassion live in the world? Recall from our previous chapter that God chose Israel to be a visible, living sacrament of God's invisible reality among the other nations. So too the new people created in Messiah and the Spirit is called to be a visible sign of invisible divine reality in the midst of the nations. The gospel does not primarily generate a new spirituality, if by that we mean a new inner life in individual believers. While that is not excluded from Paul's vision of messianic life, it is far from the center of his attention. Instead, Paul understands the gospel to generate a new *visible, bodily, public* form of life among the messianic people. Just as Israel was chosen as a social and political body to be a priestly kingdom and a holy nation, so those who live by the mercies of God are called to offer their individual bodies (*sōmata*, plural) in community as a single, living, holy offering (*thysia*, singular) that pleases God (Rom 12:1). This, Paul declares, is their "reasonable [logical] worship" (*logikēn latreian*).

Paul emphasizes the living, bodily, rational character of messianic life because he understands it to be material public life, open to public view. Living human bodies take up room in the physical world, bump into one another, and must eat, drink, and have clothing and shelter—material goods. Therefore, material, economic, and political relationships are always already explicit in the relation of every bodily being to other bodily beings, and these relationships are open to rational, critical examination. This is also true of the messianic body (the *ekklēsia*—the messianic assembly or church). When translations such as the NRSV and NIV render the Greek words *logikēn latreian* as "spiritual worship," we are all too inclined to think that Paul is imagining something that goes on "in church," largely separate from and invisible to the wider world—the weird, irrational, otherworldly practices of "religious" or "spiritual" people. Paul has a very different understanding.

For Paul, messianic worship or public service to God makes concrete demands on bodily practices (ordinary things such as eating and drinking, as we will see in Rom 14), which must accord with the *logic* of the good news. "Reasonable, thoughtful service" characterizes the presence, activity, and visibility of a community whose life in the public sphere is lived by the logic of the Messiah's own life. By its form of life the messianic community makes a specific claim within the public sphere about the nature of God, the good life, and the meaning of justice. Paul always declares the good news in public because it is meant to "bring about faithful obedience [to God] among all the nations" (Rom 1:5; 16:26). That begins with the faithful obedience of the messianic community, created by the good news to be *God's holy, public body politic* in the midst of the nations.

Paul therefore urges the messianics in Rome, "Do not conform to the sense-making scheme [*syschēmatizesthe*] of this present age" (Rom 12:2) (notice *schema* in the middle of the Greek word). With the phrase "sense-making scheme of this age" Paul indicates the sum total of the taken-for-granted (and usually not critically examined) beliefs, assumptions, concepts, images, and metaphors that a society holds about the complex, multilayered relations, institutions, systems, and powers that make society work, and about the habits and practices that confirm, conform to, and embody them in order to attain the good life. Our idea of culture partially captures this; some speak more technically of a social imaginary or form of life. It is whatever both *makes* a society and makes a society *work*. We all dwell within, conform to, live by, and embody such sense-making schemes. They are what we call *world*. Though we may be hardly aware of them, they powerfully shape our lives. We cannot live without them: for example, we now cannot think ourselves as not inhabiting a digital society.

> I have emphasized the public, visible, material, logical, rational charac-ter of the way of life Paul envisages for the messianic community. Are those some of the usual words you would use to describe your Christian life or the life of your church? If you tend to think of your faith or church life as more private, hidden, spiritual, and primarily experiential and emotional, why do you think that is so? How might the sense-making scheme of your society have pushed you into that space?

As we saw in Romans 1:18–3:20, for Paul the good news invades and interrupts our sense-making schemes like an apocalypse, calling our taken-for-granted world into question in the most fundamental way. The gospel exposes our sense-making schemes as also the fertile soil in which Sin and Death grow and begin to assert their destructive sovereignty over us. The Gentile peoples in Paul's time made sense of things and pursued well-being by acknowledging, honoring, and appeasing multiple divin-ities, spirits, magical powers, political authorities, and powers of nature that ruled the cosmos. The Judeans made sense of things according to God's law, which they understood as the structuring principle of all reality, revealed to Moses as the true form of life for the people of God living in the land of Israel. By practicing the law Judeans aligned themselves with God's will, and indeed with the truth of all creation. But, according to Paul, when seen in the revealing light of the gospel, neither the idolatrous systems of the Gentile peoples (of course) nor even the law of Moses (surprisingly) could resist being captured by the powers of Sin and Death (as we saw in Rom 2; 7).

In our own secular age in the West, we make little or no reference to divine realities or divine laws to make sense of things. Instead, democracy, science, market economy, global communications, technology, social media, film and television, advertising, and digital images altogether form our sense-making scheme and define the "real world" for us. We form our habits, practices, and patterns of thought by and around these things in our quest for the good life. Nevertheless, judged in the light of the good news, this sense-making scheme actually enslaves us, not by coercing us but by persuading us to entrust ourselves to it as the power of life and well-being, and making it difficult for us to imagine anything beyond it. Whatever the present age is—and there is always a present age with its persuasive, captivating power—the good news demands a *critical* engagement with it and a fundamental transformation of our imaginations and practices.

The God of Messiah Jesus is God of all things (Rom 11:36). The messianic people of God takes up the form of Israel's mission in the world, that is, to be a visible witness among the nations of God's reality and God's justice revealed in the gospel. That calls for a transformation in our imagining of the real and how the world really works. The real world must no longer be defined by the taken-for-granted systems of power, economy, and communication that constitute society and that seem so right and true by just being there. Imagining life otherwise is no easy thing. It requires committed rational reflection, effort, and practice, if Messiah's people are not simply to slip back into the old habits of construing and inhabiting reality. Paul intended the first eleven chapters of Romans as a fundamental redescription of the real, a revolution in how we think and practice God and all things in relation to God: sovereignties, powers, gods, allegiances, law, justice, trust, Sin, Death, Grace, life, bondage, liberation, suffering, love, creation, Israel, and the nations. The first eleven chapters of Romans are a comprehensive, mind-altering redescription of reality that cannot be had simply by observing the world around us. In fact, as we have seen, Paul received it in his own life as a divine *apocalypse*—a dramatic, world-altering *revelation* of the real. It was for him nothing less than the *death* of the real world as he had known it and the *resurrection* of a new reality defined in relation to the one God and God's Messiah. As he writes in Galatians, "the world has been crucified to me, and I to the world. . . . [What is real] is a *new creation*" (Gal 6:14-15). It cannot be less than that for us.

So for messianics there is no option: "Be transformed [*metamorphousthe*] by the renewing of your mind" (Rom 12:2)! Mind renewal requires the kind of demanding intellectual work we have already done on the first eleven chapters of Romans; it is work that cannot be ignored or avoided in favor of "practical" instructions. (For example, how often are we tempted to skip lightly over—or ignore—Rom 1-11 to get to the practical stuff in Rom 12-15?) The mandatory metamorphosis of messianic minds does not happen without serious intellectual work. Knowing God's will—knowing what is "good and pleasing and perfect" (Rom 12:2)—depends on knowing the real in gospel terms.

> How much time and effort do you typically give to the demanding intellectual work of understanding the good news? (If you have read the first nine chapters of this book, you may be more committed than many!) How does that work shape your sense of what "the real" is? How does it make you critical of the real as the present age (your current social and cultural context) understands it? Can you give an account of the real in gospel terms?

The Messianic Body Politic (Romans 12:3-13)

The gospel apocalypse of God's justice calls forth a messianic form of life. It is messianic because its form is incarnate—bodied forth—in Messiah Jesus. Jesus is the living source, power, and pattern of life in the messianic community (see Rom 6). The form of the truly human life is not laid down in law (whether Judean or Roman); it is given in Person, in the life, death, resurrection, and exaltation of Jesus. Paul knows the gospel story: it is the underlying basis of everything he writes. At crucial points that story rises to the surface in every letter he writes. Sometimes he only hints at it indirectly. Other times he explicitly summarizes it, as in Romans 1:3-4, or more fully in Philippians 2:6-11. (We who live after the New Testament have the four Gospels—much more than Paul's readers had.) So when Paul now comes to write about the form of life generated by God's justice in Jesus Messiah, the Messiah's incarnate life is the touchstone for everything.

How does a gathering of individual messianics take shape as the messianic community—the unified, visible body politic of the Messiah in the world? We can take the likely social makeup of one of the several messianic groups in Rome as a clue. An assembly of those listening to Phoebe reading Paul's letter (Rom 16:1-2) might have included a craftworker (in whose shop they might be meeting) and his family (including his wife, children, a male craftworker-slave or two, a female household slave, and perhaps a dependent relative or two); a few other householders with their families; some other individual family members, slaves, and dependents; and perhaps some homeless people and migrant workers.[1] While it is unlikely that there were high-born or wealthy social elites in the messianic assemblies in Rome, a typical Roman social hierarchy of worth was nevertheless assumed and operative there; each member knew where they stood in that hierarchy and what honor (or not) was due to them—with the male craftworker at the top of the honor scale, the female slave at the bottom (sometimes used also as a sex slave), and the others ranged between. The group was likely mostly Gentile, but there may also have been some Judeans. Among Romans (as we glimpsed in Rom 11:13-24) there was a tendency to despise Judeans, and Judeans would naturally have serious religious and moral doubts about Roman Gentiles. Ethnic tension (as we will see in Rom 14) would therefore often be either explicit or just below the surface.

When this group of diverse messianics met together in a house or shop in Rome to hear Paul's letter, the good news challenged their ordinary social and ethnic assumptions about honor, status, and worth. Paul's entire letter up to this point concludes that "all" are taken up into the justice of God in Messiah, which is in fact God's mercy (Rom 11:32). The good news for *everyone* in the gathering—high and low, Gentile and Judean—is that their worth is not conditioned by any measure that would ordinarily determine their place in the worldly social order, whether rich or poor, male or female, free or slave, Gentile or Judean. The good news of God's justice just meant

---

[1]Peter Oakes, *Reading Romans in Pompeii: Paul's Letter at Ground Level* (Minneapolis: Fortress, 2009), 96. This book is essential to understanding what the messianic assemblies in Rome might have looked like, how they met together, and the socioeconomic implications of their life together.

that their worth is given to them from God as a gracious *gift*.[2] Paul's own
life and apostleship was a gracious gift (see Rom 1:1, 5). The only measure
that counts among messianics is their "measure of trust [*metron pisteōs*]" in
God—but it is God himself who graciously "appoints" trust among them
(Rom 12:3). So if even their measure of trust comes from God, they cannot
boast about that either. The gospel of the justice of trust (see Rom 4) cuts
across all social and ethnic hierarchies and judgments, rendering them
inoperative.

The grace of God in Messiah creates a unified social body, "one body in
Messiah" (Rom 12:5), of which each person is a "[body] part" joined
in Messiah to all the others. The image of one body with its interconnected
members adds another dimension to the good news of justice. Not only is
the system of honor and status dismantled, but the disparate members of the
messianic assembly are bound together by grace into *a single social unit of
mutual dependence and benefit*. In fact, God gives grace gifts (*charismata*)
to each member of the community to offer to the body politic so that it
might thrive as a whole. Those gifts encompass a wide range of activities
necessary to sustain a robust, living community of mutual care: the proclamation of God's word (prophecy), practical services (*diakonia*), theological
instruction (teaching), encouraging presence (*paraklēsis*), financial
generosity, community leadership, joyful compassion—all of these given for
building up the one body of Messiah (Rom 12:6-8). Within the hierarchical,
status-obsessed, highly competitive society of a city such as Rome, this messianic society living by God's grace and freely sharing honor, gifts, goods,
and services would have looked odd. To some—those with a stake in maintaining the status quo—it might have looked dangerous, not such good news.
To others—those lower on the socioeconomic scale—it would have looked
very attractive, good news indeed. To Paul it looked like the assembly becoming the justice of God.

God's justice is rooted in "the love of God in Messiah Jesus our Lord"
(Rom 8:39). It is not surprising then that love is at the heart of the messianic
assembly. Anyone familiar with what Paul says about love in 1 Corinthians
knows that love is not primarily an individual feeling. It is the quality and

---

[2]John Barclay, *Paul and the Gift* (Grand Rapids, MI: Eerdmans, 2015), provides the best and most
extensive account of Paul's theology of grace and gift currently available.

practice of relationships. So too here. Those whose love will genuinely abhor evil practices and deeds, and adhere to the good (Rom 12:9). Concretely, love takes the form of loving "one another" with "brotherly affection" (Rom 12:10). That means regarding one another as members of a single, connected family of care rather than as competitive rivals in a social hierarchy.[3] If there is any competition, it should not be in *seeking* honor for oneself (a powerful shaper of Roman society) but in demonstrating honor toward the *other* (Rom 12:10): the craftworker toward the slave girl, the Roman Gentile toward the Judean, the men toward the women. As one author writes, this would mean "honour being given in all sorts of abnormal directions."[4] That kind of dynamic undoing of the normal social order would be for Paul a sign that the Spirit is at work, creating social ferment in the community, freeing each member for "slave-service" to the Lord (Rom 12:11). God's justice in Messiah generates and forms this kind of new shared life within the messianic community. And with new life comes joyful new *hope*, a hope that fosters patience and endurance among the members who must continue to serve, suffer, and pray in a world that still operates according to the old scheme of things (Rom 12:12).

To what extent does your messianic community (a.k.a., your church) reflect the economic, social, and racial divisions and disparities of your surrounding society? To what extent is the good news beginning to dissolve those divisions and disparities? What obstacles can you discern that get in the way of becoming the justice of God in your messianic community?

Paul's description in Romans 12:3-12 seems mainly to be focused on life *within* the messianic assembly. In the next verses he turns his attention to the assembly's relationships with those beyond. In Rome itself there were several messianic assemblies—not to mention many others in Greece, Asia Minor, and Judea. It was crucial that there would be a harmony of justice *among* these assemblies, and not only within individual gatherings. When Paul adds "contributing [*koinōnountes*] to the needs of the holy ones ['saints']"

---

[3]Oakes, *Reading Romans in Pompeii*, 108-10, describes some of the difficulties and complications in other relationships that might have resulted if this new kinship of messianics were taken seriously.

[4]Oakes, *Reading Romans in Pompeii*, 111.

(Rom 12:13), he is calling first for the sharing of goods and finances among the various messianic assemblies in Rome, which likely differed somewhat in their financial resources. But he would also have in mind a more global picture. In Romans 15 he writes about believers in Macedonia and Achaia who "were pleased to make a financial contribution [*koinōnian*] to the poor among the holy ones in Jerusalem" (Rom 15:26). The good news of God's justice brings about *economic leveling* in and among messianic communities— as seen dramatically in the accounts of messianic "communism" in Acts 2:43-47; 4:32-37. Serious economic disparity was endemic and normative in Roman society: only a very small minority was wealthy, and vast numbers of people lived at subsistence-level. *Koinōnia*, economic sharing, was for Paul a sure sign that the Spirit of Messiah was forming the messianic assemblies into the justice of God.[5]

So also was hospitality (*philoxenia*, Rom 12:13), that is, welcoming and loving strangers. (Note: the opposite of *philoxenia* is *xenophobia*—fear of strangers or foreigners [*xenoi*].) Sharing space and resources with strangers is often costly and difficult, and sometimes risky. *Philoxenia* may be even more demanding than *koinōnia*: it is one thing to send financial resources out to unknown others; it is another thing to welcome unknown others into one's home. Yet in the early messianic movement this was necessary, especially because being committed to Messiah (which would mean for Gentiles forsaking former gods and practices) sometimes meant being excluded from one's natural family, home, and community, and the security those provided. But Paul may also have in mind especially some Judean messianics who (along with other Judeans) had been expelled from the city of Rome a few years earlier and were now migrating back. Someone in that kind of precarious situation required shelter and support, which may have had to be provided by Gentile brothers and sisters in Messiah. In fact, Paul himself was often a migrant, depending on the financial support and hospitality of the messianic assemblies (Rom 15:24). *Philoxenia*, hospitality, was another way of becoming the justice of God.

---

[5]Bruce W. Longenecker, *Remember the Poor: Paul, Poverty, and the Greco-Roman World* (Grand Rapids, MI: Eerdmans, 2010).

Messianic Life at Street Level (Romans 12:14-18)

Surrounding the messianic believers and small messianic assemblies in Rome there was also of course the whole wider society, living according to the sense-making scheme of the present age to which messianics were not to conform (Rom 12:2). The messianic assemblies would have appeared somewhat strange and perhaps even dangerous to that society. As we have seen, the normal socioeconomic orders of Roman society were no longer to determine life in those assemblies, insofar as they lived by the justice and mercies of God. One can imagine their Roman neighbors saying, "What if everyone started living like that!? The social fabric of Rome would begin to unravel." (What if, indeed . . . !) But Paul does not envisage "everyone" living like that (even if that would be his ultimate hope). In fact, he realistically anticipates times of opposition, as he himself had often encountered in his mission of announcing God's justice in Messiah.

The question is not *whether* the messianic assemblies and their members will encounter opposition; the question is how they will *respond* when they do. Paul's instruction is clear: "Bless those who persecute; bless and do not curse" (Rom 12:14). That is the messianic pattern. When God called Abram (Gen 12:1-3), God's purpose was that through Abram and his family God would *bless* "all the families of the earth." Blessing others is a defining characteristic of God's people. In that same story of Abram's call, God recognizes the possibility that some other peoples might in fact curse Abram and his family, that is, despise or try to harm them. Yet God does *not* give Abram the right or task of cursing them back: rather, "The one who curses you *I* will curse." God retains for himself the prerogative to punish. Likewise in Paul's instruction: the messianic response to persecution is not to will or do harm to the persecutors; it is only to bless. As we will see shortly, Paul unpacks that dynamic at some length in the verses to come.

The messianics in Rome continued to live in Rome in the midst of and surrounded by their nonmessianic neighbors. While Paul imagined the likelihood of some persecution, he also imagined the likelihood of ongoing *shared life* with and among those neighbors. Far from encouraging separation from them, Paul urges the messianics to share in their neighbors' joys and sorrows, seek common ground with them, and pursue the good together (Rom 12:15-16). God's mercies invade the streets of Rome in the relationships of day-to-day living. There are no hard boundaries between messianics and others, and there are no church walls; messianic assemblies are not closed off from the world. Messianics—following the pattern of the Messiah—are called especially to seek out and share life with the humble in society rather than the high-born and not to consider themselves as "smarter" than others (Rom 12:16). The good news of God's justice makes its way in the world not only among messianics but also among those ordinary people with whom they share a daily common life.

However, common life at street level may also be life with conflict. About this Paul is also realistic. Whether within the messianic community itself or in relationships with those beyond, disagreements sometimes arise. Prejudices flare up. Animosities sharpen. Some people even intend to do harm. It is in these moments that the pattern of the Messiah must prevail and that the messianic way of justice should become most visible. Our deepest instinct in conflict is to defend ourselves and pay back. In fact, that is often what justice means for us. But for messianics the form of God's justice in Messiah interrupts our natural instincts in a fundamental way: "Do not pay back *anyone* evil for evil! Instead, thoughtfully consider what would *be seen to be good by all*" (Rom 12:17). The gospel demands that we step back rather than pay back. Stepping back creates time and space for the kind of patient, discerning thought that comes from renewed minds. It creates time and space to consider the will of God in the situation—"that which is good and pleasing and perfect" (Rom 12:2). Paul stresses the public, visible character (Greek *enōpion*) of the good that messianics seek to do, especially in times of conflict. The patience of stepping back, of nonretaliation, of looking for another way, makes our trust in God visible, and opens the door for God's justice—the justice of trust—to be done and to be seen to be done "by all."

The messianic form of life therefore brings peace to the streets. Paul does not have a grandiose vision of the messianic body politic bringing about "world peace." He does indeed have a vision of cosmic justice, reconciliation, and peace: but, as we have seen, that is what *God* accomplishes in the death of the Messiah (Rom 3:21-26; 5:1-11). However, trusting in the gracious *divine* work of peacemaking, messianics also become the embodiment of grace and peace on the street, in their direct face-to-face encounters with others. Paul does not have the naive notion that wherever messianics go, there will be no conflict. On the contrary, Romans 12:18 anticipates opposition, conflict, and sometimes persecution. The new form of life created by the gospel at times creates enemies of the gospel, when its apocalyptic disturbance of the way things are threatens to undo things such as power, status, and privilege (which operate not only among the elites but also among ordinary people—artisans, shopworkers, migrants, and slaves).

But whether they face opposition to the messianic way or are just caught up in the usual disputes that arise in day-to-day relationships, messianics are called to the way of peace—or, more emphatically, to "being peace" (*eirēneuontes*) among their neighbors. The responsibility to be at peace with all persons is not conditional on other persons being peaceable—they may not be. Nevertheless, "If it is possible, so far as it depends on *you*, be at peace with all," Paul writes. In *any* situation of hostility the call is for messianics to live the peace that they already share in by being in Messiah. They are the very form of the Messiah's peace in the midst of the disputes and hostilities of everyday life.

Does your church or denomination consider being peaceable and making peace one of its primary witnesses to the truth of Jesus Messiah? If so, what are some of its core peaceable practices? If not, what might some objections be to considering peace as a primary witness of the church? How might the good news of God's justice in Messiah engage some of those objections?

Messianics are not called out of the give-and-take of messy, sometimes conflictual life in the urban center of Rome—or any other urban or rural setting. On the one hand, they are there as the body politic of the Messiah, where the normal social competition in Roman society must give way to mutual honor and care. On the other hand, they live among a majority that does not share their altered vision of the real and its way of life. These are their neighbors, coworkers, even family members, with whom they continue to share life, space, goods and services, joys and sorrows, celebrations and controversies. Some of these neighbors do evil things; many do good (see Rom 2). Messianics *belong* in this living, dynamic, complicated, very human mess. They continue to participate in, depend on, receive from, and contribute to it. The messianic form of life is not the formation of a private club but of an open, engaging, welcoming body politic that witnesses to— becomes—God's justice, peace, and life for all. The very being of the Messiah's body politic is an invitation to all to trust in God and enter into the peaceable divine life of the Father, Son, and Holy Spirit.

11

MESSIANIC FREEDOM

IN THE PREVIOUS CHAPTER we saw that Paul described a new community "on the streets" of Rome that was to be formed by the logic of the good news. His emphasis in the first part of Romans 12 is on what I have called public service—the ways in which messianics and messianic assemblies must work not only to have their own life together shaped by the gospel but also to live among and at peace with their neighbors, seeking their good as well. In the remaining few verses of Romans 12 (Rom 12:19-21) and in Romans 13, Paul envisages a new community of public freedom, also formed by the logic of the good news. In particular, while messianics live within existing systems of law and government, their messianic life and life together is not determined by or responsible for those systems and institutions; they are free in relation to them.

As we will see, this is not because messianics are detached, anti-institutional, lawless, or against government, or can act as if these systems do not exist. It is, rather, because the fullness of justice and life they receive by grace in Messiah and the Spirit delivers them from depending on worldly institutions of law and government for justice and life, and from giving themselves in trust and obedience to those institutions. Messianics are free to live the messianic life no matter what political and judicial systemic conditions exist— conditions that in any case are often at odds with life in Messiah. As systems operating according the "sense-making schemes of the present age"

(Rom 12:2), government and law are captivated by Sin, and even frequently responsible for much injustice and evil in the world.

Messianic Patience (Romans 12:19-21)

Beyond the ordinary street-level conflicts in which messianics might be involved in everyday life (discussed in the previous chapter), there might also be disputes in which the stakes are higher and the harm done more serious. These might include serious harm to property, livelihood, core values, honor and reputation, ways of life, perhaps even life itself. In these conflicts the right and just ordering of things is under attack. We must therefore speak not simply of an offense but of an *injustice* being done, something that needs to be acknowledged as such and put right. It may appear that Paul's instructions in Romans 12:19-21 simply carry on the call (begun in Rom 12:17) to nonretaliation and peaceableness in the relationships of everyday life (which they do), but he now takes the discourse to another level: he writes, "Do not avenge [*ekdikountes*] yourselves" (Rom 12:19). You may recognize the *dik-*stem in the middle of that Greek word; it has to do with matters of justice. To avenge oneself is to attempt to get justice for oneself after experiencing an injustice. But as we have come to expect, when it comes to justice, Paul calls messianics to trust God and not to take justice into their own hands.

It is simply a natural human instinct to want to avenge a wrong, whether by retaliation, punishment, or seeking redress through authorities or law. Yet Paul's appeal to the "beloved" messianics is blunt: "Do *not* avenge yourselves." This means, to be sure, that messianics must not "take justice into their own hands" by striking back (whether literally or metaphorically). But if we take 1 Corinthians 6:1-8 into account, it also means that messianics should not immediately seek redress (in disputes among themselves) through the pagan law courts: "In fact, to have lawsuits at all with one another is a defeat for you. Why not rather suffer injustice? Why not rather be cheated? But instead you cheat and do injustice to your brothers and sisters" (1 Cor 6:7-8).

Cheating and injustice in a place such as Corinth (or Rome) was likely perpetrated primarily by those with influence in the wider public. Law courts in the Roman world tended largely to favor those of wealth and high standing; taking cases to court often worked in their favor (which is hardly only an ancient problem). Those with lower status had little chance of winning a case and were therefore less likely to take their grievances to the courts. Paul appeals to messianics in Corinth to bring their grievances before the messianic assembly, where (under the guidance of the Holy Spirit) justice rather than privilege would be more likely to prevail. It is not that Paul turns a blind eye to harm done. Rather, he asserts that the messianic community has the authority and competence within itself to adjudicate at least the "ordinary" cases of injury among messianics (1 Cor 6:2-4), which would have the effect of protecting the more vulnerable members of the community from the (often unfair) punishments of the pagan courts.

However, in Romans 12 Paul's appeal, "Beloved, do not try to get justice for yourselves," reaches beyond disputes within the messianic community. It applies also, or especially, to relationships to *enemies* (Rom 12:20), to those who deliberately intend evil against messianics. Rather than seeking to get justice against their enemies, Paul appeals to messianics to "give place to the wrath [*orgē*] [of God]; for it is written, 'getting justice [*ekdikēsis*] belongs to me; I will pay back, says the Lord' [quoting Deut 32:35]" (Rom 12:19). It is crucial to note some things here. First, Paul is not saying that getting justice does not matter. On the contrary, he is saying that justice—whatever form it might take—is assured. There will be a righting of wrong. *God* will do it. Indeed, God has done justice already in the death and resurrection of the Messiah, and the reality of that justice—God's goodness—already confronts and judges those who do evil. But whatever retributive action might be taken against an injustice (and the perpetrator) is God's work, not a work for messianics to do.

Second, when messianics "give place" (Rom 12:19) for God's justice to be done, they are doing the one thing messianics are always called to do: *trust God*. As Paul already made clear, especially in Romans 4, trust in God is how messianics share in the justice of God. It is not for them to take up the work of divine justice and make it their own human agenda. Justice is given to them through trust. In trust they already share in God's justice and justification as a gift, even in the face of injustice committed by their enemies. They are therefore free from the compulsion of demanding *visible* justice, *seeing* justice done on earth as an act of retribution or punishment. Being already justified by God, messianics are free instead to participate in God's work of reconciliation, redemption, and restoration of relationships broken by injustice. They do this when they respond to the evil done to them by doing good (Rom 12:21).

Third, the good news is that messianics, formerly enemies of God, have been delivered through the Messiah's death from bondage to the powers of Sin and Death. Paul made this clear earlier: "Now then, having been rendered just by his blood, how much more will we be delivered through him from the wrath. For if, while *we* were still *enemies*, we were reconciled to God through the death of his Son, how much more will we be saved through his life" (Rom 5:9-10). In Messiah God delivers *God's own enemies* from bondage under powers that oppose God. Therefore, messianics do not advocate or agitate for human wrath—retribution and punishment—against those who do evil. To do so would be a fundamental contradiction of their own reconciliation as enemies and their new life in Messiah. They entrust wrath to God. To do otherwise would mean to operate again according to the principles of the regime of Sin and Death. It would mean being "conquered by evil" (Rom 12:21).

What role does the idea of visible, temporal retribution and punishment play in your understanding of the meaning of justice, and in your thinking about the purpose of judicial sentences and penal systems in your state or nation? How might the fact that God's justice in Jesus reconciles the ungodly, sinners, and enemies (that is, us) to God change your attitude to the role of retribution and punishment in the meaning of justice?

Rather than acting out of wrath, messianics are freed up to become active participants in God's own grace, mercy, and kindness in Messiah. Paul quotes Proverbs 25:21-22: "If your enemy is hungry, feed him; if he is thirsty, give him something to drink; for by doing so you will heap coals of fire on his head" (Rom 12:20)—in other words, you will strike the enemy's conscience with kindness and hospitality. Engaging one's enemies with grace and kindness rather than vengeance must not be understood as a heroic stance of passive martyrdom. Rather, it is what it means to be already vindicated—justified—in Messiah; our life is even now "hidden with Messiah in God," the God whom we trust for justice. To be kind even to enemies is how messianics share in God's reconciling, restorative work of justice through Messiah Jesus. Far from being passive acceptance of injustice, this is in fact the free, active, peaceable way in which God's healing justice spreads through messianics into a world of injustice. It is the way messianics conquer evil (Rom 12:21).

Messianic Anarchy (Romans 13:1-10)

Paul's vision of how messianics change the world through kindness and nonretaliation toward enemies and evildoers is surely radical. But is it enough? What about the large-scale, global injustices that abound—poverty, corruption, oppression, slavery, organized crime, human trafficking, racism, bombings, economic sanctions, siege warfare, torture? The list could be much longer. Such injustices seem to require equally large-scale solutions, far beyond the street-level practice of nonretaliation and hospitality by small groups of messianics. Perhaps in such matters messianics could expect the "governing authorities" (*exousiai hyperechousai*, Rom 13:1)—kings and emperors, princes, presidents and potentates, overlords and commanders-in-chief, judges, juries, and jailers—to be the primary agents of justice in the world. They have the sovereign power, legal authority, and coercive instruments (the "sword," Rom 13:4) to enforce compliance or inflict punishment on those who commit large-scale crimes and injustice. Where personal vengeance is disallowed and small-scale kindness is not enough, should messianics not depend on, support, and encourage governmental and judicial authorities to get God's work of justice done? What is the relationship of the messianic community to the powers that be? What do messianics owe to the governing authorities? What should they expect from them?

When Paul writes in Romans 13:1, "Let every person submit [or, be subject to] the governing authorities," how do you understand the word *submit* [or "be subject to"]? What is included in its meaning? What does it call for from you in your relationship to your government or nation?

The most important thing to notice about Romans 13:1-7 is that Paul nowhere in these verses suggests that the governing authorities are doing the work of gospel justice when they do what they do. Rather than using gospel vocabulary such as *dikaiosynē* (justice), *pistis* (trust, loyalty, devotion), *charis* (grace), *hypakoē* (obedience), Paul returns instead to the vocabulary he used earlier (especially in Rom 1:18–3:20) to describe the world in bondage to Sin and Death: governing authorities operate according to judgment, terror, fear, sword, avenging, wrath, reward, and punishment. We have seen in Romans that *this* vocabulary characterizes the world under the power of Sin and Death. In Romans 13:1-7 it characterizes the way political authorities operate; their work as described here is not gospel work but the work of systemic bondage and opposition to the gospel. While (as we will see) God is able to *co-opt* governing authorities to God's purpose in some way, nevertheless in and of themselves the ruling powers continue to operate according to the principles of the present evil age. Paul does not discern *God's* justice among ruling authorities, nor life, nor grace, nor redemption and reconciliation; he does not find blessing, peace, or glory. He finds no promise to governing authorities that they should or would "inherit the world"—as God promised to Abraham (Rom 4:19)—despite the often ambitious desires of emperors, kings, rulers, and presidents to control human destinies and make the world their own.

How then are messianics to relate to political authorities? Paul's key verb for the relationship is *hypotassō* (Rom 13:1, 5). This Greek word is translated into English variously as "submit," "be subject to," or "be subordinate to" the governing authorities. The word is made up of two parts: *hypo*, which means "under" (think *hypo*dermic—under the skin); and *tassō*, which means "to order" (the English word *taxonomy* comes from this Greek word). Quite literally translated, then, Paul writes, "Let every soul be ordered under [*hypotassesthō*] the higher [*hyperechousais*] authorities" (Rom 13:1). What does that mean?

Hypotassō—"submit"—has *come to mean* many things. We see this already in some of the looser translations or paraphrases of Romans 13:1. The Living Bible renders it as "obey" the authorities. To obey means to do what the authorities ask, expect, or command. Most Christians, following Peter and the apostles in Acts 5:29, have stopped short of taking this as unqualified obedience: "We must obey God rather than men." But most Christians have also understood *obey* in the sense that the translation in *The Message* gives: "be good citizens." This phrase opens up, beyond mere grudging and servile obedience, a wide range of perceived *positive* responsibilities toward ruling authorities, including all of the obligations of citizenship in a kingdom or nation. It is worth exploring that range of meanings for a moment, for we are now stepping into an area of great confusion, which has also led to violence, disaster, and even apostasy throughout Christian history.

The meaning of *hypotassō* ("submit") has been inflated in many ways. Here are a few:

- It is often thought that "submit" means that Christians owe *loyal obedience and allegiance* to their political authorities and governments, come what may. Rulers and governments may therefore rightfully expect Christians, as part of their duty as good citizens, to be faithful and devoted subjects who participate in upholding and promoting political authority and institutions.

- Christians have often taken "submit" to mean *patriotism and national pride*. The idea of a people or nation is often hard to state in straightforward terms, and there may be significant disagreements about how to state it. Nevertheless, national figureheads, institutions, symbols, rituals, and liturgies are designed to transcend disagreements and create and sustain unity among a people around the *idea* of the nation. Flags, salutes, pledges of allegiance, national hymns and anthems, national holidays and celebrations, military pageants, and war memorials—these are the material things and bodily practices that establish, confirm, and mediate the sacred spiritual reality of a nation to its citizens, bind them to that reality in heartfelt devotion and acts of sacrifice, and form them as one people. Christians historically have believed that *hypotassō*—"submit"—requires their heartfelt participation in the institutions, practices, rituals, and liturgies that bind them as citizens to the spiritual reality of a ruler, nation, or empire.

- Christians have often taken "submit" to mean *to promote, advance, and defend the cause* of a people or nation and its political authorities and institutions. Particularly in times of perceived threat, governing authorities call for loyalty, devotion, and active service (including military), in order to strengthen the bonds of national unity and mobilize the people to action, especially in the face of an identified enemy. By waving flags, singing national anthems, and recalling the great sacrifices and victories of days gone by, the people gather under their leaders to defend, liberate, or expand the nation. Emboldened by popular support, the political authority issues a call to arms, orders the troops into action, rallies the people to support the troops, and exhorts the people to honor the fallen who have sacrificed their lives for liberty and justice. Christians have almost always participated enthusiastically in the wars and military liturgies of their nations, especially if the nation considers itself in some respect Christian. This too has regularly happened under the banner of *hypotassō*—"submit."

- If there is a majority of Christians in a given nation, "submit" may come to mean that Christians should strive to *become the governing authorities*. Where it is possible, Christians have often considered it important for at least some of them to attain positions of political authority—even the highest levels of authority—so that citizens might be required or encouraged to submit to *Christian* values, laws, and political systems. As part of their mission to the world, Christian rulers and governments have frequently sought to conquer and colonize other peoples of the earth, aiming to make the world a better place by establishing Christianity as the dominant religion, and thereby to bring justice, peace, and liberty for all.

"Christian" rule has been a constant factor in the history of European and American imperialism. The familiar British patriotic anthem "Land of Hope and Glory" captures this perfectly:

Land of Hope and Glory, Mother of the Free,
How shall we extol thee, who are born of thee?
Wider still, and wider, shall thy bounds be set;
God, who made thee mighty, make thee mightier yet!
(Lyrics: A. C. Benson; music: Edward Elgar, 1902)

Do you share the sentiment of this anthem with respect to your own nation? What becomes of other nations in such a vision?

Other meanings have been loaded into the word *submit*, such as believing in, upholding, and defending a nation's constitution and judicial system, demanding compliance with them, and encouraging harsh punishments for those who betray and disobey. Indeed, in some nations Christians especially are the ones who champion law and order and demand lengthy prison terms and the death penalty for transgressions and crimes.

Submit! Throughout Christian history this word in Romans 13:1 has signified for Christians either servile, unquestioning obedience or enthusiastic loyalty and devotion (or both) to political authorities, institutions, nations, and empires, from the time of the Christian Roman emperor Constantine (who ruled AD 306–337) to the present day. No wonder that some—especially those on the *outside* of worldly power and its popular support—have become deeply suspicious of that word and of Romans 13:1-7 altogether.

> As a Christian, what do you hope for from political and judicial authorities? How important do you think they are or should be for supporting, defending, and advancing the Christian way of life and mission in the world? How invested do you think Christians should be in the outcome of the next election or the next judicial appointment? How does the letter to the Romans thus far seem to support or challenge your convictions about the importance of political and judicial authorities for advancing God's cause in the world?

But when Paul writes *submit*, he means *none of things we have listed above*. Here are some things *hypotassō*—"submit"—cannot mean for Paul:

- *Hypotassō* cannot mean "obey." Paul's word for "obey" is *hypakouō*, which he uses often in Romans as a key aspect of the good news. The gospel calls us not to obey the existing political authorities, but to *obey the Messiah*. Messianics in all nations owe their loyal obedience to the sovereign Jesus Messiah (Rom 1:5; 15:18; 16:26).

- *Hypotassō* cannot mean "be loyal to" or "give allegiance to." Paul has other words for that (*pisteuō, pistis*), which, as we have seen, is central to the meaning of the good news. The good news of God calls us not to be loyal to the existing political authorities but to *be loyal to the Messiah*. Messianics in all nations owe their political trust, loyalty, and allegiance to the sovereign Messiah Jesus (Rom 1:5; 16:26).

- *Hypotassō* cannot mean "to provide military service" and "to sacrifice" one's own or one's enemy's bodies in war for the sake of political authorities or a nation. The gospel makes a radically different claim on bodies and their service and sacrifice. The gospel calls messianics to offer their bodies in unity as a "living sacrifice" *to God*, which is their "reasonable public service" (Rom 12:1). This kind of service and sacrifice deplores war; it testifies instead to the universal reality of God's justice and life revealed in the death and resurrection of Jesus, rather than to merely national visions of justice and life. Messianics offer their bodies to the sovereign Messiah Jesus, in whom and with whom they are one body, one sacrifice, one service (see 1 Cor 12:4-8). They do so for building up the one, universal, social-political body of the Messiah, and for giving themselves to saints, strangers, and enemies in works of hospitality, mercy, kindness, and blessing.

What then does Paul mean by *hypotassō*? He writes, "Let every person be ordered under [*hypotassesthō*] the higher [*hyperechousais*] authorities" (Rom 13:1). *Hypotassō* is a word about *order*. In Romans 13:1 Paul is saying (to paraphrase): "There are the 'overs,' the *hypers* (whoever they are). Acknowledge them as the 'overs'; take them as *given* in their being there (they will always be there!)—but no more! And messianics, you yourselves are therefore the 'unders,' the *hypos*. Accept that. Being the 'unders' is no disadvantage at all for you. In fact, it is *the way of being messianic in the world*" (Rom 8:17). It was the way of Abraham and Sarah, who, as nearly dead nobodies, did not strive for their place in the world but walked in trust. It was the way for the Messiah himself, who walked faithfully and humbly from Galilee to Jerusalem and did not resist the governing authorities, whether Roman or Judean, but was handed over to them and gave up his body for our sake. This is what *submit* means. There is no other meaning for those who walk the walk of Abraham's trust and who through trust share in the living reality of the crucified and risen Messiah."

It is not as if the "overs"—the governing authorities—are their own masters, even when they think they are. They typically do not offer "faithful obedience" (*hypakoē pisteōs*; Rom 1:5; 15:18; 16:26) to the crucified Messiah and operate by the resurrecting power of the Spirit of life, which is the call of the gospel; instead they operate according to their own agendas, moved by the idolatrous schemes and destructive powers of this age. Yet they continue to exist because, while God has handed over humanity to these disordered orders, he has *not abandoned* humanity to the sphere of Sin of Death. Human societies and nations continue to belong to God and to be held in being by God, because God in his sovereignty and freedom is able to, and does, work through *some* of the workings of political authorities for God's own purposes. Public works get done; infrastructure is funded, constructed, and maintained; laws are made and lawlessness curbed; sometimes even the poor, the sick, and the elderly are cared for. The governing authorities are not ultimately self-governed, but in fact *governed by the triune God* ("for there is no authority except by God's permission"— Rom 13:1); ultimately the overs are under God, and God may use them to serve God's ends, even as they usually and primarily seek to serve their own.

As we have seen, the vocabulary Paul uses to describe the role and work of political authorities is not the vocabulary of the gospel but the vocabulary of the world under the power of Sin and Death. God uses worldly political authorities because they are ordered (Rom 13:1-2) under God to be ministers (*diakonos*, Rom 13:4) of certain works of God. But as far as justice goes, their ministry is a dark and miserable one. Paul calls political authorities a terror (Rom 13:3): they administer judgment and punishment on evil with "the sword" (Rom 13:4), that is, with coercive or lethal power; they enact wrath against evil, rather than overcoming evil with good, as Paul instructs messianics to do (Rom 12:21). It is crucial to note that Paul does *not* say that God affirms every use of the sword by the authorities. When in Romans 12:19 Paul calls messianics to "give place" for divine wrath on evil, he allows that God may do a certain kind of work—wrath—by means of the ruling powers. Yet, being themselves in bondage, those powers *of themselves* are moved by and operate according to the principles of "the present evil age" (Gal 1:4). Messianics, on the other hand, have been *delivered* from bondage and the operation of the powers in this present evil age.

Being delivered from bondage, and trusting God's justice making in Jesus Messiah, messianics themselves cannot participate in politically or judicially authorized terror. They cannot be agents of wrath, wielding the sword. This means, at a minimum, that messianics must refuse to participate in or support politically authorized war and judicially authorized death sentences.

For them there is no such thing as a just war, a war that God and God's
Messiah support. Many in the early centuries of the church understood
that.[1] Anabaptists, Mennonites, and other groups throughout Christian
history understood it. Recently, even Pope Francis declared—against long-
held Roman Catholic and mainstream Christian tradition—that the death
penalty is incompatible with the gospel of life.

When Paul says, Let every messianic be ordered under the overruling
powers, he does not mean supporting, encouraging, or participating in *the
judging, punishing, coercive, violent, and warring operations of political and
judicial authorities.* Those ministries of the powers—ministries not beyond
God's rule—are precisely that from which messianics have been delivered
through their participation in the Messiah's liberating death and resurrection (Rom 5–6). They are not messianic ministries. They are not ministries
of God's justice in Messiah and the Spirit. They are ministries in bondage to
Sin and Death.

What do messianics owe political authorities and institutions? Not obedience. Not loyalty. Not flag-waving, anthem-singing devotion. Not military
service. Not participation in their ministries of punishment and death. But
also, not violent resistance or revolution (Rom 13:2). *Messianics are neither
for nor against worldly political authority.* In this sense, they might truly be
called anarchists, because for them justice and life do not depend on the
"archys"—the ruling powers of this age. Nothing truly messianic hinges on
whether the ruling powers are for or against them. Messianics are *conscien-
tious unbelievers* in worldly politics (*syneidēsin* = "conscience" in Rom 13:5).
They practice holy, peaceable anarchy because they refuse to believe in and
dedicate their bodies and souls to the political systems of this age.[2]

Messianics pay their taxes (Rom 13:6). They do so not because they believe in government but because they do not. To resist the government by
withholding taxes is to believe too much. It is to give political rulers and
institutions an authority and purpose in messianic life they do not have.
Messianics "give to Caesar" not because Caesar has his own divine mission

[1]See George Kalantzis, *Caesar and the Lamb: Early Christian Attitudes on War and Military Service*
(Eugene, OR: Cascade Books, 2012).
[2]For understanding messianic life as peaceable anarchy I am especially indebted to Vernard Eller,
Christian Anarchy: Jesus' Primacy over the Powers (Grand Rapids, MI: Eerdmans, 1987); Jacques
Ellul, *Anarchy and Christianity*, trans. Geoffrey W. Bromiley (Grand Rapids, MI: Eerdmans, 1988).

in the world but because Caesar's mission in the world has been divinely *judged, minimized, deflated, and deglorified* by God's messianic mission. When governments use taxes for the common good, this is a sign that God has not merely abandoned the political authorities to Sin and Death; they are being saved from themselves. When governments use taxes for building up militaries and prison systems they prove that they are still, nevertheless, in the grips of Sin and Death. When messianics pay their taxes and do not resist political authority, they make the simple acknowledgment—they submit—that the governing authorities are there only by the permission and patience of God. Those authorities have no transcendent origin, being, or end. They can make no transcendent claim on life. When they make such claims, they show themselves to be enslaved, and they become enslaving powers and systems and institutions of a world that is passing away. They deserve our unbelief, not our trust. For messianics, God's justice enters, rises, and moves in the world only through the governing authority of the risen, reigning Messiah and the life-giving power of the Holy Spirit.

Hypotassō—submit—is thus a *liberating* word. When messianics submit to the ruling powers, they in fact become *free of* their political claims; and they become *free for* the one thing messianics owe the governing authorities: honor (*timē*, Rom 13:7). But this is not a special kind of honor. It is only the same kind of honor—no more or greater than—that they owe to their brothers and sisters in the messianic community and to those beyond (Rom 13:7; see Rom 12:10). Indeed, they owe the authorities love, just insofar as the authorities too are their neighbors, reconciled to God by God's work of justice in Messiah.

> Consider the phrase "messianic anarchy" as defined above. How does your current relationship to political authorities compare to this phrase?

Messianics are called to live by a fundamentally different form of life and power of life from that which characterizes the ruling authorities. They become true agents of political transformation in the world by sharing in the world-transforming apocalypse of God's justice in the death and resurrection of Messiah. They "inherit the world" (Rom 4:13) by walking in trust as Abraham did. They "rule in life" (Rom 5:17) by cosuffering with Messiah in bodily solidarity with groaning creatures and hurting human beings (Rom 8:17-27). They communicate the power of God's life in the world through messianic works of love. Even love of enemies. Even those enemies who may be the ruling powers. Paul says messianics fulfill the law with one word (*logos*, Rom 13:9): "Love your neighbor as yourself." This is the single, all-encompassing earthly good to which they are called. It is how they share in and manifest the messianic justice of God in the world, and it is how that justice makes its way in the world, with or without access to or help from judicial and political authorities.

The one word of love is a word of messianic-political fullness, abundance, and power. It is pregnant with political possibility. It opens up to an infinite range of local engagements, peaceable practices, timely interventions, solidarities, cosufferings, and advocacies, especially with and for the weak and lowly of the world. It interrupts the political world of idolatry, ungodliness, and injustice (Rom 1:18), of pride, power, and greed, of infidelity, lovelessness, and mercilessness (Rom 1:29-31), with truth, reconciliation, grace, hospitality, and peace—that is, with the good news. There is no end to this one word.[3]

Messianic Time (Romans 13:11-14)

Messianic anarchy operates beneath the governing powers because it does not need them to pursue and fulfill its political calling. It does not seek out and strive after the high places but the low. It walks in the Abrahamic trust that God reckons as justice. But such messianic trust is not about sleepwalking through the time of trouble! It is not naive about or disengaged from the disordered and destructive state of the world or the nations or the neighborhood. It is not the lazy thought that "somehow good things will happen," or that "everything will be all right in the end," as if some benevolent power of progress is intrinsic in history. It is not. Indeed, as Paul writes to the Corinthians, "the present scheme of this world is passing away" (1 Cor 7:31).

Messianics live by another scheme, the "fullness of time" (Gal 4:4) of the Messiah. Jesus Messiah is *already* "declared to be Son of God in power

---

[3]For accounts of messianic action in practice, see the numerous stories told by Ronald Sider in *Nonviolent Action: What Christian Ethics Demands but Most Christians Have Never Really Tried* (Grand Rapids, MI: Brazos, 2015).

according to the Spirit of holiness by resurrection from the dead" (Rom 1:4), and *already* reigns over all times and nations. Whatever is going on in the horizontal history of the world and nations is never separated from the nearness and power of God's liberating justice in Messiah (Rom 13:11). Things do not "work out in the end" because "things" do not have the power of their own redemption. Only God is able to bring about good in the workings of history, and he will indeed do so (Rom 8:28; 11:32). Living in the radical nearness of God's salvation, in which alone they trust, messianics are wide awake to the present moment, the *kairos*, which is a moment full of both dangers and possibilities (Rom 13:11).

The dangers are real. There is always the temptation to numb oneself to the moment, to drown out the demanding word, "Love your neighbor as yourself." The temptation to numbness was all around in Paul's time (especially among the social and political elites), as it is in ours: parties, entertainment, drunkenness, sexual immorality, pornography, violence, fighting, and jealousy (Rom 13:13). These are the sins of sleepwalkers, those who do not know or forget that they live in the now-time of the Messiah, the time of God's justice and judgment. They shut themselves off from God's gracious nearness, and therefore also from their neighbor and the suffering world, by self-indulgence, diversions, excess, exploitation, envy, and strife, until clock-time winds down.

But for those who have "put on the Lord Jesus Messiah" (Rom 13:14), the *kairos*, the hour, the day of salvation, is "nearer now than when we first believed" (Rom 13:11). The Messiah is near, now! Messiah's imminent arrival is not determined by some shorter or longer span of historical time, but by his own sovereign decision to seize *any moment* of historical time and transform and fulfill it with the justifying, resurrecting power of the Spirit of holiness. The day of Messiah's arrival is today! Therefore "knowing the time," messianics "put away the works of darkness" and "walk in the day" (Rom 13:11-13).

Messianic time is not determined by the self-declared epochs and calendars of rulers, empires, and nations. Messianics live in the pregnant moment, the moment in which it is always time to fulfill the one word: Love your neighbor as yourself. Not being timed by the ticking of the down-winding clock, or numbed by distractions, or lulled by dreams of historical progress, they are alive to the present, to the gift that comes in the moment, to the neighbor or stranger who shows up, to struggling against the powers of darkness, to doing good, even to enemies. In other words, they share in the justice of God apocalypsed in Jesus Messiah.[4]

As a Christian you are probably not (one hopes) passing the time in self-indulgence, excess, sexual immorality, or violence (but what about those video games?). Instead, perhaps you are striving to do something important and fulfilling in the world, to make a difference—not just any difference, but one that will be effective, evident, noticeable. How does the thought of *dwelling in* and *living from* the fullness of Messiah's time, and *in* the difference Messiah makes—God's justice—challenge your mode of being in the world? How might it make you more available and open to the moment of Messiah's arrival in your neighbor, a stranger, or even an enemy?

We live in an age—probably not really unlike others—in which our gaze is constantly being drawn to the ruling powers; not only the political ones but also all those powers—technology, the economy, the media, the crowd—that would grab our attention and call us to celebrate their glory and greatness. It is hard not to believe that they, rather than the lowly, have inherited the earth. It seems obvious. But the whole of the letter to the Romans draws our gaze elsewhere—to the justice of God in the crucified and risen Messiah Jesus and the power of life in the Spirit. By the standard of what counts as great in our world, this often seems like next to nothing. Where are the visible signs of the Messiah's power and glory? Where are the measurable outcomes?

But Paul's letter calls us to "hope for what is not seen" (Rom 8:24). The good news inserts itself, mostly unnoticed, into the world of the powers—in fact, into the center of worldly power in its worldly time—and proclaims (also *to* the powers!) an *other* word, an *other* form of power, an *other* mode of world-historical influence. Messianic freedom neither affirms nor opposes nor hankers to become the *exousiai hyperechousai*, the "ruling authorities,"

---

[4]A powerful reading of Rom 13:8-14 is provided by L. L. Welborn, *Paul's Summons to Messianic Life: Political Theology and the Coming Awakening* (New York: Columbia University Press, 2015).

the movers and shakers of history. In the freedom and power of the Spirit of life, messianics carry on according to their own messianic mode of operation, on the streets and in the neighborhoods, in marketplaces and offices, in public squares and policy rooms, in homes and schools. Even, perhaps— there is no imperative here, just freedom in Messiah, and considerable danger—even, perhaps, in some seats of political authority. But, as messianics, their authority and way of doing things even there can be none other than Jesus Messiah–like. Wherever and whenever they are, messianics testify to and live the good news that justice, peace, and life for all comes from God alone, through God's grace in Jesus Messiah, in the freedom of the Holy Spirit, to those who trust.

12

MESSIANIC SOLIDARITY

PAUL DOES NOT LOOK for justice in the halls of political and judicial power. Messianic justice begins at the dinner table, where people eat and drink together. That is not surprising. It is also where injustice began, according to Genesis 3, where eating divinely forbidden food signaled the fundamental break in creational harmony. Paul writes a lot about what goes on at the table (Gal 2:11-14; 1 Cor 8–10; 11:17-34). The whole of Romans 14 is devoted to it. The work of the Messiah and the Spirit in the world happens first at the table and moves out from there.

Reflect on your dining practices (if *dining* is not the wrong word!). How does your eating and drinking, and with whom you eat and drink, manifest your core Christian convictions, especially your convictions about justice?

How messianics dine, with whom, and what goes on during the meal may seem like small matters. Why would a treatise on justice that is theological, cosmic, and world historical in scope arrive here, to deal with how a few Gentiles and Judeans eat and drink together in someone's shop in a back street of Rome? Some scholars have taken the "practical" issues addressed in Romans 14 to constitute the whole point of Paul writing the letter in the first place. That is surely an exaggeration. Yet for Paul the table is precisely where God's justice in Messiah creates something new, a new form of human life. It is the place where messianic witness to God's justice begins. If ethnic, religious, social, economic, and political barriers to human unity and solidarity are not dealt with here, in the immediacy of face-to-face encounter over ordinary food and drink, how can we expect that they will be dealt with in the imperial halls, congresses, courts, and parliaments of the world? The apocalypse of divine justice generates messianic life first at the dinner table. It spreads from there. It doesn't work the other way around.

Whose Table? (Romans 14:1-12)

We might recall the story of Genesis 2–3. The garden was the original table, and everything for human flourishing was provided there: "Out of the ground the LORD God made to grow every tree that is pleasant to the sight and good for food, the tree of life also in the midst of the garden. . . . And the LORD God commanded the man, 'You may freely eat of every tree of the garden'" (Gen 2:9, 16 NRSV). Whatever was available at this table was provided by the Lord God. It was his table. So, too, the table in the craftworker's shop in Rome is the table of God. Whoever is there, Paul says, "God has welcomed them" (Rom 14:3). When Paul urges, "Welcome the one who is 'weak in faith'" (Rom 14:1), he is requiring nothing more or less than to follow God's lead and share in God's own welcome. Disharmony at the table over who is there and what there is to eat forgets that.

There is a great deal of scholarly debate over who the "weak" (Rom 14:1) and the "strong" (Rom 15:1) are in this section of Paul's letter. Generally speaking, most scholars take the discussion of the weak and the strong to be addressing the relationships between Torah-observant Judeans (whether messianic or not) on the one hand (the weak), and non-Torah-observant messianic Gentiles (the strong) on the other. Among the weak there may also have been some Gentile God-fearers who observed Torah. In Rome (as in other cities in Paul's mission) Judeans, messianic Judeans, Gentile God-fearers, and messianic Gentiles continued to associate, meet together in synagogues, and share common meals. Those meetings and meals could be places where persisting tensions between Gentiles and Judeans surfaced, tensions that would be especially present in close encounters at the dining table. As we know from Romans 16, Paul was familiar with the situation of the messianic assemblies in Rome through his many contacts there. Whether tensions were at a crisis level in Rome is not known, but Paul addresses the Judean-Gentile relationship throughout the letter. The common meal was the natural flashpoint for dealing with this matter.

Paul wrote the letter to the Romans specifically for messianic *Gentile* readers. We saw in Romans 11 that Paul directly confronts and challenges the attitude of sociocultural superiority and condescension that (some) Gentile messianics in Rome held toward Judeans. The widespread opinion among Romans that Judeans were an inferior people may well have been carried over into the messianic assemblies. Further, in AD 49, a few years before Paul sent his letter, Judeans (including messianic Judeans) were expelled from Rome, ostensibly for causing unrest in the city. They soon began to move into the city again, but their numbers were depleted, and the Gentiles came to dominate the messianic assemblies in both numbers and influence. The Gentile members appear to have been especially critical of Judeans who did not confess Jesus as Messiah. In Romans 11 Paul wrote emphatically to these Gentiles: "Do not boast over the 'branches' of the tree of Israel that have not believed in Jesus Messiah—their salvation is ultimately assured; but your salvation as Gentiles depends on you being 'branches' grafted into the tree of Israel. So do not be proud" (Rom 11:17-18 paraphrased).

The designations "weak" and "strong" in Romans 14 signify groups and persons in the assembly with more or less *social power*. The strong—Roman Gentile messianics—had the numbers and the social sensibilities of the wider society on their side. Romans ate meat. The Judeans—a minority immigrant group—avoided the meat available in Rome because they believed it may have been tainted by idol worship. They were few in number and out of step with Roman society; it is not surprising that they felt intimidated at the dinner table. The terms *weak* and *strong* designate this imbalance of social power. As we will see, Paul will later subvert these categories for the sake of solidarity and unity at the table.[1]

---

[1] For what follows, I have been influenced by Mark Nanos, *The Mystery of Romans: The Jewish Context of Paul's Letter* (Minneapolis: Fortress, 1996).

Paul nowhere in Romans 14 expects or requires the so-called weak in faith to give up their Judean convictions and practices about what they eat and drink, or which special days they observe (e.g., the Sabbath and other holy days). On the contrary, he urges them to remain firm in them: "Let each person be fully convinced in their own mind" (Rom 14:5). For Paul, this is what it would mean for the Judeans to be strong; they would not submit to pressure to give up their particular Judean practices. The socially dominant Gentile messianics, on the other hand, think being strong means that the Judeans should become just like them, should give up their Judean convictions and practices and effectively become Gentiles. That would be one way to resolve the dining-table tensions; it would also be another colonizing victory for Romans, even in the messianic assembly. But it would be a contradiction of the good news, which is not about assimilation in either direction but about respect and reconciliation in the midst of real differences. The point of the good news is not that the "conservative" Judeans should make a "progressive" journey toward the "liberal" convictions and practices of the Roman messianics. Rather, the good news is that both groups are at the table only because it is God's table, and because God welcomes both Judeans and Gentiles to the table through the Messiah's reconciling death (Rom 3:21-26). Unless everyone at the table grasps *this* point, they will only descend into passing judgments on one another's opinions in an effort to establish social dominance.

Paul begins with a sort of caricature of the two positions: "One person believes it is acceptable to eat *every* kind of food [every kind? really?], while another only eats greens [only greens? really?]." Well, good! "But the one who eats everything must not despise the one who does not; and the one who does not eat everything must not judge the one who does. For God has welcomed them both!" (Rom 14:2-3 paraphrased). It is worth noting the difference in the verbs Paul uses: on the one hand, the omnivorous Roman diners are tempted to despise (*exoutheneō*) the Judean vegetarians (who abstain from meat because it is not kosher or because of its possible association with idolatry). On the other hand, the Judean vegetarians are tempted to judge (*krinetō*) the omnivorous Romans. The verbal difference signals not only that there is a disagreement about diet but also that the socially dominant Gentiles adopt an imperious, condescending stance toward the Judeans; they not only judge, they despise.

Paul rules out both despising and judging. Yet, he does *not* ask the two groups at the table to practice one diet. Each must stand on their different convictions. In fact, the Lord will *enable* each to stand (Rom 14:4). For whether it is about eating and drinking or observing special days, each group must do what they do "to the Lord" and in doing so "give thanks [*eucharistei*] to God" (Rom 14:6). Each group "lives to the Lord" and "dies to the Lord" (Rom 14:8). "For this is why Messiah died and lived, that he might be the sovereign of both the dead and the living" (Rom 14:9). The eucharistic table is the place where everyone meets in the presence of the one Lord and gives thanks to him.

If there is any judging to be done, it will not be by either Judeans or Gentiles (or any other polarized groups) toward one another (as Paul already made clear in Rom 2:1-16), but by God himself through Jesus Messiah: "For we will all stand before the judgment seat of God" (Rom 14:10; see also Rom 2:16). Judean and Gentile alike will bow to God alone. God alone will receive their common praise. To God alone everyone will give an account (Rom 14:11-12). When despising and judging are taken off the table, everyone is free to dine on the food that is there, each according to their own convictions. Therefore, welcome!—Gentiles and Judeans, messianics and nonmessianics, rich and poor, high and low—to the common messianic table. Share the meal!

> Which types of people are welcome at your dining table? Which types are not? On what basis do you make those judgments? When it comes to the messianic table (the Lord's Supper, Communion, the Eucharist), which types of people are there? Which are not? What conditions would someone have to meet to be there?

Mutual honor and respect toward one another, in and with profound differences, begins in the common eucharistic space and time that does not belong to any group but to the God and Lord who has welcomed all into his own space and time. At God's table harmony is created once again, as in the beginning.

Whose Food? (Romans 14:13–15:6)

The peaceable table is created by the welcoming God, the only one allowed to judge those who gather. Nevertheless, Paul calls for a clear-eyed analysis of the barriers that exist and threaten to divide. When two cultural groups gather at a common table, food is more than food. Food embodies a wide range of cultural meanings, associations, and identities: we know we are at home with our people when the food is familiar. Food is a sacrament of a certain form of life. Even the prevalence of fast-food joints in our time signals something important about our society. For faithful Judeans, food (along with Sabbath keeping and circumcision) signified the whole form of life defined by the written and oral Torah. The dietary rules were given to them by God as a sign of God's holiness and of their own existence as a distinct (holy) people among the nations. Food marked them off from the nations—made them "uncommon." For Judeans to eat the common (*koinos*, "unclean," Rom 14:14) food of the Gentile peoples would be to forsake their own God-given distinctiveness among the nations. It would be for them to become common or unclean.[2]

It has been tempting for interpreters to think that Paul simply wants the Judeans to get over it—to stop being "weak" (in other words, Judean)—and start eating whatever is on the table like the "strong" do. It is true that Paul (like Peter in Acts 10:9-16) affirms "in the Lord Jesus that nothing is unclean [*koinon*] in itself" (Rom 14:14). But the point of this is not that Judeans—even such as Paul and Peter—may or must now eat everything that Gentiles eat. For example, there is no indication in Acts 10 that, after his threefold vision of the net full of unclean foods, Peter gave up his kosher ways and started eating everything. At the end of the vision the net was "taken up to heaven" (Acts 10:16). Peter actually *eating* unclean foods was not part of the vision. The point of Peter's vision was that "God has shown me that I should call *no one* common or *any person* unclean" (Acts 10:28) and that "God shows no partiality, but in every nation anyone who fears God and does justice is acceptable to him" (Acts 10:34-35).

---

[2]As the Greek word *koinos*—"common," usually translated "unclean"—indicates, the characterization of some foods as unclean is not a *moral* assessment about the foods, or even necessarily about those who consume them. It simply characterizes the foods that God has not made available for Judean consumption but are otherwise available for common Gentile consumption.

Further, Peter was now free to associate with the Gentile Cornelius and his family and "to remain several days" in his home (Acts 10:48). While we do not know for certain, it is fair to assume that during those days Peter kept kosher while Cornelius continued to eat everything. The difference in their ways of life signified by foods remained intact, even as Peter and Cornelius shared life in the common confession of Jesus Messiah, the common gift and experience of the Holy Spirit, the common baptism, and the common table (Acts 10:43–48). According to Paul's account in Galatians, Peter continued to "eat with the Gentiles" in Antioch—note: not to "eat what the Gentiles eat"—until he felt pressured by "certain people from James" to "draw back and separate himself" from Gentile messianics. Paul opposed Peter in this because he and other Judeans *broke the solidarity* of the common table (Gal 2:11-13).

In Romans Paul is clear: though he is persuaded that no foods are unclean, that does not imply that Judeans should give up their kosher diet. On the contrary, he insists that "if any one considers something to be unclean, for that person it *is* unclean" (Rom 14:14). That "nothing is unclean in itself" simply means that Gentile food is clean *for Gentiles*. They need not eat kosher. But there is no warrant for the so-called strong to despise the weak and expect them to assimilate to Gentile food culture. To do so would be to fail to walk in love and to forget that Christ died for Judean and Gentile alike (Rom 14:15). God's justice is indeed at stake at the dinner table, but it is not in what food and drink is consumed by either group. It is in the communion in Messiah that God creates at the table: "For the kingdom of God is not eating and drinking but justice and peace and joy in the Holy Spirit" (Rom 14:17). That is the ultimate messianic purpose that those gathered at the common table serve. Not only is such communion "well-pleasing to God," but it is also the way God's justice, peace, and joy in the Holy Spirit—messianic life—becomes visible and *attractive* (*dokimos*) to others (Rom 14:18). When messianic communion happens at one dinner table, it is likely to spread to others.

So then, Paul concludes, "Let us pursue the things that make for peace and for mutual upbuilding. Do not for the sake of food destroy the work of God" (Rom 14:19-20 NRSV). Each person at the table must eat and drink according to their own convictions about whatever meat, vegetables, and wine are on the table, and not impose those convictions on the others gathered there. Further, no one at the table need allow others' convictions to cause them to doubt their own. The whole point is this: everyone must be strong in their own convictions "before God" (Rom 14:22), because dining at the common table is not about everyone becoming culturally the same, but about each person *honoring the other* in their convictions.

Paul writes, "Now we, 'the strong,' ought to bear [*bastazein*] the weaknesses [*asthenēmata*] of the 'not strong' and not please ourselves" (Rom 15:1).

The translation of *asthenēmata* as "failings" in both NRSV and NIV implies a negative judgment on these "weaknesses." But the noun here harks back to the participle *asthenounta*—"being weak"—in Romans 14:1, which does not mean "failing." Further, the NRSV translation of *bastazein* as "put up with" rather than "bear" is inexcusable; it simply confirms the idea that the "strong" are in the right and have good reason to feel superior to those whose "failings" they must nevertheless "put up with." Nothing could be further from Paul's meaning. See Galatians 6:2: "Bear [*bastazete*] one another's burdens; thus you will fulfill the law of Messiah."

Now the meaning of *weak* and *strong* has shifted. The not strong are not those who observe kosher food laws; rather, they are those who *waver in their convictions* before God about what they are eating. That wavering could be among the Judeans, whom some Gentiles despise, but it could also be among some Gentiles, who feel the judgment of the Judeans and feel pressure to conform. Those who, like Paul, are really strong in their convictions—whoever they are—must "bear the weaknesses" of those who waver. They must *stand in solidarity with the weak*, rather than reproach (Rom 15:3) them or exploit their weaknesses. Everyone at the table must work to build up the convictions of those who are wavering: "Let each one of us please the neighbor for their good, for building them up" to become strong (Rom 15:2). Let Gentiles encourage Judeans to be faithful as Judeans; let Judeans encourage Gentiles to be faithful as Gentiles, "each according to the measure of faith that God has appointed" (Rom 12:3). For the "strong" to "bear the weaknesses of those who are not strong" means to stand in messianic solidarity with them; far from tolerating them (which implies a condescending judgment), it means to reject condescending criticism and instead to build them up in their convictions.

> What aspect of the Christian life does the celebration of the Lord's Supper (Communion, Eucharist) in your church focus on? Sin and forgiveness? Personal relationship with Jesus? How aware are you of who is celebrating with you and how they are similar to or different from you—socially, culturally, politically? What difference would such awareness make to the meaning of the celebration?

Food is indeed a sacrament of a form of life. When Judeans and Gentiles eat their *different* foods at the *common* table, their eating and drinking together in mutual upbuilding becomes a sacrament of life in Messiah, according to the form of the Messiah, through the work of "the God of endurance and encouragement" (Rom 15:5). It is a sign of the kingdom of God, which is justice and peace and joy in the Holy Spirit. Indeed, it is a sign of creation *healed* and brought to the end for which it was made in the beginning, sharing in divine life.

Recall that earlier in Romans Paul wrote about how the apocalypse of the good news of God also disclosed the fundamental sin of humanity: "though they [the nations] knew God, they did not glorify him as God or give thanks to him" (Rom 1:21); "you who boast in the law [of Moses] dishonor God" and cause God's name to be "blasphemed among the nations" (Rom 2:24); "all have sinned and come short of the glory of God" (Rom 3:23). But at the eucharistic table of God—where each person *with the others* eats and drinks in full conviction "to the Lord" and "gives thanks to God"—the alienating, enslaving, divisive power of Sin is undone. Those gathered at this table do what they were created to do: "with one heart and with one voice" they "glorify the God and Father of our Sovereign Jesus Messiah" (Rom 15:6). In this moment of communion and praise to God, the gospel of justice is fulfilled and creational harmony is restored. The healing of the nations has begun.

Interlude: The Table of *In*justice—A Brief History

We have already noted that starting at Romans 12:1 Paul set aside the language of justice and turned to addressing messianic life on the ground and in the streets. He does not propose a justice agenda for messianics, either through social activism in their neighborhoods or political activism in the offices and halls of power. But in the middle of his discussion of life at the dinner table the term *justice* returns for the last time in the letter: "the kingdom of God is justice [*dikaiosynē*] and peace and joy in the Holy Spirit" (Rom 14:17). The justice of God apocalypsed in the good news "to the Judean first and also to the Greek" (Rom 1:16-17); the justice of God disclosed and enacted in the atoning death of the Messiah for Judeans and the nations (Rom 3:21-31); the justice of God that graciously comes on those who trust God, whether circumcised or not (Rom 4:1-25); the justice of God fulfilled in the life, death, and resurrection of one human being, Jesus Messiah (Rom 5:12-21)—this divine-human *justice* is shared in, enacted, and realized at the messianic table, where Judeans and Gentiles dine together in peace and joy, in thanksgiving and praise to God. The kingdom of God arrives in that moment.

It is no accident that the central sacrament of God's liberating, reconciling, healing justice is not the coronation of a monarch, the writing of a constitution, or the passing of a law, but rather the eucharistic or Communion table. The practice of regularly eating and drinking together face-to-face in remembrance of the Messiah constitutes the very meaning of the *ekklēsia*—the assembly or gathering otherwise known as church. Yet precisely in this meal the church over two millennia has rarely moved much beyond where the church in Rome was when Paul wrote his letter. From early on and throughout much of its history, the church has been anti-Judaic, against Paul's explicit warnings and instructions in Romans 11 and 14. The church quickly became predominantly Gentile and the "strong" continued to despise the "weak" as they had in Rome, rather than building them up. For the first millennium of the church, while there was (almost) only one eucharistic table, messianic Jews *as Jews* were excluded from it; they were required to give up their Jewish ways in order to participate. The Jews as a people (whether messianic or not) have been regularly shunned, persecuted, expelled, and exterminated by Christians, or with Christian approval. This is the church's original sin. But it is not the last.

With the great schism of AD 1054 between the Eastern and Western traditions, there were now (at least) two tables and separated communions. While that separation was ostensibly theological, the fact is that political, ethnic, and linguistic differences were as much or more at the heart of it. From the Reformation and beyond, Communion tables multiplied exponentially with the explosion in numbers of different denominations. Churches were also divided according to their regional loyalties to kings, princes, and nation-states. Christians regularly found themselves killing other Christians in the service of these "higher" loyalties (see the previous chapter), rather than gathering at the common table in loyalty to the one Lord in whose life and death they were reconciled.

For generations in places such as South Africa, the southern United States and elsewhere, racial and ethnic differences demanded divided tables. White Christians despised black Christians and made them eat at another table. In our highly mobile modern Western world, Christians can locate themselves in neighborhoods and drive to churches where members share the same economic status, political commitments, social values, ethnic backgrounds, and tastes in music and worship style, separated from and despising those who differ on these terms. In many churches only those who are baptized (the badge of membership) are welcome to eat and drink at the table.

In your church or denomination, who (if anyone) would be refused (explicitly or implicitly) access to the Lord's Table and to the bread and wine? On what basis would they be refused? If the grounds are biblical-theological, what are they?

The table of the Lord has functioned and continues to function like a private dining club that requires the equivalents of dues, membership cards, secret handshakes, and following the club rules. Despising and judging others around the table is the order of the day. The fact that at the eucharistic table "*God* has welcomed them" and that it is "the *Lord's* Supper" is forgotten. Denominational barriers and institutional gatekeepers block the way to open access and harmonious communion. At the table of gathering—the central sign of God's justice in Messiah for *all*—churches perpetuate the injustices of the world by their "unworthy manner" of eating and drinking, by honoring old divisions between human groups and even creating new ones. As Paul says in 1 Corinthians, it is therefore "not really the Lord's supper you eat" (1 Cor 11:17-34). That Christians cannot eat and drink together in solidarity and harmony across worldly lines of division stands as the surest testimony that the good news of God's justice is not being fully believed and practiced. If the good news is irrelevant at the dining table, how can it be relevant in the larger spheres of life where injustice reigns?

God's justice in the world begins with God's welcome to God's own table. It begins when the church receives, practices, and celebrates God's hospitality at the table by living in messianic solidarity and harmony. The good news of God's justice spreads out from there.

Justice Rising: A New History of the Nations (Romans 15:7-13)

As the prophet Isaiah announced in his own proclamation of the good news, the messianic dining table signals the final hope of Israel and all nations: "On this mountain the LORD of hosts will make for all peoples a feast of rich food. . . . He will swallow up death forever . . . The disgrace of his people [Israel] he will take away from all the earth" (Is 25:6-8 NRSV). In the next few verses of Romans 15 Paul stretches the vision of God's welcoming, reconciling justice to the furthest horizons of human history. From the beginning of the letter Paul made clear that the good news is not only or even primarily about individual persons and their final destinies. It is "the power of God" (Rom 1:16) for salvation for all peoples, which brings about faithful obedience among the Judean people first (that is, beginning with them as God's elect people), and also among all the nations (Rom 1:5). Peaceable unity among all nations was always God's will, but that unity was destroyed through the warring idolatries of the Gentile nations and the legal-cultural insularity of the Judeans. Sin and Death took over the meaning of history. History became a story of the—usually violent—triumph of the strong over the weak, invariably under the banner of good over evil.

God's apocalyptic act of atoning justice in Jesus Messiah marks *the fundamental break* with that destructive history and creates a new history through the power of resurrection life. To gather in unity at Messiah's table is to share in God's way of healing history, to see it become real and visible in the midst of all nations. "Therefore," Paul writes, "welcome one another, just as Messiah welcomed you, to the glory of God" (Rom 15:7). Mutual welcome and harmony in Messiah at the eucharistic table *is* what it means to bring glory to God, that is, to make manifest *in history and as history* the glorious reality of the triune divine life in perfect communion with the glorious destiny of human life. The power of God in history is realized in the divine-human Messiah, the servant who is sovereign, and in the life together in the Spirit of those who gather in Messiah's name.

> Do you have a vision of God redeeming nations at all? If so, what might that look like? If not, why not? What role, if any, does Israel play in your understanding of how God works in history to redeem and heal the nations of the world? As you answer that, what do you mean by "Israel" (for example, the collection of all individual Jews, the people Israel, the modern nation-state of Israel, etc.)?

What follows in Romans 15:9-12 is a powerful declaration of the Messiah's universal sovereignty. But—following the same logic we find in Philippians 2:6-11—Paul first emphasizes that Messiah came as a *servant* (*diakonos*, Rom 15:8). As God's servant who arrives within history, the Messiah engages the elemental historical difference between Israel and the nations, a difference with which Paul opened his letter and of which he has never lost sight. "For I declare that Messiah has become *a servant of the circumcision* for the sake of the truth of God in order to confirm the promises [God made] to the forefathers" (Rom 15:8). The Messiah himself is the substance of the promise made to Abraham, as Paul made clear in Galatians: "Now the promises were made to Abraham and to his seed . . . that is, to the one seed, which is Messiah" (Gal 3:16).

We might say on the one hand that Israel as Israel, as God's chosen people in history, takes place within the singular promised Messiah. In turn, God's promises are proved to be true when Messiah takes place within Israel, to serve Israel, redeem Israel, and confirm Israel as God's chosen people among the nations. The Messiah's sovereignty over *all* is not an undifferentiated sovereignty, for he came first as a servant of Israel; and *therefore also* he came to serve the Gentile peoples: "and that the nations [*ethnē*] might glorify God for his mercy" (Rom 15:9). As Paul made clear in Romans 11, the destiny of the Gentile peoples has always been bound up with the destiny of Israel; if Israel is not finally redeemed, neither are the Gentile peoples. Isaiah's prophesied great gathering of Israel and the nations begins—but only begins—in the eucharistic gathering of Judeans and Gentiles in Messiah.

That is the truth at stake when messianic Judeans and Gentiles gather at the common table in mutual welcome. At that table they testify to the world-historical sovereignty of Messiah over Israel and all nations anticipated in the Torah, Psalms, and Prophets, which Paul now quotes.

In each of the four quotations from the Old Testament in Romans 15:9-12 it is essential to translate *ethnē* as "nations" rather than "Gentiles" (as both NIV and NRSV do), because Paul is now clearly thinking in *geopolitical* rather than personal terms. This is obvious in Romans 15:10-11, where *ethnē* is paralleled with *laou autou* ("his people"—i.e., Israel, Rom 15:10) and *laoi* ("peoples" [of the earth], Rom 15:11). But this also clear in Romans 15:12, where the geopolitical scope of *ho anistamenos archein*, "the one who rises to rule," cannot be missed.

Paul first aligns his own confession and praise with that of David in 2 Samuel 22:50 (LXX version, repeated in Ps 18:49): "Therefore I will confess you among the nations [*ethnesin*] and I will sing praise to your name" (Rom 15:9). In a sense this quote from the psalm sums up Paul's whole mission (as an Israelite) to declare the reality of God among the nations. The name that Paul (with David) confesses and praises is none other than "the God and Father of our Sovereign Jesus Messiah," the triune God, whom the messianic assemblies of Judeans and Gentiles also "glorify with one heart and one voice" (Rom 15:6).

In the next quote (from Deut 32:43 LXX) God calls the nations to join God's people (Israel) in the joyful song of praise: "Rejoice, O nations [*ethnē*] with [God's] people [*laou*]!" (Rom 15:10). With this quote Paul emphasizes both the distinction between the nations and Israel, and the fact that they are called by the good news to a common end, the joyful praise of God. Indeed, issuing that call is the very heart and burden of Paul's mission to the nations from beginning to end. He invokes another declaration from the Psalms: "Praise the Lord [*kyrion*], all the nations [*ethnē*], and let all the peoples [*laoi*] praise him" (Rom 15:11, quoting Ps 117:1). Here the emphasis is on *all* (*panta*) nations and peoples brought together in a single act of worship.

For his final quotation Paul draws from the prophet Isaiah, this time not to call the nations to praise God, but to make a declaration about the Sovereign who reigns over all nations and draws them together to a single hope. "The root of Jesse will come, even the one who rises to rule the nations [*ethnōn*]; the nations [*ethnē*] will put their hope in him" (Rom 15:12, quoting Is 11:10 LXX). This quote is rich with significance for Paul, taking us back even to the very first sentences of Romans in order to close the circle of meaning that was opened there.

- In Romans 1 Paul wrote of "the good news of God, which he promised beforehand through his prophets in holy writings" (Rom 1:2). In Romans 15 Paul invokes the holy writing of Isaiah, the greatest prophet of the good news, as testimony to that promise.

- In Romans 1 Paul wrote that the good news of God is about God's Son, "who has come from the seed of David according to the flesh" (Rom 1:3). In Romans 15 Isaiah testifies that the coming ruler is indeed a descendent of David, "the root of Jesse."

- In Romans 1 Paul wrote that David's descendant "was declared Son of God in power according to the Spirit of holiness by resurrection [*anastaseōs*] from the dead" (Rom 1:4). In Romans 15 Isaiah testifies to the resurrection by announcing "the one who rises [*anistamenos*] to rule the nations."

- In Romans 1 Paul declared that his apostolic mission was to "bring about faithful obedience among all the nations to the name [of Jesus Messiah our Sovereign]" (Rom 1:5). In Romans 15 Isaiah testifies to the sovereign authority of the one who rises up "to rule the nations" (*archein ethnōn*).

- In Romans 1 Paul announced all of this as "good news" (*euangelion*) for the nations. In Romans 15 Isaiah testifies that the nations are right to "put their hope" in the one who comes.

If we want to know the ultimate destination in all the twists and turns of Paul's journey through Romans, it is summed up here in Romans 15:7-13. The hope of the good news is Jesus Messiah, descended from David, resurrected from the dead, and now reigning over Israel and all nations, calling for their unreserved trust, faithful obedience, and joyous praise. The Messiah has not achieved his universal rule by conquering and subjugating peoples, but peaceably, by his own faithfulness, self-offering, and love, which alone is the justice of God. Because of this, Paul can confidently pray that "the God of hope" will fill messianics with joy and peace in trusting, and that they may "abound in hope" through the same power that raised Jesus from the dead and enables him to rule the nations in love—the power of the Holy Spirit, the Spirit of life. The reign of Messiah is the hope of Israel and all nations—hope for a new history of humankind. Justice rising.

13

MESSIANIC SPREADING

PAUL'S—AND ISAIAH'S—VISION of the reign of the Messiah is cosmic and world historical in scope. It is good news for everyone; it must be proclaimed everywhere. Paul knows himself to be God's chosen emissary for getting this news out to all the nations. He is intense, passionate, and always on the move in fulfilling his apostolic mission. In a significant sense the letter to the Romans is written not only for the sake of providing a clear and comprehensive account of the gospel of God's justice but also for the sake of moving the good news along in the world. With the letter Paul is paving the way for a sojourn in Rome, where he hopes to build up the messianic assemblies with his presence and teaching. But ultimately he plans to launch a mission from Rome to the far western limits of the Roman Empire.

Given the universal scope of the message, the enormity of Paul's apostolic calling, the sheer geographical reach of all the nations, and Paul's own personal character, we might expect him to be manically driven, opportunistic, relentless, and results-oriented in accomplishing his mission. But the opposite is true. For Paul, *how* the good news gets out is intrinsic to the very meaning of the good news. The *means of spreading* the news of God's justice must share in and accord with the fundamental character of God's justice. If it does not, it is not God's justice that is being spread.

Messianic Patience (Again) (Romans 15:14-24)

The fact that Paul paused in Corinth—it was a *significant pause*—to write this letter to the Roman assemblies is already an indication that he believed there was time for it. Paul wrote earlier in the letter, "You know what time [*karion*] it is. The hour [*hōra*] is already here for you to wake up from sleeping, for now [*nyn*] our salvation is nearer than when we believed. The night is ending; the day is at hand" (Rom 13:11-12). There is a persistent opinion that these sentences reveal that Paul was driven by a heightened consciousness that the end time was near, and this explains his frenetic (so it is thought) missionary activity. Yet everything about *this* letter suggests that Paul took time—a great deal of time—carefully and patiently to consider its words, sentences, movements, structures, overall shape, beginnings and endings, and so on, in order that *in itself* the letter would be the good news. Paul expected it to arrive and be read among the Roman assemblies as the power of God for salvation (Rom 1:16), effecting among them the divine work of "goodness," "knowledge," and "mutual instruction" (Rom 15:14).

It would not be wrong to think of Romans as in some sense a work of art (literature), that is, a work that is not merely a means to an end—a piece of propaganda—but a work in which the (divine) end, the word of God, is present *as* the text when it is read in the assemblies. Taking time and care to *compose* the letter is itself a labor of messianic peace and patience, and it requires peace, time, and patience to hear it, meditate on it, receive its power. To know what time it is, is to know that there is also time for this labor of writing and reading. In his seemingly urgent and daunting world-historical mission, the apostle to the nations nevertheless took the time he needed—the time given to him—to compose letters: "I have written to you— sometimes boldly—to remind you [of the good news] because of the grace given to me by God" (Rom 15:15).

In a world filled with so many injustices, it seems there never is or will be enough time for all that needs to be done. Is it irresponsible, then, to take time for art, for careful composition of a treatise, for patient meditation on truth, goodness, and beauty? How would these things help? What good news would justify such things?

While at first glance it may seem otherwise, Paul's description of his mission thus far (Rom 15:16-21) also reveals his messianic patience. We might imagine many ways to achieve a goal of world-historical proportions, many of which have been tried and even proven successful on their own terms: military conquest; diplomatic strong-arming; market takeover and monopoly; propaganda and mass communications; effective global advertising, and so on. What makes these means nonmessianic is the intent to outmaneuver, overpower, outsell, and captivate everyone, or as many as possible, and as soon as possible—because everyone is an object of conquest or control, and the time is short. Competition, control, and impatience characterize such world-historical missions, most of which are justified on the basis of making the world a better place. By extreme contrast, Paul has no plans for a takeover; he has all the time he needs.

Paul understands himself to be a "servant of Messiah Jesus to the nations," "because of the grace given to me by God" (Rom 15:15-16). As a servant (*leitourgos*) Paul's emissarial task is defined by the one who commissions him—defined not only in terms of what he is to do but also how he is to do it: by grace. The mission and the method are one: they are defined by the gracious mission and method of the Messiah himself. Everything about the Messiah rules out a missional mandate characterized by competition, control, and impatience, and the zero-sum relationships that accompany these. Paul's mission is moved by "the grace given to [him] by God"; if his emissarial ministry were not likewise gracious, it would contradict the character of his calling.

Paul's work therefore is not about achieving outcomes measured by the number of people he has reached and evangelized, but about carefully preparing an offering to God as a priest would do (Rom 15:16), an offering of good news–believers from among the nations. What makes this offering acceptable is not the quantity but the sanctity of lives, which itself is not

Paul's achievement but the work of the Holy Spirit. The kind of mission in which Paul is engaged is anything but grand, frenetic, and results-oriented. It is slow and small, patient and peaceable. In fact, it looks meager by most reckonings of successful world-historical missions. There is not much to boast about. So Paul instead "boasts in Messiah Jesus," who has commissioned him to this work, and "about what Messiah has accomplished" by grace through his ministry (Rom 15:17-18).

> Were you to go or be sent on a mission to proclaim the good news of God, how would you assess whether your mission was successful? How might those supporting you assess it?

What *had* Paul accomplished over the course of his labors up to the point of writing Romans? A Roman geopolitical map from Paul's time would have put the city of Rome in the center, with the various regions of the Roman Empire stretching along the north coast of the Mediterranean Sea from Syria in the east to Spain in the west, and including the regions along northern Africa on the south coast of the Mediterranean.[1] If we imagine a journey east to west from Judea through Asia Minor (current-day Turkey), Greece, Italy, Gaul (France), and Spain, and then circling back west to east along the north coast of Africa to Egypt and north again to Jerusalem, we can say that at the time of writing Romans (from Corinth) Paul had covered about a quarter (or less) of that journey along the northeast of the Mediterranean. We know, of course, that he did not do that in one trip but three, sometimes by land, sometimes by sea. Along the way he proclaimed the good news of God and God's Messiah, and established a number of messianic assemblies in the cities of Asia Minor and Greece. The total number of Gentile messianics in those cities is not known, but altogether there would not likely have been much more than a thousand. Yet Paul did not simply rush to the next region on his next trip. As much as he could, he returned to those small assemblies to teach them further and build them up in the good news. He also wrote letters to them. Before writing Romans he had already written 1-2 Thessalonians, Galatians, and 1-2 Corinthians.

---

[1] A description of such a map is provided by Robert Jewett, *Romans: Hermeneia—A Critical and Historical Commentary on the Bible* (Minneapolis: Fortress, 2007), 912-13.

What did Paul think he had accomplished? He provides no head count of Gentile messianics at all; instead, he claims that Messiah has "accomplished through" him "the obedience of Gentiles," that is, their faithful obedience to God and the sovereign Jesus Messiah (Rom 15:18; see Rom 1:5). The number does not matter. What matters instead is *how* their obedience was won. The Greek verb translated "accomplished" ("what Messiah has accomplished through me") in some contexts bears the sense of overpowering or conquering (as it does in Eph 6:13). Paul believes that is what has happened *in some sense* in his mission among the Gentile nations, since some Gentiles are now obedient to the Sovereign who has conquered them.

But *in what sense* has the Messiah through Paul conquered the Gentiles? In no sense by threat, coercion, or military might! Rather, by fundamentally different means: "by word and deed [*logō kai ergō*], by the power [*dynamei*] of signs and wonders, by the power [*dynamei*] of the Spirit of God" (Rom 15:18-19). These are the instruments of power with which the messianic mission makes its way in the world (see Eph 6:10-17). This is how messianic justice spreads. It spreads by *divine* power, which is always only *grace and peace*. The good news that is God's justice is not only *what* spreads; it is *how* it spreads. Justice spreading by any other means is not good news. It is not justice.

What did Paul think he had accomplished (or rather, the Messiah through him)? Enough, thus far, and more than enough. "From Jerusalem and as far around as Illyricum I have completed the good news of Messiah" (Rom 15:19). Illyricum was just east across the Adriatic Sea from Italy, so Paul's mission had reached the doorstep of Rome, the center of the world. Remarkably, Paul believes he has "completed the good news of Messiah" in the entire northeast quadrant of the Roman Empire, so much so that he declares a few sentences later that there is "no longer any place for me in those regions" (Rom 15:23). It is time for him to go west, to stop first in Rome and then to be sent on from there to Spain (Rom 15:23-24).

This is a strange kind of universal mission. Simply in terms of a percentage of the population in those regions, hardly anyone had heard the good news, and even fewer had believed it. Yet Paul sees no need to stay on there; he is determined to move on "to announce the good news not where Messiah has already been named, so that I might not build on someone else's foundation" (Rom 15:20). There are still three quadrants of the empire that must hear the news of the justice of God. His mission to those farthest regions would fulfill what the prophet Isaiah wrote about the suffering Servant of God: "Those who have not been told about him will see; and those who have not heard will understand" (Rom 15:21, quoting Is 52:15).

Paul's mission as apostle to the Gentile nations was unique. The geographical extent of the nations to which he was sent seemed to cover at least the same territory covered by the Roman Empire. To announce the name of Messiah throughout this territory meant for Paul to declare that the Messiah lays sovereign claim to it and calls for the obedience of the nations. Yet that claim and call are only realized *on the ground*, through the patient, peaceable work of the itinerant apostle, among ordinary people who hear and believe the message. God's justice spreads like that.

Geopolitical Good News (Romans 15:25-33)

Though he "eagerly aspires" (Rom 15:20) to move on to Spain and the next sphere of his mission, Paul is not in a hurry. He has other important work to do first that will take him in the opposite direction, back to Jerusalem. Indeed, because this work is a concrete, material sign of God's justice at work among the nations, he must take time for it too. We learn much more about this "ministry to the saints" (Rom 15:25) in Jerusalem from 2 Corinthians 8–9 than we do from Paul's brief description in Romans 15. Very early on in his mission to the nations Paul began collecting funds from the Gentile messianic assemblies to take back to the Judean messianic assemblies in Jerusalem that were experiencing poverty (for reasons which are not clear).[2] In fact, one scholar has called the collection of funds for Jerusalem Paul's obsession.[3] It was as important to him as proclaiming the good news; or rather, it was important because it was *intrinsic* to the good news he proclaimed, a manifestation of the effective power of the gospel:

- The collection for Jerusalem was a material sign of God's own gracious generosity and abundant blessing in Messiah toward the Gentile nations (2 Cor 8:1-7).

---

[2]For an account of the collection and its significance see Scot McKnight, "Collection for the Saints," in *Dictionary of Paul and His Letters*, ed. Gerald Hawthorne, Ralph Martin, and Daniel Reid (Downers Grove, IL: InterVarsity Press, 1993), 143-47.

[3]McKnight, "Collection for the Saints," 143.

- The collection was intended to meet the real bodily needs of those who were suffering. It was messianic care and love in action (2 Cor 8:14-15, 24).

- The collection was a material sign of sharing in Messiah's life: "For you know the generous grace of our sovereign Jesus Messiah, that though being rich, he became poor for your sake, so that you by his poverty might become rich" (2 Cor 8:9).

- The collection was a material sign of thanksgiving and obedience to God by Gentiles; in other words, precisely what Paul's apostleship was meant to bring about among the nations (2 Cor 9:11-13).

- The collection was material evidence that God's justice in Messiah was bringing forth justice in the relationship between the Gentile peoples and Judeans (2 Cor 9:8-10).

It is especially this last aspect that Paul focuses on in Romans 15:26-27. Throughout the letter Paul never loses sight of the fact that God's redeeming justice in Messiah is aimed at healing the relationship between Judeans and Gentiles, between Israel and the Gentile peoples. For Paul that healing could never simply remain a "spiritual" reality. We saw in the previous chapter just how important it was for him that every local gathering of Judeans and Gentiles should materially manifest the gospel in mutual welcome, respect, and honoring of their different traditions at the Lord's Table. The collection for Jerusalem represents the same thing in the larger geopolitical arena of Israel and the nations: "Macedonia and Achaia have been pleased to share their resources with the poor among the saints at Jerusalem" (Rom 15:26 NRSV).

It is significant that Paul uses the regional names, Macedonia and Achaia, rather than, say, "believers from" those places. The regional names signify larger ethnic-political entities. The collection from those *ethnē* to Judea represents something fundamental: the *sharing of life* (*koinōnia*, Rom 15:26) between peoples who, on other grounds, would see each other as in competition for the means of life (land, labor, resources, etc.). This kind of material sharing between the Gentile nations and Israel, represented in the collection, is a geopolitical realization of the good news, unimaginable apart from it. "They [Macedonia and Achaia] were delighted to do this [share their resources] and indeed they saw it as repaying a debt; for if [through Israel] the nations have come to share in [Israel's] spiritual realities, so also the nations ought to serve [Israel] in material things" (Rom 15:27). Everything that Paul argued for in Romans 11 comes to material, economic fruition in the collection for Jerusalem. Therefore when he delivers the collection, Paul says, he will have secured the fruit of the good news (Rom 15:28).

So important is the collection that Paul is prepared to suspend his ambitious plan to carry on his mission to Spain and travel instead from Corinth—nearly next door to Rome—all the way back to Jerusalem to deliver the collection. In terms of time, this is a costly venture, which Paul nevertheless plans to take time for. It is also a risky venture. While Macedonia and Achaia are eager about this *koinōnia* (sharing of resources), it is not at all clear to Paul that the messianic assembly in Jerusalem is ready to receive it. He anticipates possible threats to his safety in Judea and possible rejection in Jerusalem. (According to Acts 19:21; 21:15-36, his concerns were well-founded.) He begs the messianics in Rome to pray that he will be kept safe and that the "saints" in Jerusalem will accept this work of sacrificial service from the Gentile peoples. If all goes well he will come to Rome and carry on to Spain (Rom 15:30-32).

In the meantime, Paul leaves the Romans with a prayer: "Now may the God of peace be with you all. Amen" (Rom 15:33). The whole letter has proclaimed the reality of God's peace in Messiah Jesus. The proclamation now becomes the prayer—"Amen"—that it will be so among the Gentile and Judean messianics in Rome.

Messianic Friendship (Romans 16:1-23)

Romans 16 seems like a fairly simple list of greetings that Paul wants to send to the Romans. It is a list of greetings, to be sure, but scholars have found it to be far from simple. In fact, a great deal of information can be gained from this chapter about the messianic assemblies in Rome and Paul's relationship to them. For example, it is likely that Phoebe (Rom 16:1-2), one of Paul's financial supporters in Cenchreae (near Corinth), was not only the bearer of the letter to Rome but also the one who read and interpreted it in the assemblies there. She was the first interpreter of Romans.[4] Carefully analyzing the many names in this chapter yields further results: some are Latin, some Greek, some Jewish; some names signify higher social status, others lower. There are women and men, elders and youth, relatives and strangers in the list. Some are leaders with significant roles in the assemblies, including the woman Junia who is said to be "notable among the apostles" (Rom 16:7). We could go on.

But what does any of this list of greetings have to do with the good news of God's justice in Messiah? Indeed, all of it does! The messianic reality in Rome does not exist as a crowd or collective. It exists in and among *persons* with *names* embedded in multiple complex *relationships*. The good news has spread among these persons, creating something new. While some of Paul's birth relatives are mentioned (Andronicus and Junia [Rom 16:7], Herodion [Rom 16:11], and some other kin relationships [Rom 16:10, 11, 15]), most of the relationships among the messianics and between them and Paul have been brought about by the good news: the phrases "in the Lord" and "in Messiah" are frequent (Rom 16:3, 7, 9, 10, 11, 12, 13) and define the whole. Phoebe is a "sister," a "minister" (*diakonos*) of the assembly in Cenchreae and a benefactor of Paul and many others. Prisca and Aquila are Paul's coworkers in Messiah Jesus who risked their lives for Paul and now host an assembly in their house in Rome (Rom 16:3). Others are also identified as coworkers: Mary (Rom 16:6); Urbanus (Rom 16:9); Tryphaena, Tryphosa, and Persis (Rom 16:12); and Timothy (Rom 16:21). Striking is Paul's frequent use of the word "beloved" (*agapētos*) with respect to Epaenetus (Rom 16:5), Ampliatus (Rom 16:8), Stachys (Rom 16:9), and Persis (Rom 16:12).

Love pervades the greetings in other ways, both in the evident devotion of these people to Paul and in Paul's devotion to them: "Greet Rufus . . . and his mother, who is also a mother to me" (Rom 16:13). Paul refers to all as "brothers [and sisters]" (Rom 16:14, 17). He concludes the greetings by urging the messianics in Rome to "greet one another with a holy kiss" (Rom 16:16). And, while God's gracious, reconciling, uniting justice in Messiah creates these bonds of affection throughout the assemblies in Rome, they also stretch well beyond Rome: "*All* the assemblies of Messiah greet you!"

---

[4]This is suggested by Beverly Roberts Gaventa, *When in Romans: An Invitation to Linger with the Gospel According to Paul* (Grand Rapids, MI: Baker Academic, 2016), 9-14.

(Rom 16:16), which includes Paul's relatives, associates, and "the whole church" in Corinth (Rom 16:21-23).

The point is that these greetings reflect *how* the cosmic, world-historical reality of the Messiah's sovereign reign of justice spreads on the earth and throughout the empire: it spreads through ground-level networks of newly created bonds of affection in and among communities created by God's justice. So the word of warning that Paul inserts at this point is to guard against anyone who would seek to destroy these bonds of affection by causing divisions and offenses. Such people undermine "the teaching you have learned," namely, the whole gospel of justice (Rom 16:17). Their favorite target is the simpleminded, whom they attempt to deceive, which is why Paul puts such stress on teaching and learning here. The surest defense against such divisive people is a robust understanding of the good news. Paul's letter is nothing if not robust!

If you are an activist for God's justice in your neighborhood or in the wider world, what role does friendship have in your work for justice? Are friends primarily means to justice-ends? Are friends intrinsic to the meaning of justice? What is the relationship between justice and friendship?

As I just wrote, God's justice spreads in the world through ground-level networks of newly created bonds of affection in and among communities of God's love. Everyone within the messianic assemblies was also related in multiple complex ways to many others beyond those assemblies. The messianic gatherings in Rome were not closed-door affairs; there certainly was not a "church" building. Sometimes they met in the synagogues. But the homes and shops in which they usually met for common meals and worship were attached, and open to alleys, streets, and squares, as well as to observers, the curious, and passersby.[5] The gatherings were quite publicly visible, and from them relational networks spread out into the neighborhood like rhizomes. Paul's greetings give us a glimpse into the early

---

[5]Detached homes were not part of the reality of the city of Rome. Countryside villas were the property of only a very few elite. See Peter Oakes, *Reading Romans in Pompeii: Paul's Letter at Ground Level* (Minneapolis: Fortress, 2009).

rhizome-like movement of God's grace, manifest especially in newly created harmonies around the common table. Paul even claims that the obedience of the Romans "has reached out to *all* so that I rejoice over you" (Rom 16:19). People are taking notice. New life in Messiah and the Spirit has become *a real presence* on the streets of Rome.

For this reason Paul utters an astonishing word to the Romans: "The God of peace will soon crush Satan under your feet" (Rom 16:20). How can the language of divine peace and the militant "crush under your feet" hold together in the same short sentence? Paul here invokes the apocalyptic image of cosmic warfare between God and his enemy Satan. He assures the Romans that this war will soon be won. The enemy will be crushed. But how? And how will the God of *peace* be manifest in this victory?

The whole of the good news is ultimately the good news of peace—peace brought about through God's reconciling justice mission in Messiah. It is Satan who alienates, divides, and conquers, among people and in history, through pride, greed, violence, and warfare. God crushes Satan by destroying enmity through the *peacemaking death and resurrection* of Messiah. When that divine peacemaking reality hits the ground on the streets of Rome, and around the table of the messianic gathering, where people once at odds eat and drink in mutual respect, solidarity, and friendship, Satan is indeed crushed under their feet! Satan's power among them is destroyed by the divine grace of the gathering. So Paul invokes that conquering grace in a concluding messianic blessing: "The grace of our Sovereign Jesus Messiah be with you" (Rom 16:20).

Doxology: Just Worship (Romans 16:25-27)

Paul concludes the letter with a beautiful and complex hymn of praise to God, which amounts to nothing less than a recapitulation of the good news he has announced throughout the letter.[6]

"Now to the one who is powerful to strengthen you according to the good news . . ." From the beginning (Rom 1:16-17) Paul announced the good news as God's *power* to bring about justice for all who trust him, for Judeans and Gentiles, for Israel and the nations.

---

[6]While there is a good deal of debate about the authenticity and placement of these verses, I simply take them here in their received canonical form.

"The proclamation of Jesus Messiah . . ." The entire letter is a declaration about Jesus Messiah: his Davidic lineage; his resurrection, exaltation, and divine sonship; his atoning death apart from law; his justice and obedience as the truly human one; his living reality through resurrection and the Holy Spirit; his ongoing presence to and coming justice for Israel; his living body in the messianic assembly; his ultimate sovereignty over Israel and all nations. Jesus Messiah *is* God's justice. He *is* the good news. With the Father and the Holy Spirit he is one God blessed forever.

"According to the apocalypse of the mystery which was kept hidden from eternal times, but is now manifested . . ." The eternal reality of the divine Son was apocalypsed in time; God arrived in person in Jesus Messiah. The arrival of the divine Son as the human Jesus is the event in which the mystery of both God and humanity is made known to all. This apocalyptic arrival and manifestation also shines searing divine light on how humanity has distorted divinity into idolatry, become enslaved to destructive powers, and enacted a long history of enmity, violence, and injustice. The apocalypse of God's Messiah is the apocalypse of God's right-making justice for all humanity, for Israel and the nations. The arrival of Messiah in the midst of Israel reveals the mystery of Israel's messianic purpose and destiny as God's chosen people among the nations, and the justice and faithfulness of God toward Israel in the promise of Israel's once and coming Deliverer. In him Israel—and the nations—can trust.

"Through the prophetic writings . . ." The arrival of the Messiah opens up the Scriptures of Israel, such that they all in some way or another testify to the reality of God's Messiah and God's justice.

"According to a command of the eternal God . . ." God himself is the source, power, and reality of the good news. Because God *is* in the unity of Father, Son, and Holy Spirit, there is good news. Good news happens because the eternal triune God wills it to happen. God is the *subject* of Romans in both senses of the word: it is a letter *about God*, and it is a letter through which *God speaks* his powerful word of justice.

"For faithful obedience to all the nations . . ." God brings about justice through the faithful obedience of the Messiah in order that all the nations might render faithful obedience to God through the Messiah. Romans—the good news—is relevant not only to messianic assemblies throughout the world but to every government and nation on the face of the earth as well. Peace and justice for all depends on it.

"To the only wise God through Jesus Messiah . . ." Jesus Messiah is the strange wisdom of God, a wisdom that cannot be grasped apart from the Messiah. While this wisdom will count as foolishness according to worldly criteria of rationality, power, justice, and security, this wisdom is the world's only hope of personal, political, economic, ecological salvation. We must call the world to this wisdom.

"To whom be the glory unto the ages . . ." The absolute and eternal reality of the triune God is the one true object of glory and praise; yet the living glory of the Father, Son, and Holy Spirit is also our glory and the glory of all creation, the gift of justice and life.

SUGGESTIONS FOR FURTHER READING

THE LITERATURE ON PAUL and the letter to the Romans is, of course, vast and varied in purpose, perspective, and accessibility. In what follows I have included books that, to my mind anyway, provide helpful entries into Paul and Romans, and important background and perspectives on some of the issues I deal with in this book. Most resources I list are accessible to an engaged wider readership, but I have also included some that presuppose some scholarly background and will take the reader deeper into the material. These latter I have indicated with an asterisk.

General Treatments of Paul, His Times, and His Letters

Barclay, John M. G. *Paul: A Very Brief History*. London: SPCK, 2018.
———.*Paul and the Power of Grace*. Grand Rapids, MI: Eerdmans, 2020.
Benedict XVI, Pope. *Paul of Tarsus*. London: Catholic Truth Society, 2009.
Campbell, Douglas A. *Paul: An Apostle's Journey*. Grand Rapids, MI: Eerdmans, 2018.
*Gaventa, Beverly Roberts. *Our Mother Saint Paul*. Louisville, KY: Westminster John Knox, 2007.
Gorman, Michael J. *Reading Paul*. Eugene, OR: Cascade Books, 2008.
Longenecker, Bruce W., and Todd D. Still. *Thinking Through Paul: A Survey of His Life, Letters, and Theology*. Grand Rapids, MI: Zondervan, 2014.
Suchet, David. *In the Footsteps of St. Paul*. DVD. RLJ Entertainment, 2014.
*Westerholm, Stephen, ed. *The Blackwell Companion to Paul*. Malden, MA: Wiley-Blackwell, 2011.

Literary, Historical, Social, and Political Backgrounds to Paul and Romans

Elliott, Neil, and Mark Reasoner. *Documents and Images for the Study of Paul*. Minneapolis: Fortress, 2011.

Oakes, Peter. *Reading Romans in Pompeii: Paul's Letter at Ground Level.* Minneapolis: Fortress, 2009.

Books and Commentaries on Romans

*Barth, Karl. *The Epistle to the Romans.* 6th ed. Translated by Edwin C. Hoskyns. London: Oxford University Press, 1933.

Gaventa, Beverly Roberts. *When in Romans: An Invitation to Linger with the Gospel According to Paul.* Grand Rapids, MI: Baker Academic, 2016.

Keck, Leander E. *Romans.* Abingdon New Testament Commentaries. Nashville: Abingdon, 2005.

Reardon, Patrick Henry. *Romans.* An Orthodox Commentary. Yonkers, NY: St. Vladimir's Seminary Press, 2018.

Rutledge, Fleming. *Not Ashamed of the Gospel: Sermons from Paul's Letter to the Romans.* Grand Rapids, MI: Eerdmans, 2007.

Toews, John E. *Romans.* Believers Church Bible Commentary. Waterloo, ON: Herald, 2004.

Justice and the Nations in Romans

Elliott, Neil. *The Arrogance of Nations: Rereading Romans in the Shadow of Empire.* Minneapolis: Fortress, 2008.

Gorman, Michael J. *Becoming the Gospel: Paul, Participation, and Mission.* Grand Rapids, MI: Eerdmans, 2015.

On Apocalyptic and Messianic in Paul, Romans and Theology

*Agamben, Giorgio. *The Time That Remains: A Commentary on the Letter to the Romans.* Translated by Patricia Daley. Stanford, CA: Stanford University Press, 2005. (On messianic)

*Gaventa, Beverly Roberts. *Our Mother Saint Paul.* Louisville, KY: Westminster John Knox, 2007. (Pages 79-160 on apocalyptic)

*Martyn, J. Louis. *Theological Issues in the Letters of Paul.* Nashville: Abingdon, 1997. (On apocalyptic)

*Welborn, L. L. *Paul's Summons to Messianic Life: Political Theology and the Coming Awakening.* New York: Columbia University Press, 2015. (On messianic)

Yoder, John Howard. *He Came Preaching Peace.* Scottdale, PA: Herald, 1985. (Sermons on messianic)

*————. *The Politics of Jesus: Vicit Agnus Noster.* 2nd ed. Grand Rapids, MI: Eerdmans, 1994. (On messianic)

*Ziegler, Philip G. *Militant Grace: The Apocalyptic Turn and the Future of Christian Theology.* Grand Rapids, MI: Baker Academic, 2018. (On apocalyptic)

GLOSSARY AND TRANSLATIONS

THE FOLLOWING SOMEWHAT UNFAMILIAR TERMS are used frequently throughout this book. Here are brief definitions.

apocalypse, apocalyptic: the Greek verb *apokalyptō* is usually translated "to reveal," and the Greek noun *apokalypsis* is translated "revelation." To capture the dynamic, dramatic, and self-and-world changing character of these words in Paul's letters, I have retained the words in their (roughly) Greek form, including using the word *apocalypse* as both a noun and a verb: e.g., God *apocalypsed* himself to Paul in the risen Jesus. In this event God did much more than "reveal" or show himself to Paul; the *apocalyptic* event fundamentally revolutionized Paul's self (Gal 2:19-20; Phil 3:4-11), Paul's world (Gal 6:14-15), and indeed all things, bringing about new creation (2 Cor 5:16-17).

christos/Messiah: I have regularly translated the Greek word *christos*, usually translated "Christ," with *Messiah*. Messiah with reference to Jesus is not a "second name" but a title signifying Jesus's connection with the messianic prophecies of the Old Testament, his descent from the royal line of David, and his exalted sovereign rule over Israel and all nations. Paul declares Jesus's messiahship in this sense immediately in Rom 1:1-5 and concludes with it in Rom 15:7-13, and this meaning is assumed throughout Romans.

Diaspora: This term refers to those Judeans (see below) who lived outside the land of Judea, in regions to the East (Persia, Babylon) and in cities and regions around the Mediterranean. The word *diaspora* means something like "seeded abroad" or scattered. In our time it can refer to any ethnic people-group living in a region or city outside of its native land.

222 GLOSSARY AND TRANSLATIONS

dikaioō, dikaios, dikaiōsis, dikaiosynē: this set of Greek words, each beginning with *dik-*, has usually been translated into English with words such as "justify," "righteous," "justification," "righteousness," and so on. All of these English words have over time taken on theological meanings—often individualistic, moralistic, and religious—that are a long distance from the meanings of "just," "justice," and so on—those words we commonly use to signify rightly ordered relationships in the social, economic and political realms. As a result, when we read Romans, we think it has little or nothing to do with these latter meanings. But when Paul uses the *dik-* words, he is far from limiting their meaning only to the right-standing of an individual before God. I consistently translate those words with "just-" words and meanings in order to lead beyond the individualistic, religious meanings we usually associate with them. Romans is about *justice* (*dikaiosynē*).

ethnos, ethnē: These words (singular and plural) are regularly translated in English bibles as *gentile* and *gentiles*, signifying one or more than one non-Judean individuals. Sometimes that is the right translation. But often the translation *nation* or *nations* is more appropriate, since Paul often (along with the Old Testament) is thinking along the lines of political regions, people-groups, or peoples, rather than individuals. For example, it is difficult to make sense of Romans 15:7-13 without thinking of *nations*. The same must be said about Romans 9–11. Paul's gospel vision is far more political-global than we are in the habit of thinking.

Judeans: Where English bibles almost always translate *Ioudaios, Ioudaioi* as "Jew," "Jews," I almost always translate these words as *Judean, Judeans*. I do this to prevent the reader from thinking that Paul is writing primarily about a "religion" (Judaism) and "religious" people (Jews). This loses touch with the thought that Judea is a region, a *land*, populated by a *people* in the ethnic-political sense, and that even most Diaspora Judeans were more than "religious"; they sustained an attachment to the land of Judea (or Israel) as their geographical, political *home*, which in the time of Jesus and Paul was unjustly occupied by the Romans. Paul would certainly have hoped someday for a liberation of the land of Judea, with the law of Moses as the law of the land. Paul was a Judean.

messianic: I use *messianic* as both an adjective and as a noun. As an adjective (e.g. *messianic* life) it indicates participation in the reality and conformity to the pattern of the Messiah, Jesus. As a noun (e.g. the *messianics* in Rome), it means those who have been claimed by, participate in, and conform to Jesus Messiah, his life as written in the gospels, his self-offering death, his resurrection, and his sovereign rule over Israel and all peoples. We would normally say *Christian* and *Christians* today, but this often simply means something like belonging to the Christian religion.

pisteuō, pistis: As a verb and a noun, these words are usually translated "to believe," "to have faith in," and "faith." These translations are not so much wrong as narrow in range. The Greek words could indicate trust, loyalty, allegiance, devotion, and so on. A Roman citizen would have *pistis* in relation to the Caesar. That did not mean that he believed in the Caesar as an object of "religious faith"; rather, he owed the Caesar, as Lord (sovereign), his devotion, loyalty, and allegiance. That is what messianics owe to the Sovereign Messiah. In Romans 4, on the other hand, *pistis* means primarily utter confidence and trust in God and God's promise.

power over: One of the core meanings of sovereignty in our normal usage is the capacity and means (often coercive) to exercise controlling *power over* a subject or subjects. Yet in Romans Paul consistently declares the sovereignty (lordship) of the Messiah Jesus. The question of the meaning of sovereignty is central in the message of Romans. What does sovereignty mean if it is *defined* by Jesus's "ruling"? It must mean something fundamentally different than our normal usage, something fundamentally different from *power over*, which, for Paul, is a primary manifestation of Sin (see below). Jesus's absolutely unique sovereignty (that is, the sovereignty of God) is the Good News, and it is a sovereignty the Messiah doesn't hoard to himself, but bestows on messianics—as the only kind of sovereignty they are to exercise in their life in the world.

Septuagint, LXX: The Septuagint is the Greek translation of the Old Testament (completed in the century before Christ) that was effectively *the Bible* for Paul. When Paul quotes from "the scriptures" or "the law and the prophets" he almost always quotes from the Septuagint. The abbreviation for the Septuagint is **LXX** (Roman numeral for 70), for reasons which are not necessary to describe here. Google Septuagint.

Sin, Death, Flesh, Law: These words are frequently written with upper case letters, especially Sin and Death. This is to signify that for Paul these are *oppressive powers* at work in the world *under which* humans are held in bondage. Sin is not merely individual transgressions; it is an anti-God power which "entered" into the world scene and started "lording it over" human beings, as Paul writes in Romans 5:12-21. It is the same with Death (not merely dying), which accompanies Sin in its enslaving power. Flesh (upper case *F*) is not human organs and muscles; rather it is human being and willing held captive under the powers of Sin and Death and thus powered by them, rather than by the Spirit (see Romans 8). Law (upper case *L*) signifies how even something good, like law, can be captured and used by Sin and Death to serve injustice and oppression, thus itself becoming a power opposed to God (see Romans 7). These powers opposed to God are defeated in the apocalypse of God's power in the death, resurrection, and exaltation of Jesus Messiah.

SCRIPTURE INDEX

Finding the Textbook You Need

The IVP Academic Textbook Selector
is an online tool for instantly finding the IVP books
suitable for over 250 courses across 24 disciplines.

---

ivpacademic.com
